# Evaluating the Financial Performance of Pension Funds

# Evaluating the Financial Performance of Pension Funds

Richard Hinz, Heinz P. Rudolph,
Pablo Antolín, and Juan Yermo
*Editors*

**THE WORLD BANK**
**Washington, D.C.**

1818 H Street NW
Washington DC 20433
Telephone: 202-473-1000
Internet: www.worldbank.org
E-mail: feedback@worldbank.org

ISBN: 978-0-8213-8159-5
eISBN: 978-0-8213-8160-1
DOI: 10.1596/978-0-8213-8159-5

**Library of Congress Cataloging-in-Publication Data**

Evaluating the financial performance of pension funds / Richard Hinz ... [et al.], editors.
    p. cm. — (Directions in development)
    Includes bibliographical references and index.
    ISBN 978-0-8213-8159-5 (alk. paper) — ISBN 978-0-8213-8160-1
    1. Pension trusts—Evaluation. 2. Rate of return—Evaluation. I. Hinz, Richard P. II. World Bank.
    HD7105.4.E93 2010
    331.25'24—dc22

                                                                                        2009043702

Cover photograph: Aziz Gökdemir
Cover design: Naylor Design

# Contents

## Figures

## Tables

# Preface and Acknowledgments

This volume is the product of a partnership organized by the World Bank that includes the Organisation for Economic Co-operation and Development (OECD), two private sector entities with worldwide pension-related business and a significant interest in public policy—the ING Group headquartered in the Netherlands and BBVA with headquarters in Spain—and VB, the Dutch Association of Industry-wide Pension Funds. Although not formally members of the partnership, the American Council of Life Insurers (ACLI), which provided funding, and the U.K. Department for Work and Pensions, through a staff secondment to the OECD, also supported the work. The partnership represents a promising approach to organizing and financing policy research on issues of importance to international policy and research institutions and the business community.

The project originated with a proposal from ING to engage in a research partnership with the World Bank, first made in 2002. It exemplifies the Dutch ideal of collective effort and public-private cooperation. Over the course of the ensuing two years, the partnership that was formed was extended to include the other institutions, and a program of research emerged from the discussions among its members.

This work was initially directed toward a comparative analysis of the financial performance of the many forms of funded pension arrangements that have emerged over the last several decades in an attempt to assess the quality of investment management and to discern any factors that may have been responsible for differences in their performance. As the effort progressed, it became readily apparent that neither the necessary data nor a feasible methodology was available that could support a cross-national comparison of financial results. It also became evident that to do this in a meaningful way would require the development of some type of country-specific benchmark that was developed in consideration of the income replacement and consumption-smoothing objectives of a pension system. This refocused the work of the partnership on the consideration of the many risk and other factors that must be considered in the construction of such a benchmark; also examined were the methods that might be used to derive the benchmark for the unique pension systems and operation of the financial markets in developing countries.

The work presented in this volume is the result of the efforts of many individuals who worked cooperatively in the spirit of the partnership over several years. The partnership was initially organized by Richard Hinz of the World Bank, Frans van Loon and Hasko van Dalen of ING Group, and Juan Yermo of the OECD. Robert Holzmann of the World Bank and André Laboul of the OECD provided management support in their respective institutions. The research program and publication were planned and overseen by a Coordination Committee that included Pablo Antolín and Juan Yermo of the OECD; Richard Hinz, Heinz P. Rudolph, and Roberto Rocha of the World Bank; Violeta Ciurel and Hasko van Dalen of ING; Carmen Pérez de Muniain and Patricio Urrutia of BBVA; and Renske Biezeveld from VB.

Many others, whose work does not appear in this book, made important contributions to the effort by undertaking research that ultimately was not included in the volume and by providing ideas and thoughtful commentary that greatly contributed to the direction and the quality of the resulting studies. These scholars include Solange Berstein, Gonzalo Camargo, Agnieszka Chłoń-Domińczak, Joaquín Cortez, Piotr Denderski, Leonardo Díaz Barreiro, Sandra Gómez, Esteban Jadresic, Ross Jones, Con Keating, Niels Kortleve, Mariusz Kubzdyl, Barthold Kuipers, Lorena Masias, Alberto Musalem, Theo Nijman, Ricardo Pasquini, Stephanie Payet, Fons Quix, Tony Randle, Ambrogio Rinaldi, Clara Severinson, Jean-Marc Salou, José Siesdedos, Dariusz Stanko, Fiona Stewart, Waldo Tapia, and Tomas Wijffels, as well as the many participants in several research forums and seminars in which the work was presented and discussed.

The establishment and operation of the partnership was also supported by many individuals who overcame the many bureaucratic hurdles required for this type of endeavor to succeed; they include Andrea Stumpf, Jane Kirby-Zaki, Sophia Drewsnowski, Nancy Pinto, and Richard Zechter at the World Bank. The publication was ably supported by Paola Scalabrin, Denise Bergeron, and Aziz Gökdemir, who, in addition to managing the many details of the publication, generously contributed the cover photo.

In addition, the work could not have been undertaken without the strong support of many people within the respective institutions who provided the necessary support to enable the commitment of time and energy to make the project possible. These include Jan Nijssen, formerly the Global Head of Pensions at ING Group; Eduardo Fuentes, the Global Head of Pensions and Insurance at BBVA; Peter Borgdorff, formerly the Director of VB; Frank Koster and Guillermo Arthur at ING Group; and Brad Smith at the ACLI.

# Abbreviations

| | |
|---|---|
| bp | basis point |
| CCAPM | consumption capital asset pricing model |
| CDC | collective defined contribution |
| CEE | Central and Eastern Europe |
| CIEBA | Committee on the Investment of Employee Benefit Assets |
| CVaR | conditional Value at Risk |
| DB | defined benefit |
| DC | defined contribution |
| DYNASIM | Dynamic Simulation of Income Model |
| EBRI | Employee Benefit Research Institute |
| FTSE | *Financial Times*/London Stock Exchange |
| GDP | gross domestic product |
| GFD | Global Financial Database |
| ICI | Investment Company Institute |
| IIT | integrative investment theory |
| IRA | individual retirement account |
| LTL | long-term local |
| LTU | long-term U.S. |
| MINT | modeling income in the near term |
| MRG | minimum return guarantee |

| OECD | Organisation for Economic Co-operation and Development |
| PAYGO | pay as you go |
| PENSIM | Pension Simulation Model |
| RP | risk premium |
| RWA | return weighted average |
| S&P | Standard & Poor's |
| SDF | stochastic discount factor |
| SIPP | Survey of Income and Program Participation |
| SR | Sharpe ratio |
| STL | short-term local |
| STU | short-term U.S. |
| T-bill | Treasury bill |
| T-bond | Treasury bond |
| TDF | target-date fund |
| TIPS | Treasury inflation-protected security |
| VaR | Value at Risk |
| VB | Vereniging van Bedrijfstakpensioenfondsen (Dutch Association of Industry-wide Pension Funds) |

All dollars are U.S. dollars unless otherwise stated.

CHAPTER 1

# Evaluating the Financial Performance of Pension Funds

## Heinz P. Rudolph, Richard Hinz, Pablo Antolín, and Juan Yermo

### Background and Motivation for the Research Program

Since the early 1980s, the structure of arrangements to provide retirement income has gradually moved from defined benefit (DB) systems to various types of arrangements in which the provision of pensions is backed by assets, either in individual accounts or in collective schemes. This change has been motivated principally by governments seeking to lessen the fiscal impact of aging populations and to diversify the sources of retirement income. One of the key results is that many pension systems are now in the process of becoming asset backed. This increasingly links retirement incomes to the performance of these assets, resulting in participants being exposed to the uncertainties of investment markets to determine the level of benefits that they will ultimately receive. The potential consequences of this have never been more evident than during the recent global financial crisis.

Despite the abysmal performance of investment markets in 2008 and early 2009 and the effect on pension funds, most governments have remained steadfast in their commitment to the concept of funded arrangements. The rapid decline in asset values, however, has renewed debate regarding the underlying principles of linking benefits to asset performance and has led to considerable attention to enhancing the organization and operation of the arrangements currently in place. A small number of countries have reacted by reverting to traditional arrangements or by reducing or suspending contributions to mandatory funded pension schemes, but these actions appear to have been primarily motivated by short-term fiscal considerations and are not admissions of the failure of the new arrangements.

Underlying much of the recent policy debate is the increasing recognition that pension fund assets have important differences compared with other forms of collective investments. Pension funds have the objective of providing income replacement in retirement, whereas other forms of collective investments are primarily concerned with short-term wealth maximization. The differences in objectives result in different time frames over which performance should be considered and different attitudes to risk. Despite these distinctions, the performance measures that are typically applied to pension funds are identical to those used to evaluate the performance of other types of investments.

To date, the debate on optimal investment strategies and performance evaluation of defined contribution (DC) pension systems has taken place largely in the academic literature, although its impact on practical policy recommendations has been relatively limited. This is understandable given the relative infancy of funded systems in most countries and governments' urgency in addressing other basic problems, such as the high cost of the systems, governance issues, and approach to supervision.

Recognizing the emerging importance of measuring the performance of these funded pension systems, the World Bank and the Organisation for Economic Co-operation and Development (OECD) established a partnership with three private sector entities, (BBVA, ING, and the Dutch Association of Industry-wide Pension Funds [VB]) in late 2005 to undertake a program of research on these issues. This introductory chapter provides an overview of the issues and motivation for this work and summarizes the studies that were conducted and their main findings. It concludes with policy-related observations that arise from the overall consideration of the research program. The remainder of the volume contains a selection of the studies undertaken through the partnership that focus on developing approaches to evaluate performance of pension funds and concludes with observations and commentary from four noted experts in the field on the issues raised by this work and the interpretation of the findings.

## The Importance of Appropriate Measures of Performance

The spectacular losses experienced by many pension funds since the onset of the financial crisis in late 2008 have been widely noted and debated. The OECD estimates the losses of pension funds in OECD countries to be $5.4 trillion or about 20 percent of the value of assets in these countries in 2008 (Antolín and Stewart 2009). The returns of pension funds in Latin America and Central Europe in 2008 were two-digit negative.

A focus on short-term nominal returns on investments, however, hides the fact that returns are only one of several factors that will determine the performance of pension funds to provide retirement income to their members. Others factors include administrative and investment management costs, the density of contributions, and the behavior of participants in choosing a retirement age.

The other factors that drive pension benefits in an asset-backed setting have received much research and policy attention in recent years. For instance, countries have designed a variety of mechanisms to reduce costs, including the imposition of caps on fees (Central and Eastern European countries), centralization of collections and the use of blind accounts (Latvia and Sweden), lotteries that allocate new contributors among funds (Chile and Poland), and paperless transactions (Estonia). Policy makers are aware of the alternatives available, and the challenge is to ensure that the alternatives chosen are properly implemented.[1] Collective pension arrangements established by employers and employee associations can also be an effective way to keep costs low, especially when the funds established achieve sufficient scale (for example, Denmark, Iceland, and the Netherlands).

Density of contributions is also an important factor that has affected the pension benefits in countries with large informal sectors. Individuals with a low density of contributions are likely to face low accumulated assets at retirement age, and therefore are likely to have low retirement incomes. The retirement age is also an important factor that affects the performance of pension funds. Because the accumulation period is shorter in countries that allow individuals to retire earlier, individuals are likely to receive lower retirement income. As a consequence, governments in some countries have been raising the official retirement age or have introduced incentives to delay retirement. The capacity of funded individual account systems to deliver retirement income will be further challenged in this respect as life expectancy continues to increase in virtually all countries.

Although these factors are important in the overall performance of pension funds, the focus of this book is on investments and investment performance. It is primarily directed to evaluating what can be learned about the comparative investment performance of pension funds and consideration of how to undertake investment performance measurement within a framework that is derived from the particular characteristics and objectives of pension systems. Developing a performance measurement framework that is specific to pension funds is a relatively new topic in the literature. Since the seminal work of Campbell and Viceira (2002), many other papers have explored the issue of developing an optimal asset allocation for pension funds, which is derived from the principles of life-cycle savings and risk management. The applied research presented in this book represents an initial attempt to link the main themes of the more theoretical academic literature with the available data on the financial performance of pension funds to support the development of practical policy recommendations.

The traditional approach of performance of pension funds has put excessive emphasis on short rates of return. Because the objective of mandatory funded systems is to ensure adequate retirement income to individuals, monthly or annual returns of pension are not totally meaningful if they are not measured against a benchmark or against an objective. In addition, once the alternatives faced by investors are different, international comparisons of returns or other measures of performance such as the Sharpe ratios might not be totally meaningful.

Some policy makers might be less interested in the performance measurement because they expect the market to provide the optimal asset allocation. Also, some governments have the implicit belief that the presence of competition in open DC pension systems helps to optimize the pensions of individuals. Pension fund managers will compete for funds, and individuals will select pension funds that optimize their own risk-reward preferences.

This competitive model assumes that contributors have the ability to identify factors that will determine the capacity to provide retirement income, evaluate the investment performance of pension funds against these factors, and make choices that optimize outcomes in relation to their individual circumstances. In practice, these factors are not readily available or easily understandable by the typical contributor. The information that is provided is usually limited or is a proxy for the relevant factors and, when available, is not easy to understand for most members.

In addition, considerable evidence exists of inertia, decision avoidance, and excessive risk aversion by participants in making choices. Because of the complexity of defining the optimal portfolio allocation, some governments have promoted other sources of competition, which may be irrelevant to the long-term financial performance of funds.[2] Some countries have considered mandating higher levels of information to the public to improve the capacity of contributors to make informed decisions, but these efforts could be wasted because contributors have a limited capacity to understand the complexities of the systems.[3] This problem may be solved in part by improving the financial literacy of individuals, but it may take decades before the average contributor is in a position to make an informed decision about his or her asset allocation.

In the absence of more relevant long-term measures of performance, the existing emphasis on short-term returns creates incentives for pension fund managers to focus their efforts on maximizing short-term returns. However, the funds with better short-term performance are not necessarily those best aligned with the long-run performance of a pension system. The literature on strategic asset allocation provides numerous examples of cases in which short-term asset allocation conflicts with longer-term objectives, including selection of the risk-free asset, international portfolio diversification, and currency hedging strategies. In general, no assurances can be given that competition in the short-term will result in long-term optimal asset allocation (Campbell and Viceira 2002).

Regulatory restrictions on pension fund performance, such as the minimum return guarantee, may create additional disturbance in the equilibrium portfolio allocation that is reached in a competitive framework.

Policy makers have only partially addressed the issue of the investment performance of pension funds. As a way of increasing the contributors' responsibility for their own retirement income, some governments have opened up the number of investment opportunities through the creation of lifestyle pension funds that provide varying asset allocation approaches intended to produce different risk and return outcomes. The assumption implicit in this approach is that participants will be able to assess their own circumstances and select the fund best aligned with their longer-term objectives and risk capacity. However, these actions have not been accompanied by guidance to contributors on strategies that they can employ to optimize their expected pension funds at retirement age.[4] Although lifestyle funds are a step forward in recognizing the heterogeneity in the preferences and needs of individuals, the systems that permit lifestyle funds fail to recognize the complexity of the portfolio decision for the contributors. Governments are not comfortable giving recommendations on portfolio allocation. Although this reluctance is understandable, it is likely to result in individuals making suboptimal portfolio selections and ultimately receiving low levels of pensions in retirement. As documented by Campbell (2006) and Benartzi and Thaler (2007), when unable to make decisions, people tend to rely on simple heuristics that may end up being suboptimal.

One alternative that has developed to try to address the limited ability of participants to assess their optimal risk and return objectives and make adjustments as their age or other circumstances change has been the introduction of what have become known as life-cycle funds. The research presented in this volume provides a strong argument that defining an investment portfolio (and by extension a relevant performance benchmark) that is consistent with the objective of providing a reliable level of income at retirement is a complex challenge that requires consideration of a variety of factors that will vary among individuals on the basis not just of their age but a range of other factors as well. This suggests that to improve the long-term performance of pension funds, regulation will have to move beyond the current reliance on market forces that function through competition and short-term incentives.

The need to rebalance the equilibrium between the government and the market in traditional DC pension systems is an important policy conclusion that can be extracted from this book. A likely way to address the challenge that emerges from the research would be to create a model set of life-cycle pension funds, which can serve as benchmarks against which the performance of pension fund managers can be measured. This would move the basis of competition from short-term returns to trying to beat the benchmark on the model sets. The asset allocation would depend not only on age, but also on other parameters, including contribution rates, density of contributions, benefits from other social insurance programs, patterns of lifetime earnings, risk preferences, and correlations among these factors and asset returns. This suggests a challenging process through which these optimal portfolios for individuals with different characteristics could serve to inform investment choices and provide benchmarks against which the performance of pension fund managers could be measured. It is interesting to observe that such an approach is broadly consistent with the manner in which the control of investments is exercised in a hybrid DB system, such as in the Netherlands, in which asset allocations are regulated in consideration of the targeted, although not guaranteed, benefit stream. As such, it would represent a continuation of the convergence that has begun to render the distinction between traditional DB and DC system increasingly irrelevant.

In this approach, governments will be required to take greater responsibility in defining long-term investment strategies for pension funds. The implication of this interpretation is that by not defining guidelines for investment strategies, governments leave participants subject to day-to-day uncertainty, which diminishes the overall performance and may end up affecting the long-term viability of funded pension systems.[5] The need for moving forward in the creation of life-cycle pension funds can be reinforced by the recent interest in Central European governments in granting some sort of guarantee on the real value of contributions to pension funds. It is postulated that the design of optimal portfolios and benchmarks may help to reduce the cost of these guarantees.[6]

## Overview and Summary of the Book

This book is an effort to bring together the limited information available on the performance of pension funds across a broad range of settings with some of the latest developments in the theoretical literature regarding portfolio allocation to consider how the design of pension systems can be improved to address these limitations. A few policy conclusions can be extracted from this exercise. At the most basic level the work indicates that rates of returns are a very limited indicator of pension fund performance and that the reliance on this indicator can be counterproductive; second, competition may not bring pension portfolios toward the optimal long-term allocation; and third, pension funds need to measure performance against optimal long-term benchmarks, the design of which is essential for optimizing the value of the benefits received at retirement. Finally, it is argued that governments can play an important role in setting up these optimal benchmarks but should not interfere in asset allocation.

The book comprises six main chapters that present a selection of key work undertaken in the research project and four short essays together in a final chapter that provide additional policy observations and reaffirm the analysis in the context of the financial crisis. This introductory chapter summarizes the main issues raised by these studies and key aspects of their findings. The other chapters are organized in a way to allow the reader to move from a review of the available data to a policy discussion about the development of pension-specific benchmarks that are needed to support more meaningful evaluation of pension fund investment performance. The short essays provide observations and commentary about interpretation of the work and about challenges of life-cycle funds in the context of the financial crisis.

After the introductory chapter, the book begins with a chapter by Pablo Antolin and Waldo Tapia. This chapter provides a brief summary of the effort undertaken by the OECD to compile information on privately managed pension funds. This effort yielded data from 23 countries for which data on the financial status and performance of pension fund were available,[7] including a mix of personal and occupational pension systems, as well as DB and DC pension systems.

This chapter provides basic descriptive information on the various pension systems design parameters as well as a summary of the different approaches to investment regulation. The chapter's findings indicate a range of regulatory frameworks that might influence investment outcomes with the various countries imposing limits by instrument category, limits by issuer, limits by risk, minimum return guarantees, and limits on foreign holdings. The descriptive data indicate that among the OECD countries included in the sample, investment regulation is less prescriptive and based on prudent person principles. The information on asset allocation indicates that pension portfolios in Latin America and Central Europe are heavily dominated by allocation to bonds, which, in some cases, reaches above 90 percent of the value of the pension funds. Pension portfolios in industrialized countries show a greater balance between equities and bonds.

The chapter then provides estimates of the real returns for the pension systems of the countries included in the sample, for the period 2001–05, and calculation of the standard deviation of these estimated real returns.

In chapter 3, Eduardo Walker and Augusto Iglesias extend the evaluation of performance using a risk-adjusted sample of returns from pension funds in 11 countries for which adequate data are available to support such an exercise. Their chapter begins with a brief discussion of the applicability of standard measures of financial performance that focuses on the potential use of the Sharpe ratio to measure the ability of pension fund managers to provide a risk premium from the active management of the fund. The authors argue that pension fund performance should be focused on evaluating the value added by portfolio managers with respect to benchmarks. They clarify that performance measures are relative measures, and that to be meaningful they need to be compared against passive investment strategies. Simple measures of performance, such as returns, do not provide any point of reference and therefore are not informative with respect to the value added by managers. High returns of pension funds, for example, might be related to high interest rates in the economy or a country-specific risk premium arising from lack of development of the domestic capital market. Walker and Iglesias discuss different indices that can be used to measure performance and attribution of pension funds. These indices measure the value added by pension funds with respect to a portfolio of the same style, but they do not analyze whether pension portfolios chosen by the managers are optimal or efficient from the perspective of the ability to provide a future level of income replacement.

Walker and Iglesias also counsel against international comparisons of traditional performance measures, including returns, volatility, and Sharpe ratios. They argue that in addition to the differences in investment alternatives, including different risk-free interest rates and different investment alternatives, pension fund managers in different countries are subject to different risks, including exchange rate risk and real interest risk, which make comparisons not meaningful. The authors argue that volatility cannot be considered as a comprehensive measure of risk, because intrinsic risk elements are found in countries with different levels of development. For example, Sharpe ratios tend to vary overtime and across asset classes, and therefore comparing pension funds that have invested differently or in different time frames may not always be relevant.

Walker and Iglesias use monthly data to calculate the Sharpe ratio for the pension funds of a sample of 11 countries.[8] Performance is calculated against four proxies for the risk-free rate: a short-term local rate, a local long-term rate, a short-term U.S. Treasury bills rate, and the annual return on long-term U.S. Treasury bonds. They find that nearly all of the pension systems that they are able to examine have been able to deliver a significant risk premium over short-term local and U.S. interest rates, but the evidence is more mixed when the premium is evaluated against long-term interest rates. Two countries in the sample reported negative value added against long-term benchmarks, because pension funds invested in short-term assets in periods in which long-term interest rates were falling.

Chapter 4 begins the discussion of the development of benchmarks by examining the potential impact of imposing minimum return guarantees, such as are currently in place in several countries. This addresses one of the threshold questions regarding the common belief that competition would drive portfolios toward optimal levels. In this chapter Pablo Castañeda and Heinz P. Rudolph analyze the equilibrium portfolios that can be reached when pension fund managers are subject to performance restrictions, such as minimum return guarantees. The analysis is based on a standard model of dynamic portfolio choice but includes strategic interaction among portfolio managers through relative performance constraints. The model follows the seminal work of Basak and Makarov (2008), which analyzes the portfolio equilibrium in the absence of restrictions and finds that portfolio allocation without performance measures can lead pension portfolios to single equilibrium, multiple equilibria, or no equilibrium at all. In this literature a pension system with multiple options in which individuals have limited capacity to understand the available options is likely to end up in multiple equilibria, suboptimal asset allocation, and low pensions for individuals in the future.

The equilibrium portfolios in the model used by Castañeda and Rudolph are a weighted average of portfolio policies that are optimal for different possible scenarios. The scenarios correspond to cases that are not restricted by the minimum return guarantees and in which at least one manager is restricted. The model shows that relative performance concerns play a crucial role in determining the optimal portfolios.

Depending on the relative performance constraints, Castañeda and Rudolph conclude that pension fund managers can move portfolio allocations to suboptimal levels. The authors suggest that in the presence of minimum return guarantees, and when pension fund managers are too prone to relative return standards, portfolio allocation may converge toward myopic portfolio allocation. In these circumstances the use of exogenously defined single-index benchmark portfolios can help to move pension portfolios toward optimal allocations. The main policy lesson that can be extracted from chapter 4 is that competition does not guarantee equilibrium with optimal portfolio allocation, and the presence of a minimum return guarantee may exacerbate the divergence with an optimal portfolio.

Chapter 5 by Olivia Mitchell and John Turner discusses the impact of human capital risk on the design of optimal portfolio allocation of pension funds. The authors suggest that employment volatility and fluctuations in labor earnings may have different effects on human capital accumulation and income replacement targets that will show an important impact on the way in which pension portfolios are designed.

Mitchell and Turner open the discussion with the need to define properly the concept of income replacement rate, which they perceive as the ultimate outcome measure relevant to evaluating the performance of pension funds. Income replacement rates are defined as the amount of income that a retiree receives from his or her pension compared with some level of pre-retirement income. This measure requires comparison of workers' pre-retirement income flows and the resulting or expected flows in retirement. However, there is still disagreement about the correct measurement of this ratio, including the period to cover with regard to the earnings in the denominator (whether it is income immediately before retirement, in a few peak years, or entire average pay), net or gross income, and the indexation rule of the benefits. In addition, Mitchell and Turner discuss the impact of other factors, including labor income shocks, and how they will have differing effects in DB systems and DC systems. This discussion highlights the importance of differences in the regulatory framework, which are especially important in how they may affect portability of benefits in DB systems when participants change jobs, the potential risks of bankruptcy of the pension plans, and the uncertainty about how shocks to labor income influence benefit payments within different system designs and regulatory regimes. This chapter also discusses the importance of the density of contributions on the future level of pensions in DC systems.

Chapter 5 explores how human capital risks translate into pension outcomes in different types of system designs, including DB, DC, and the recently emerging collective DC systems. Mitchell and Turner analyze the effects of wage-related shocks (skill obsolescence, health shock, disability shock, and labor force shock) and employment shocks (reduction of working hours, retrenchment, and retirement) on these pension systems. The analysis highlights that the typically assumed "classic humped-shape earnings profile" may not be empirically sustainable and that the effects of different earning distributions may have an important effect on portfolio allocation. This leads to the conclusion that the diversity of patterns in wage distribution should be taken into consideration when pension portfolio allocations are decided. Mitchell and Turner suggest that to create a more realistic picture of the variability in labor earnings and employment patterns over the life cycle, countries will need to invest in longitudinal surveys of earning and employment patterns to obtain the information tracking individual workers over time that is necessary to inform the development of portfolios that are suited to the significant variations in human capital.

The focus of attention in chapters 6 and 7 is on developing methods to incorporate the ideas introduced in the earlier chapters into the formulation of a portfolio allocation that optimizes the ability of pension funds to smooth consumption and hedge the impact of human capital volatility to better achieve the income replacement objective of pension funds.

Optimal portfolio allocation requires a sophisticated approach that includes an intertemporal optimization of pension portfolios, which needs to take into consideration numerous variables, including the risks of the different financial instruments, age of individuals, human capital risk, and individual preferences. Policy makers in some countries feel confident that defining a limited number of lifestyle pension funds (typically between three and five) differentiated by boundaries on equity exposure is enough to design an optimal path of accumulation of pension funds. These chapters show that lifestyle funds are insufficient to create an optimal path of retirement savings but can create the illusion to contributors that they are doing so.

To put these two chapters in perspective, life-cycle funds need to be built on well-defined benchmarks, and, consequently, regulations that solely impose maximum limits on different asset classes might not be enough to optimize the future pensions of individuals. For example, in a world where all equity instruments are homogenous, the only decision of individuals is the allocation to equities versus fixed-income securities. The lifestyle approach does not solve the problem of how much equity contributors need at each moment of time.[9] In current practice, the maximum exposure to equity tends to vary by country, being, for example, 80 percent, 50 percent, and 30 percent for the cases of Chile, Estonia, and Mexico, respectively.[10] The maximum exposure to equity in these countries has not been derived from any optimization model and therefore cannot guide the decision of participants about the level of equity exposure that they should seek. Because lifestyle models also do not provide guidance about the preferred portfolio allocation, contributors are subject to the risk of underperforming returns.

The introduction of heterogeneity into the equity component complicates the situation even more. As many countries have experienced, pension funds may overinvest in equity in emerging economies, which might be optimal from a short-term perspective but suboptimal from the perspective of optimal portfolio allocation. Walker (2006) argues that in the late 1990s Chilean pension funds had invested about 70 percent of the equity portfolio in the energy sector in Chile, which implies a high level of concentration in one particular sector, which is suboptimal from any perspective. Simple restrictions on maximum equity exposure without issuer or sector limits by pension might not prevent poor diversification of portfolios.

Examples can be given of short-term asset allocation not optimizing long-term portfolios and, consequently, acting against the long-term objectives of pension funds. Where the interest rate yield curve has been in backwardation and with the incentives that focused on short-term returns, many pension fund managers in convergence countries preferred to take short-term positions contrary to the objectives of the funds and, with few exceptions, have performed significantly worse than had they invested in long-term positions. Chilean pension funds between 2003 and 2007 experienced an economic climate of favorable terms of trade and the evolution of other macroeconomic aggregates, resulting in the domestic currency's appreciating against the dollar. During this period Chilean pension funds hedged most of their currency exposure to maintain returns that were comparable with their competitors. In the second half of 2008, during the global crisis, the local currency depreciated by about 30 percent, and the main equity indices collapsed by about 40 percent. Pension funds were not able to benefit from the currency depreciation and suffered the cost of the collapse of the international stock prices, apart from the implicit cost of the currency insurance. The literature (Campbell, Serfaty-de Medeiros, and Viceira 2009) shows that global falls in stock prices are correlated with appreciations in reserve currencies, and therefore pension funds should have kept unhedged currency positions. Finally, it is interesting to see that DC pension funds that mark to market their portfolios tend to avoid investing even a small part of their portfolio in instruments with longer maturities, such as venture capital. The risk of these instruments is not the main impediment for investing in them, but the fact that returns in these instruments can typically be expected only after the fifth year. A pension fund that cannot show immediate results would be disadvantaged compared with its competitors that can show better short-term returns simply by investing in short-term deposits. There is therefore a bias against investing in instruments that cannot provide an immediate return.

Chapter 6 by Fabio Bagliano, Carolina Fugazza, and Giovanna Nicodano addresses a number of methodological issues necessary to develop a life-cycle model for optimal asset allocation of pension funds. The chapter also explores the relationships between strategic asset allocation and the degree of investor risk aversion and level of replacement rates. The model uses one riskless and two risky assets and introduces a positive correlation between equity returns and labor income. It reaches a key finding that income risk and correlation of equity returns to income shocks result in reductions to the optimal allocation of equities at any age.

The model is calibrated with parameters that are typically used in the United States and is used to predict an optimal portfolio allocation for

DC pension funds. One interesting finding of Bagliano, Fugazza, and Nicodano is that the presence of idiosyncratic labor income shocks generates substantial heterogeneity in the pattern of financial wealth accumulation over time. Consequently, there is a potentially wide dispersion of the optimal portfolios across individuals of the same age. However, the dispersion tends to decrease as individuals approach retirement age. The results suggest that the optimal allocation needs to be implemented through diversified investment options that will vary by multiple parameters, including occupation, age, and risk aversion.

The results suggest that the welfare losses of grouping individuals along a defined set of benchmarks might not be as high as expected. Although models suggest an optimal asset allocation for each individual, this chapter validates the alternative of grouping individuals among benchmarks. Chapter 6 also discusses the welfare implications of suboptimal strategies; an age rule, which allocates (100 − age) percent to the risky portfolio; and the $1/N$ strategy, in which the portfolio is simply distributed equally among the available asset classes. The results confirm that applying these simple rules would have welfare costs in the range of 2–3 percent, but the cost varies depending on the degree of risk aversion, the financial wealth of individuals, and the correlation between retirement income and equity returns. In any case, simulations show consistently that welfare costs are lower in the case of the $1/N$ strategy compared with the age strategy. It is also noted that, using a proposed metric, the welfare loss for these presumed passive strategies is similar if not less than the costs of active management.

Chapter 6 proposes that the performance of pension funds should be measured against a benchmark, but in terms of welfare, as opposed to simple returns. Traditional methods for performance evaluation of mutual funds are based on returns compared with the benchmark. These methods rely on the concept that a higher return to risk differential maps into better performance, overlooking the pension fund's ability to hedge labor income risk and pension risk of plan participants. In traditional methods of performance evaluation, it is not easy to identify whether performance is due to strategic asset allocation or short-term timing and security selection. Bagliano, Fugazza, and Nicodano suggest computing welfare ratios as the ratio of the worker's ex ante maximum welfare under optimal asset allocation, with his or her welfare level under the actual pension fund asset allocation. The advantage of measuring performance in terms of welfare is that higher welfare may be due not only to a higher return per unit of financial risk earned by the pension fund, but also to a better matching between the pension fund portfolio and its members' labor income and pension risks.

Chapter 7 by Luis Viceira summarizes the policy recommendations that come out of the literature about strategic asset allocation for individuals. It suggests that asset allocation depends on a number of factors, including age, human capital, correlation between labor income and equity returns, the rate of contribution, and the presence of other sources of retirement income. The literature on strategic asset allocation assumes that individuals want to have the same asset allocation at all times, but the allocation takes into consideration not only financial wealth but also human wealth. The wealth of individuals is composed of both financial wealth and human capital wealth. Unlike financial wealth, human wealth in not tradable, and working investors can monetize only the dividends paid out by their human wealth, which are their labor earnings. Because they have not yet had the opportunity to accumulate savings, human wealth of young individuals typically represents the largest fraction of their wealth. For individuals close to retirement age, the opposite is true. Because the human wealth of individuals with safe jobs is equivalent to holding an implicit bond, young individuals are likely to compensate for this with a greater proportion of equity in their portfolios.

These findings are generalized through a discussion about the effects of the correlation between labor income and equity returns on portfolio allocation, which suggests that the higher this correlation, the lower should be the proportion of equity in pension portfolios. Viceira conducts a useful discussion about the effects of other sources of retirement income on portfolio composition of mandatory pension funds, which may help to explain differences in portfolio allocation across countries. Because the structure of benefits offered by public retirement systems (Social Security) could be seen as equivalent to a bond, in terms of individual wealth, contributors in countries with multipillar systems are expected to have a higher proportion of equity compared with countries with mandatory funded systems as the only source of retirement income. The author also observes that the rate of contribution is an important factor explaining the portfolio allocation among countries, and therefore two similar countries that differ only in terms of the contribution rate are expected to have different portfolio allocations if both aim to have similar replacement rates.

Viceira observes in chapter 7 that no fixed-income instrument is fully adequate for pension portfolios. Although cash instruments, such as Treasury bills, are a risk-free asset for short-term investments, they are not risk-free assets for long-term investors, as are pension funds, because of the reinvestment risk and inflation risk. Although government long-term bonds provide protection against reinvestment risks, they do not protect the real value of the investments. Inflation is a still a major threat to the value of assets in both developed and emerging markets. Therefore long-term inflation-indexed bonds are the only true riskless asset for long-term investors.

Several key issues of asset management relevant to implementing optimal portfolios are addressed in the chapter. Although inflation-indexed bonds provide the safest investment option for working investors, in the absence of these instruments it is suggested that pension funds hold short-term bonds denominated in foreign currencies in countries with stable inflation and real interest rates. In the case of equity, the author observes that the evidence about the long-term benefits of investing in equities is not associated with a particular instrument but to international well-diversified portfolios. National equity markets are subject to country risk, and therefore excessive reliance on local equity markets imposes a risk on the value of the pension funds.

The question of currency exposure is also discussed. The conventional practice of fully hedging currency exposures is optimal only when excess returns to equity are uncorrelated with those to currency. However, currencies in emerging economies tend to be negatively correlated with the dollar and tend to appreciate when global stock markets fall. Therefore, contrary to conventional practice, pension funds in most emerging economies should keep unhedged positions in their equity exposure. The short-term volatility created by unhedged currency positions is more than compensated by the natural hedge and returns that are achieved in the medium and long term.

Chapter 7 concludes with an application of these concepts to an emerging economy and compares performance of multiple portfolios, including full investment in government bonds, full investment in domestic equity, full investment in global equity, and life-cycle pension funds. The analysis explores the benefits of inflation-indexed bonds and international equity diversification, as well as the advantages of life-cycle funds over alternative strategies, such as constant positions along the life-cycle and lifestyle pension fund line. The analysis shows that life-cycle funds do not perform worse and in most cases perform better than alternatives, such as lifestyle funds, in terms of the expected asset accumulation at retirement and the volatility that they can provide. Simulations are run with nominal and inflation-indexed instruments. In addition, the simulations suggest that the volatility of the resulting income is higher when nominal bonds (instead of inflation-indexed bonds) are considered in the portfolio. The analysis is supported by numerous simulations that consider nonstochastic labor income, stochastic labor income uncorrelated with equity returns, and stochastic labor income correlated with equity returns.

Viceira states that the optimal design of the glide path for life-cycle pension funds is sensitive to the risk tolerance of the plan participant. In particular, participants with low risk tolerance experience welfare losses if they are forced to adopt life-cycle funds with the average high-equity allocations that are optimal for medium risk tolerance participants. This leads to the conclusion that, on the basis of risk tolerance, life-cycle funds dominate other strategies, including lifestyle funds. The chapter further concludes that contributors can fully exploit the benefits of funded systems by having a well-designed asset portfolio allocation and, therefore, properly designed default investment options that can reduce the risks and potentially improve the long-term expected asset accumulation of contributors.

The last chapter comprises four essays that summarize the views of well-known experts on pension policy and pension fund management who participated in a January 2009 seminar in Mexico City, in which the research work from the partnership was presented and discussed. These commentaries are focused on factors that will influence the performance of pension funds and the future of optimal portfolio allocation in the context of the financial crisis.

In the first essay, Keith Ambachtsheer addresses the importance of well-designed "retirement income systems." He emphasizes the need not only to develop effective asset management methods but also to create institutions that are able to deliver value to their stakeholders, noting in particular the need to better provide for the payout of benefits in retirement. He views the financial crisis as revealing weaknesses not only in portfolio strategies but also in the overall effectiveness of pension systems. Olivia Mitchell similarly focuses on the need to effectively define the desired outcome and measurement metrics for pension systems. She notes that consumption smoothing is ultimately the purpose of any pension system, and she identifies the challenges attendant to measuring consumption and integrating this into system outcome metrics. She views the recent financial crisis as revealing a variety of challenges before pension policy makers, including holding down fees and expenses, creating system designs that are consistent with the level of financial literacy among their members, implementing the pay-out phase, and effectively managing portfolio risks.

Luis Viciera's commentary provides practical advice about how to effectively implement life-cycle strategies in funded systems. After emphasizing the importance of controlling costs and creating a proper institutional design for pension funds, he outlines the limitations of standard performance measurement methods when they are applied to pension funds. This provides a foundation for exogenously designing meaningful long-term benchmarks for pension funds. He suggests the creation of expert panels to define these benchmarks.

The final commentary, by Zvi Bodie, initially emphasizes the theoretical appeal of the life-cycle approach to portfolio design but then moves on to outline the practical challenges in implementing such an approach. He concludes that the benefits obtained from the life-cycle approach are unlikely to warrant the costs and complexity; he suggests instead that the relatively simple approach of investing in inflation-indexed bonds would potentially achieve similar net results.

## Policy Implications of the Research Findings

The research highlights the potential to improve the effectiveness of pension funds to achieve their ultimate objective of providing income replacement in retirement by developing portfolio strategies that adopt a long-term horizon and consider the influence of a range of human capital and other preferences in the formulation of asset allocation strategies. These optimal portfolios could provide a useful benchmark to evaluate the performance of fund managers that would considerably improve the value of performance measurement in relation to the methods now used that are derived from evaluation of other types of investment management with very different attributes from pension funds. Without portfolio design and performance measurement criteria that are explicitly derived from consideration of the particular nature of pension funds, the theory and evidence presented in this volume indicate that reliance on market competition with minimal criteria for investment strategies will not result in an investment portfolio that will effectively achieve the goal of consumption smoothing and income replacement.

This suggests the need to find a better balance between the role of the market and the role of the government in enhancing the performance of pension funds and reducing the risks of pension shortfalls due to inefficiencies in portfolio allocation. Consequently, governments and their pension supervisors should consider a more active role in evaluating and proposing the long-term objectives of pension funds for various categories of workers and defining benchmark portfolios that can be used to guide the design of funds, facilitate choice among funds, and provide more meaningful performance evaluation. This could lead to important improvements in establishing default options. Although this imposes a more explicit responsibility on governments (because they will share in the pension outcomes), the increase in responsibility is largely illusory.

Simply offering a large number of lifestyle pension funds might not be enough to achieve the full potential of funded retirement savings arrangements because most individuals do not have the capacity to understand the complexities of intertemporal asset allocation, which may take into consideration various parameters, including age, human capital risk, other sources of revenue, and risk aversion. Furthermore, cost considerations need to be addressed. In this context, collective schemes offer a balanced alternative to some countries. Even more so, lifestyle pension funds may also misguide individuals about their portfolio decisions because an asset allocation considered to be aggressive at a certain age can be considered conservative at a different age. Significant gains can accrue from providing individuals with appropriate benchmarks that enable them to evaluate the performance of the funds offered in relation to a strategy that considers a broader scope of relevant factors. For example, in the case of mandatory collective programs, investments do not rely on the financial literacy of individuals, but on investment professionals with well-aligned incentives.[11] Given the well-documented limitations of the majority of participants in funded pension systems to interpret financial performance information and make choices consistent with their need to manage risks and achieve optimal levels of retirement income, default choices are essential to the operation of a pension system that offers individual choice. The experience of countries with mandatory lifestyle funds shows that individuals tend to rely heavily on default options.[12]

The evidence provided in this volume demonstrates that the technical aspects of determining the strategic asset allocation of the default options impose a difficult, but not impossible, task. The main challenge is likely to be to ensure that any performance benchmarks are created without political interference. One approach that merits consideration would be to utilize a body of independent experts, with enough resources to conduct analytical studies on the strategic asset allocation for pension funds, to define optimal strategies and the associated benchmarks for different characteristics and attributes of workers. The benchmarks would be expected to be set for long periods but might need to be reviewed if major changes occur in investment markets. The easiest way to design benchmarks for life-cycle funds would be to connect them to the retirement age of different cohorts. To reflect the heterogeneity in the risk tolerance of individuals belonging to the same cohort, it would be necessary to define a limited number (two or three) of benchmark portfolios for each cohort.[13]

This would require the adoption of a risk-based approach to supervision and necessitate a strong reliance on reliable disclosure to market participants to provide simple and reliable signals to individuals about the funds best matching their requirements and the performance of those funds. Because the performance of pension funds would be measured relative to the benchmark, the supervisory authorities would need to have in place a mechanism that would allow them to measure the risks of the pension fund system in a comprehensive manner.

The welfare analysis proposed by Bagliano, Fugazza and Nicodano in chapter 6 can be translated into the design of a "traffic light system" for monitoring the performance of pension funds. The traffic light system is one of the simplest ways of encouraging proper market surveillance of pension funds. Traffic light systems are easy to understand but require clear parameters and explicit models that can identify the risks of the portfolio allocations that differ from the benchmarks.[14]

Pension funds would be assigned a rating (color) that reflect their performance and the risk management capacity of the pension fund managers. Green light pension funds are those that have a portfolio structure aligned with the benchmark and have a good risk management system. The yellow light pension funds are those with weaker risk management systems and a higher probability of deviating from the benchmark. Funds assigned a red light would be those with portfolio structures substantially different from the benchmark or with weak enough risk management that they would have a high probability of substantial deviations in the future. The supervisor should be empowered to impose restrictions on pension funds in the yellow and red zones and mandate improvements within a certain period of time. Pension funds in the red zone must present a plan for moving to the green zone and should not be allowed to bring in new contributors until they have addressed the deficiencies identified by the supervisor. Clients should be made aware when a pension fund migrates from one zone to another. In a more advanced model, these ratings would also be different in relation to individuals of different age or other attributes for the same fund.

In countries that choose individual DC systems, people should be free to select the life-cycle portfolio that best accommodates their risk appetite, but the default options for individuals who do not opt for a particular pension fund should be carefully designed. Governments are encouraged to use age and scoring mechanisms to identify the default options for individuals who do not select a particular fund.[15] It is unrealistic to assume that it is cost effective to design pension funds that may fit in the characteristics of each individual, but the benchmarks for the same cohort should provide a broad approximation to the individual's preferences. The development of the scoring method is an important challenge to allocate individuals into the different benchmarks.

In summary, through the creation of a commission of wise persons, governments should assume responsibility for setting up benchmarks that may optimize the expected pensions of individuals. Pension funds should compete on the basis of these benchmarks within a similar risk structure. This book addresses the challenges of constructing these benchmarks and the variables that should be considered. To some degree this will be determined by the availability of financial instruments; however, notwithstanding the level of financial market development, these benchmarks should consider the following factors:

a. The presence of other sources of retirement income, including the income from public retirement schemes
b. The age of individuals
c. The rate of contributions
d. The target replacement rate and its downside tolerance
e. A matrix of correlations between labor income and equity returns[16]
f. The expected density of contributions for different categories of workers
g. The type of retirement income in the payout phase, in particular the risk tolerance of pensioners in the payout phase (for example, real fixed annuities, variable annuities, and phased withdrawals)
h. A parameter that reflect the risk aversion of policy makers.

Introducing a system of performance benchmarks that are based on parameters that specifically consider the ability of the fund's investment strategy to deliver retirement income will significantly improve the efficiency of retirement savings. The optimal portfolios derived from this process can both serve as guidelines for default investment choices that are better aligned with the needs of different groups of participants and provide benchmarks that permit meaningful evaluation of the performance of fund managers. The use of pension investment performance benchmarks would represent one of the more important innovations in pension systems and further advance the increasing convergence of DB and DC designs.

## Notes

1. Valdes (2005); Calderón, Domínguez, and Schwartz (2008); and Impavido, Lasagabaster, and Garcia-Huitron (2009) have addressed the issue of costs.
2. For example, competition on the quality of service in the case of Chile.
3. For example, in 2007 the Lithuanian Association of Asset Managers proposed to make available to the public the Sharpe ratios.
4. Lifestyle funds or balanced funds are funds that rebalance their holdings automatically toward a target asset mix that remains constant over time. Life-cycle pension funds change the asset allocation over time toward more fixed-income instruments as individuals get closer to retirement age.
5. Experiences such as that of Argentina in 2008 reflect the view that governments may take a short-term view of market risk in DC pension systems.
6. These guarantees may be expensive and subject to moral hazard if they are managed in the context of lifestyle funds, but they can be much less expensive and with minimum moral hazard if they are offered in the context of optimal life-cycle benchmarks.
7. The sample includes Argentina, Bolivia, Brazil, Chile, Colombia, Costa Rica, El Salvador, Mexico, Peru, and Uruguay from Latin America; the Czech Republic, Estonia, Hungary, Kazakhstan, and Poland from Central and Eastern Europe; Australia, Canada, Japan, the Netherlands, Sweden, the United Kingdom, and the United States from the OECD; and the Hong Kong economy.
8. Chapter 3 includes the following countries: Argentina, Bolivia, Chile, Estonia, Hungary, Mexico, the Netherlands, Peru, Poland, the United Kingdom, and Uruguay.
9. Leaving that decision to contributors, who are clearly unable to make an informed decision.
10. In the Mexican case, starting from a maximum equity exposure of 30 percent of the fund, the regulation requires 27-year-old contributors to start moving to more conservative portfolios.
11. Collective systems have the additional advantage of requiring changes in the contribution rates, depending on the performance of the funds.
12. For example, in Chile, about two-thirds of contributors have opted for the default option since lifestyle funds (multifunds) were introduced in 2002. In Sweden about 90 percent of new entrants are selecting the default options.
13. As the number of benchmarks increases, the capacity to compare funds decreases.

14. On a more restricted basis, the Danish Financial Sector Authority applies a traffic light system to supervise life insurance companies and pension funds in Denmark. See Van Dam and Andersen (2008).

15. Although some countries have moved in the direction of creating a role for financial advisers to advise contributors, the authors see that approach as more expensive and inefficient.

16. The correlation with the returns of other financial instruments might also be considered.

## References

Antolín, Pablo, and Fiona Stewart. 2009. "Private Pensions and Policy Responses to the Financial and Economic Crisis." OECD Working Paper on Insurance and Private Pensions no. 36. Organisation for Economic Co-operation and Development, Paris.

Basak, Suleyman, and Dmitry Makarov. 2008. "Strategic Asset Allocation with Relative Performance Concerns." Working Paper, London Business School.

Benartzi, Shlomo, and Richard Thaler. 2007. "Heuristics and Biases in Retirement Savings Behavior." *Journal of Economic Perspectives* 21 (3): 81–104.

Calderón-Colín, Roberto, Enrique E. Domínguez, and Moisés J. Schwartz. 2008. "Consumer Confusion: The Choice of AFORE in Mexico." Draft, Consar Mexico.

Campbell, John Y. 2006. "Household Finance." *Journal of Finance* 61: 1553–1604.

Campbell, John Y., Karine Serfaty-de Medeiros, and Luis M. Viceira. 2010. "Global Currency Hedging." *Journal of Finance,* forthcoming.

Campbell John Y., and Luis Viceira. 2002. *Strategic Asset Allocation: Portfolio Choice for Long-Term Investors.* Oxford: Oxford University Press.

Impavido, Gregorio, Esperanza Lasagabaster, and Manuel Garcia-Huitron. 2009. *Competition and Asset Allocation Changes for Mandatory DC Pensions: New Policy Direction.* Washington, DC: World Bank.

Valdes, Salvador. 2005. "Para aumentar la competencia entre las AFP." *Estudios Públicos* 98 (autumn): 87–142.

Van Dam, Rein, and Erik B. Andersen. 2008. "Risk-Based Supervision of Pension Institutions in Denmark." In *Risk-Based Supervision of Pension Funds: Emerging Practices and Challenges,* edited by G. Brunner, R. Hinz, and R. Rocha, 95–134. Washington, DC: World Bank.

Walker, Eduardo. 2006. "Benchmarks, Risks, Returns and Incentives in Defined Contribution Pension Funds: Assessing Alternative Institutional Settings." Draft, Pontificia Universidad Católica de Chile.

# CHAPTER 2

# Investment Performance of Privately Managed Pension Funds: Overview of the Available Data

## Pablo Antolín and Waldo Tapia

This chapter provides an overview and basic tabulations and initial analysis of the data collected by the Organisation for Economic Co-operation and Development (OECD) on the aggregate investment performance of pension systems in the countries for which meaningful data series were available.[1]

It begins with a description of privately managed pension funds that are contained in the database. The chapter describes the types of pension funds and the regulatory environment in which they operate and compares the various pension systems according to the total assets under management and the allocation of investments among fixed-income and equity instruments. This is followed by a brief discussion of the challenges and limitations imposed by the way in which the data are reported by different countries and tabulations of the reported returns and standard deviations that are calculated from the data. The chapter concludes with observations derived from review of the data.

## Description of Privately Managed Pension Funds around the World

Sufficient data are available from a variety of sources to provide an initial assessment of the financial performance of privately managed pension funds in Latin America and Central and Eastern Europe, as well as selected OECD countries (Tapia 2008b). The reported data collected by the OECD in 2007 provide a comparative description of the privately managed pension funds in 23 countries. For this purpose, they classify the countries in terms of (1) whether the pension funds are mainly occupational or personal,[2] (2) the prevalence of defined benefit (DB) or defined contribution (DC) pension plans, and (3) the nature of investment regulations to which pension plans are subject. Second, it presents an international comparison of the privately managed pension funds in terms of the total value of pension assets under management, the level of assets as a percentage of the economy, and the allocation of pension assets among the major asset categories. The way in which the value of assets is presented is then described. The last part of this section presents an initial overview of the investment performance of the privately managed pension funds. It provides annual real rates of return and annual geometric and average real returns for all countries for the period for which data are available (December 2000–December 2005). The data on reported returns are asset-weighted average gross investment returns across countries in nominal and real terms in the local currency.[3]

The first step in the effort was to compile data on investment performance of pension funds across countries. This was done by collecting information from each country's regulators and pension fund associations on membership, total assets under management, portfolio composition, investment return, and commissions and fees charged. In addition, information was collected on the investment regulations, asset valuation, and the methodology used to calculate investment returns. Unfortunately, the available data are not complete. Data on returns are provided only on a monthly basis for a few (mostly, Latin American) countries. Most other countries report only annual data. The available data on commissions and fees are very limited and do not allow distinguishing between the different costs, for example, investment costs.

### Types of Privately Managed Pension Funds Included in This Chapter

A large variety of pension arrangements are seen across countries (table 2.1).[4] Pension provision through privately managed pension

**Table 2.1 Privately Managed Pension Funds Included in This Study, by Country and Form of Provision**

| Area | Country | Date | Mandatory Occupational | Mandatory Personal | Voluntary Occupational | Voluntary Personal | % DB | % DC |
|---|---|---|---|---|---|---|---|---|
| Latin America | Argentina | 1994 | | ✓ | | | 0 | 100 |
| | Bolivia | 1997 | | ✓ | | | 0 | 100 |
| | Brazil | 1977 | | | ✓ | | 0 | 100 |
| | Chile | 1981 | | ✓ | | | 0 | 100 |
| | Colombia | 1994 | | ✓ | | | 0 | 100 |
| | Costa Rica | 2001 | | ✓ | | ✓ | 0 | 100 |
| | El Salvador | 1998 | | ✓ | | | 0 | 100 |
| | Mexico | 1998 | | ✓ | | | 0 | 100 |
| | Peru | 1993 | | ✓ | | | 0 | 100 |
| | Uruguay | 1996 | | ✓ | | | 0 | 100 |
| CEE | Czech Republic | 1994 | | | | ✓ | 0 | 100 |
| | Estonia | 2002 | | ✓ | | | 0 | 100 |
| | Hungary | 1998 | | ✓ | | ✓ | 0 | 100 |
| | Kazakhstan | 1998 | | ✓ | | | 0 | 100 |
| | Poland | 1999 | | ✓ | | | 0 | 100 |
| North America | Canada | 1965 | | | ✓ | | 84 | 16 |
| | United States | 1947 | | | ✓ | | 71 | 29 |
| Western Europe | Netherlands | 1952 | ✓ | | | | 95 | 5 |
| | Sweden | 1967/2000 | ✓ | | ✓ | | 90 | 5 |
| | United Kingdom | 1834 | | | ✓ | | 79 | 21 |
| Asia - Pacific | Australia | 1992 | ✓ | | | | 10 | 90 |
| | Hong Kong economy | 2000 | ✓ | | | | 0 | 100 |
| | Japan | 1944 | | | ✓ | | 99 | 1 |

*Source:* Tapia 2007b, OECD, Global Pension Statistics.

plans is through systems that are both mandatory and voluntary, and pension plans are linked through an employment relationship, making them occupational pension plans, or are solely on an individual basis and classified as personal plans. Moreover, pension systems are organized on a DC or DB basis.

Occupational pension plans are dominant in Western Europe, North America, Asia-Pacific countries, and Brazil. These plans are voluntary in the United Kingdom and the United States, mandatory in Australia, and quasi-mandatory (that is, most workers are enrolled as a result of employment agreements between unions and employers) in the Netherlands. Latin American and Central and Eastern European (CEE) countries, on the other hand, rely mainly on mandatory personal pension arrangements.

Occupational pension plans in OECD countries have traditionally been structured as DB plans. However, recent years have seen a pronounced shift from DB to DC plans, in particular in the United Kingdom and the United States. In these countries, companies have closed or frozen their DB plans or have converted them to DC plans. In contrast, occupational pension plans in the Netherlands and Sweden have mainly preserved their DB character, although in recent years many plans have introduced DC features. Occupational systems in Australia and the Hong Kong, China economy offer mainly DC plans. Unlike the variation in occupational pension provision, personal pension plans are entirely of the DC type. These include the Swedish personal pension plans (the Premium Pension System), which are a fully funded DC system based on individual accounts. The characteristics of the pension systems included in the study are shown in table 2.1.

### The Regulatory Investment Environment

Portfolio regulation for privately managed pension funds can follow the prudent person principle or be based on quantitative portfolio restrictions (or a combination of the two). The prudent person focuses on regulating the decision-making process and behavior of investment managers rather than imposing specific restrictions on permissible investments or limits by investment category. The quantitative approach prescribes various investment limits not only in terms of allowing types of investments but also in relation to asset allocation that investment managers are obliged to follow in managing the portfolio of pension funds. Table 2.2 summarizes the main differences in investment regulation across the different countries. Pension funds in Anglo-Saxon countries generally follow the prudent

**Table 2.2  Investment Regulations**

| Area | Country | Investment only in authorized instrument | Limits by instruments | Limits by set of instruments | Limits by issuer | Limits by risk | Minimum return guarantees | Foreign limits |
|---|---|---|---|---|---|---|---|---|
| Latin America | Argentina | ✓ | ✓ | | ✓ | ✓ | ✓ | ✓ |
| | Bolivia | ✓ | ✓ | | ✓ | ✓ | | ✓ |
| | Brazil | ✓ | ✓ | ✓ | ✓ | ✓ | | ✓ |
| | Chile | ✓ | ✓ | ✓ | ✓ | ✓ | ✓ | ✓ |
| | Colombia | ✓ | ✓ | ✓ | ✓ | ✓ | ✓ | ✓ |
| | Costa Rica | ✓ | ✓ | ✓ | ✓ | ✓ | ✓ | ✓ |
| | El Salvador | ✓ | ✓ | ✓ | ✓ | ✓ | ✓ | ✓ |
| | Mexico | ✓ | ✓ | ✓ | ✓ | ✓ | | ✓ |
| | Peru | ✓ | ✓ | ✓ | ✓ | ✓ | ✓ | ✓ |
| | Uruguay | ✓ | ✓ | ✓ | ✓ | ✓ | ✓ | ✓ |
| CEE | Czech Republic | ✓ | ✓ | | ✓ | | | ✓ |
| | Estonia | ✓ | ✓ | | ✓ | | | ✓ |
| | Hungary | ✓ | ✓ | | ✓ | | | ✓ |
| | Kazakhstan | ✓ | ✓ | | ✓ | | | ✓ |
| | Poland | ✓ | ✓ | ✓ | ✓ | | | ✓ |
| North America | Canada | ✓ | ✓ | | ✓ | | | |
| | United States | | | | | | | |
| Western Europe | Netherlands | | | | | | | |
| | Sweden | | ✓ | | ✓ | | | |
| | United Kingdom | | | | | | | |
| Asia – Pacific | Australia | | | | | | | |
| | Hong Kong economy | | | | | | | |
| | Japan | | | | | | | |

*Source:* Tapia 2007b.

person principle, whereas Latin American and CEE countries have tended to adopt a quantitative limit approach as their core regulatory mechanism.

The investment regulation of private funds is typically associated with the level of development of the respective capital markets and other related factors. For example, the relatively underdeveloped capital markets in Latin American and CEE countries are linked to the strict investment regulation in these countries. On the other hand, pension funds in countries with better-developed capital markets generally are associated with the more flexible prudent person regulatory framework. Additionally, mandatory retirement savings arrangements impose greater responsibility on the government than do voluntary arrangements. Under mandatory arrangements, governments typically assume a higher degree of responsibility for the outcomes of the systems, and hence there is a "stronger" case for a more stringent regulatory approach. Finally, countries with DB pensions often perceive themselves to have less need for specific investment limitations because employers stand behind the promised pension benefit. This contrasts with the detailed regulation of the portfolio in DC pensions, in which the outcomes and resulting level of members' retirement income depends more closely on fund performance.

### Total Assets and Asset Allocation

The total amount of assets held by privately managed pension funds as a share of gross domestic product (GDP) varies significantly across the countries studied (figure 2.1). By the end of 2005, total assets in the 23 countries covered in this study amounted to over $15 billion, ranging from around 100 percent of GDP in some OECD countries to less than 10 percent in most Latin American and CEE countries. The relatively small size of accumulated assets in Latin America and CEE countries is partly explained by the recent implementation of their private systems, which, with the exception of Chile, have been in place for less than 10 years.

Asset allocation between equity and bonds shows a wide dispersion among different countries (figure 2.1). In some countries, pension funds hold their entire portfolio in fixed-income securities, whereas in others the funds have no or only a few fixed-income holdings. Equity investments also vary widely from 0 percent to over 98 percent of the asset allocation depending on the country. These differences in asset allocation can be partly explained by the liability structure (DB occupational plans) and by investment regulations (DC personal plans). Other variables affecting strategic asset allocation could include factors such as the age structure of

**Figure 2.1  Total Assets and Asset Allocation, 2004**

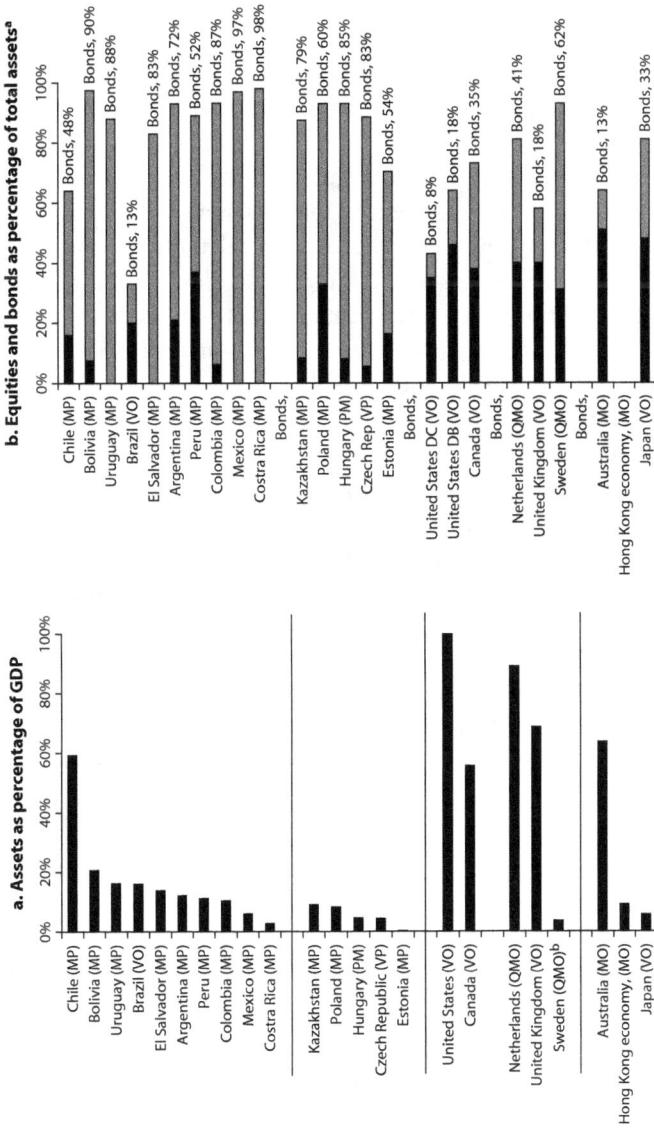

**a. Assets as percentage of GDP**

**b. Equities and bonds as percentage of total assets[a]**

*Sources:* OECD, Global Pensions Statistics.

a. Share in bonds provided. The other bar correponds to the share in equity. The difference from 100% corresponds to investment in other asset classes.

b. Includes information only from Alecta.

MO = mandatory occupational plans; MP = mandatory personal plans; QMO = quasi-mandatory occupational plans; PM = mandatory personal plans; VO = voluntary occupational plans; VP = voluntary personal plans.

members,[5] historical reasons, a sponsor's particular preferences, or varying forecasts of future capital market returns.

## Methods to Value Pension Funds' Assets and to Report Investment Returns

The assets of pension funds are typically valued at market prices. Additionally, the approach to reporting investment returns varies across countries (Tapia 2008a, b) Personal pension plans in Latin American and CEE countries have detailed regulations defining the methodology for calculating returns. This regulation is usually established by the supervisory authority, either as the official calculation or as a control, verifying the asset managers' calculations. Calculation methods are even more important in those countries that regulate the performance of the portfolio through minimum or relative rate-of-return guarantees. In contrast, the definition of and criteria for calculating and reporting total return among Western Europe, North America, and Asia-Pacific countries can vary considerably depending on the investment policy and methods used by the asset manager. Another difference in return calculation methodologies across countries is the treatment of management fees. Most Latin American countries report returns gross of fees, whereas some OECD countries report them net of some fees (for example, administrative fees).

## Reported Returns and Standard Deviations

As a result of these differences in reporting and regulatory frameworks, as well as differences in the time frame of reporting periods along with a variety of other idiosyncratic characteristics of individual pension systems,[6] comparison of the investment performance across countries based solely on reported values and returns should be approached with considerable caution. Keeping in mind these limitations, however, it is useful to examine the distribution of reported investment returns across countries, which, in the absence of fully comparable data, provides an initial view of the variations across the different pension and regulatory settings Table 2.3 reports average real returns (nominal returns in local currency less price inflation) and the standard deviation of the returns for the countries in the database. These are presented in the first set of columns for the entire period for which data are available for the country and in the last two columns for the latest five-year period for data are available, December 2000–December 2005.[7]

**Table 2.3  Basic Statistical Information on Real Investment Returns by Economy[a]**

| Country | Data since | Entire period | | | Dec. 2000–Dec. 2005 | |
|---|---|---|---|---|---|---|
| | | Geometric mean return | Arithmetic mean return | Standard deviation | Average return | Standard deviation |
| **Latin America** | | | | | | |
| Argentina (MP) | 1995 | 9.7 | 10.2 | 11.6 | 7.3 | 15.0 |
| Bolivia (MP) | 1998 | 10.1 | 10.2 | 4.6 | 9.6 | 5.9 |
| Brazil (VO) | 1995 | 5.7 | 5.9 | 6.3 | 2.7 | 4.8 |
| Chile (MP) | 1982 | 9.5 | 9.8 | 8.5 | 6.1 | 2.7 |
| Costa Rica (MP) | 2002 | 5.8 | 5.9 | 3.3 | 4.6 | 3.3 |
| El Salvador (MP) | 1999 | 5.7 | 5.8 | 4.5 | 3.7 | 2.5 |
| Mexico (MP) | 1998 | 7.3 | 7.3 | 3.8 | 6.5 | 4.0 |
| Peru (MP) | 1994 | 14.3 | 14.6 | 8.8 | 15.0 | 6.1 |
| Uruguay (MP) | 1997 | 14.7 | 15.3 | 13.0 | 19.2 | 16.4 |
| **Central and Eastern Europe** | | | | | | |
| Czech Republic (VP) | 1995 | 1.0 | 1.1 | 1.6 | 1.5 | 1.5 |
| Estonia (MP) | 2002 | 5.2 | 5.3 | 4.5 | 4.1 | 4.5 |
| Hungary (MP) | 1998 | 2.3 | 2.4 | 5.4 | 3.1 | 5.8 |
| Kazakhstan (MP) | 1999 | 7.9 | 8.4 | 12.7 | 2.3 | 5.3 |
| Poland (MP) | 2000 | 8.7 | 8.7 | 4.9 | 9.6 | 4.8 |
| **North America** | | | | | | |
| Canada (VO) | 1990 | 6.2 | 6.2 | 3.2 | 3.5 | 1.9 |
| United States (DB) (VO) | 1988 | 7.1 | 7.5 | 9.6 | 1.5 | 13.9 |
| United States (DC) (VO) | 1988 | 6.1 | 6.5 | 8.7 | 0.7 | 13.1 |

*(continued)*

**Table 2.3 Basic Statistical Information on Real Investment Returns by Economy[a]** *(Continued)*

| Country | Data since | Entire period | | | Dec. 2000–Dec. 2005 | |
| --- | --- | --- | --- | --- | --- | --- |
| | | Geometric mean return | Arithmetic mean return | Standard deviation | Average return | Standard deviation |
| **Western Europe** | | | | | | |
| Netherlands (QMO) | 1993 | 6.1 | 6.4 | 8.2 | 2.0 | 10.3 |
| Sweden (QMO) | 1990 | 6.2 | 6.6 | 9.7 | 1.0 | 10.4 |
| United Kingdom (VO) | 1982 | 8.7 | 9.5 | 12.5 | 1.9 | 16.5 |
| **Asia-Pacific** | | | | | | |
| Australia (MO) | 1990 | 8.9 | 9.1 | 5.7 | 4.9 | 8.4 |
| Hong Kong, China (MO) | 2000 | 2.1 | 2.7 | 13.2 | 1.7 | 13.2 |
| Japan (VO) | 1990 | 3.4 | 3.7 | 8.9 | 4.8 | 13.9 |

*Source:* OECD calculation from Tapia 2007b.

a. Calculation since the data in the column headed "Data since" and for the last five-year period. Higher returns do not entail better performance because these data do not take into account several dimension (see main text) to allow performance comparisons.

MO = mandatory occupational plans; MP = mandatory personal plans; QMO = quasi-mandatory occupational plans; VO = voluntary occupational plans; VP = voluntary personal plans.

## Additional Problems with the Data Reported on Investment Returns

Before attempting to make any observations about the reported data, it is important to consider further the full range of challenges imposed by the reporting methods. In addition to the very basic problems outlined above—different valuation methodologies, differences in expenses charged to the funds, and differences in the legal environment (for example, investment restrictions)—a range of other limitations are related to the way that investment returns are averaged across pension funds and over the year that potentially will affect the ability to undertake comparative analysis across the countries. These issues are discussed further in the following chapter.

Additionally, some countries (such as Colombia) provide overlapping returns (for example, a 36-month moving average return). Returns reported in this manner cannot be worked back into monthly, quarterly, or annual rates of return. One of the more severe problems when comparing investment performance across pension funds and countries is the lack of a clear portfolio composition separation between the different asset classes. The data reported by pension funds and regulators also suffer from survival bias, which arises when constructing weighted averages across pension funds using only data from existing funds. Using only funds that remain in business without accounting for those funds that did not survive over the period analyzed will bias the returns upward. This bias will make it impossible to compare investment performance across countries and pension fund groupings when pension funds' survival rates differ.

## Preliminary Observations from the Initial Data Review

As an introduction to the following chapters, which will discuss in more detail empirical and theoretical issues regarding the measurement of the financial performance of privately managed pension systems, this chapter has discussed the available data to assess investment performance and has provided initial tabulations of the financial performance of pension funds that are derived from these data. This review indicates that although data are available from a wide range of different pension systems, important limitations are imposed by the way in which the data are reported and presented that limit ready applicability to undertaking cross-country comparative analysis of the investment performance of pension funds. Most important among these are differences in the reporting methodologies, varying time frames for which information is reported, and differences in the manner in which returns are adjusted for fees and expenses.

Keeping in mind the important caveats regarding comparability of the data across countries, initial tabulations of reported financial results can be derived from the collected data. These indicate considerable variation in both the level of real returns and the standard deviation of the reported returns among the countries that vary from a geometric annual mean return of as low as 1 percent real returns per year to one country that has reported returns of nearly 20 percent between 2000 and 2005. The standard deviations of the reported returns indicate show a similar degree of variation ranging from below 2.0 percent to above 16 percent over the five-year period.

Looking at the relationship between reported returns and their standard deviation for a five-year time period (2000–05) for which data are available for all 23 counties in the sample indicates no clear relationship between the reported level of returns and the variance around them. It is interesting to note that most countries have had relative low average returns and relative low volatility (table 2.3). However, some countries achieved relatively high returns with relatively high volatility (Uruguay and, to some extent, Argentina and Peru), whereas others achieved relative high returns with low relatively volatility (Bolivia and Poland). Some, however, such as Hong Kong, China; Japan; the United Kingdom; and the United States, report relatively low average returns over the five-year period yet indicate relatively high volatility. Finally, the standard deviation of returns in OECD countries is larger than in non-OECD countries.

On balance, the initial effort to collect and evaluate data on the financial performance of pension funds across countries indicates that considerably more work is required to support any meaningful evaluation of the results and to produce measures that provide useful comparison across countries or that can begin to explain the differences observed. This leads to the conclusion that further comparative analysis should be limited to an exploratory effort to measure the reported returns on a risk-adjusted basis, which is presented in the following chapter, and to direct subsequent research work toward making progress toward developing individual country benchmarks to evaluate returns in relation to a retirement income-related standard, which is addressed in the other chapters of this publication.

## Notes

1. This chapter borrows substantially from the background documents prepared for this project by Tapia (2008a, b).
2. According to the OECD pension taxonomy, an occupational pension plan is linked to an employment or professional relationship between the plan

member and the entity that establishes the plan (plan sponsor). They may be established by employers or groups thereof (for example, industry associations) and labor or professional associations, jointly or separately. The plan may be administered directly by the plan sponsor or by an independent entity (a pension fund or a financial institution acting as pension provider). Personal pension plans, on the other hand, are not linked to an employment relationship. However, the employer (for example, the Slovak Republic) or the state (for example, the Czech Republic) may nonetheless contribute to personal pension plans.

3. It is important to use real returns when comparing pension funds' investment performance across countries because nominal returns can be higher in one country just because inflation is higher. To compare investment performance, *ideally* one should compare returns net of investment management costs. These issues are discussed later in the chapter.

4. Table 2.1 does not describe all the different types of privately managed pension plans available in all countries, only those included in this study. For example, all OECD countries have voluntary personal pension plans, but they are not included in this study.

5. Pension funds with younger participants tend to have more equity exposure, whereas more mature pension funds tend to have more fixed-income investments.

6. Some of these aspects are specific to pension funds, such as the investment horizon and the existence of future commitments; others are specific to the regulatory framework in each country, including the investment regulatory regime, the criteria for valuing portfolio, and the methodology used for pension funds to calculate investment returns. Finally, some aspects are related to the level of development and the performance of the local financial market. See Tapia (2008a) for more information.

7. Tapia (2008b) reports the complete time series of investment returns, detailed basic statistics, and a detailed description of the different sources of information used from each country.

## References

Tapia, Waldo. 2008a. "Private Pension Systems across Countries." OECD Working Paper on Insurance and Private Pensions, No. 21. OECD, Paris.

———. 2008b. "Comparing Aggregate Investment Returns in Privately Managed Pension Funds." OECD Working Paper on Insurance and Private Pensions, No. 22. OECD, Paris.

# CHAPTER 3

# Financial Performance of Pension Funds: An Exploratory Study

## Eduardo Walker and Augusto Iglesias

### Introduction and Overview of Findings

This chapter considers alternative methodologies that can be used to analyze the risk-adjusted financial performance of privately managed pension funds. Selected methodologies are applied to the countries for which data have been compiled by the Organisation for Economic Co-operation and Development (OECD), which were presented in the preceding chapter. It begins with a discussion of the most commonly employed measure of risk-adjusted investment performance, the Sharpe ratio, and its potential uses and limitations in the performance evaluation of pension systems. This is followed by an overview of alternative approaches and potential variations of the Sharpe ratio as well as an assessment of their applicability to the performance evaluation of funded pension systems. This overview considers the limitations that are imposed by the available data and proposes methodologies for developing benchmarks that are specific to the particular characteristics of pension funds. The background discussion notices that, if there are no data limitations, comparing performance measures between countries is difficult and not always meaningful.

Keeping in mind these important caveats, the chapter uses the variations of the Sharpe ratio in an exploratory effort to provide an initial evaluation of pension fund performance in 11 countries with sufficient data available. This allows assessing the degree to which fund managers have been able to deliver investment results that are commensurate with the risk levels assumed. This is done through comparisons against feasible local and foreign benchmarks that provide proxies for a risk-free rate of return. This approach allows assessing the extent to which portfolio restrictions and decisions have affected the performance of pension systems in different countries and considers whether such restrictions have had significant effects. Conscious that it is not feasible to simply rank performance by country, a comparison across them is undertaken with the purpose of detecting commonalities.

With only a few exceptions the analysis finds that the pension systems have been able to deliver a significant risk premium per unit of volatility with respect to short-term local and U.S. interest rates. A significant premium per unit of excess return volatility is found less often when the benchmark of long-term fixed-income wealth index returns (local and U.S.) is used as a reference for the risk-free rate, which indicates that there has been a bias toward short-term instruments in a period of falling interest rates. Finally, performance is assessed with respect to multiple indices representative of several asset classes. This approach finds significantly positive extra returns or alphas, which implies that portfolio decisions by managers have added value, that the evolution of portfolio restrictions has had a positive impact on portfolio performance, or both.

## Portfolio Performance Measurement

In general, the purpose of measuring portfolio performance is to determine whether portfolio managers add value with respect to passive or naive investment strategies, typically represented by feasible and well-diversified benchmarks. Under the assumptions of the Efficient Markets Hypothesis, it is difficult for managers to add value, so it should not be surprising to find that the different pension systems have had performances similar to their benchmarks.

In considering the performance of aggregate pension funds by country, an important question is whether portfolio restrictions (given by regulations and the level of capital market development), jointly with the aggregate portfolio decisions, have added value with respect to feasible alternative investment strategies. Unfortunately, it is not possible to separate the impact of investment decisions from the impact of investment restrictions, which jointly affect performance.

An important point to keep in mind is that all performance measures are relative measures that have to be compared against some kind of benchmark. To see if a pension system is doing a reasonable job in terms of the welfare offered to its members, using a (set of) benchmark(s) for comparison purposes is unavoidable.

### Sharpe Ratios

The Sharpe (1966) ratio (SR) remains at the core of modern portfolio theory.[1] If every investor combines a single riskless asset (supposedly well defined) with the portfolio whose performance is being evaluated, and assuming that the relevant risk measure is the same for all investors (volatility), then the unique measure of performance that should be used to rank alternative investment opportunities is the SR. For the SR to provide a meaningful ranking, every investor should view risk in the same way. This requires that the following assumptions, among others, hold: (1) there are no short-sale restrictions for the risk-free asset, (2) all investors have the same planning horizon, (3) there are no other sources of wealth, and (4) consumption goods prices are uncorrelated with asset returns.

Under these assumptions investors should choose the portfolio with the highest SR, as illustrated by the line with the steepest slope in figure 3.1,

**Figure 3.1    The Sharpe Ratio**

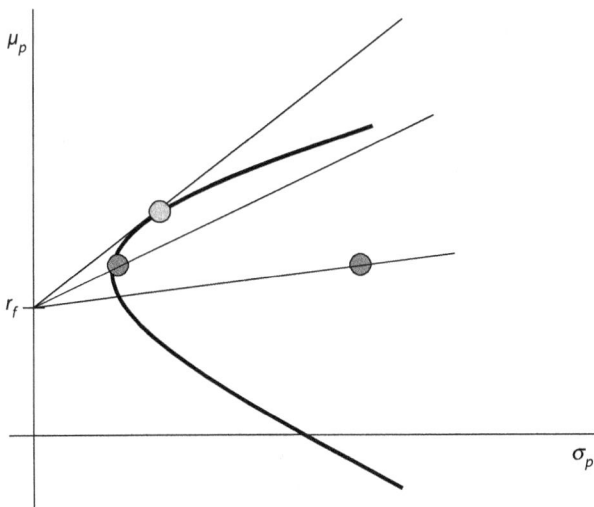

because it allows investors to maximize expected return per unit of total risk. Preferences are assumed to be increasing in expected returns and decreasing in volatility. The SR measures the line's slope coefficient.

It is important to realize that under the above assumptions the SR is a monotonically increasing transformation of welfare: if an investor can achieve a higher SR, this automatically implies improved welfare. However, it is also important to keep in mind that if an investor cannot combine the risky portfolio with the riskless asset used for calculating the ratio (for example, in an all or nothing case), comparisons based on the SR are not necessarily meaningful. Perhaps from the perspective of managers, who indeed combine low-risk securities with riskier ones, this comparison could still make sense.

The SR as a performance measure tends to be different from others because the rest try to measure the return (or value) added by a portfolio manager, for instance, whether he or she offers higher returns without commensurate increases in risk, in the context of a benchmark portfolio. Because the SR corresponds to a risk premium per unit of risk, comparisons are slightly more involved, but it should still be useful for ranking different risky portfolios, under the assumption that they will be combined with the riskless asset used in the calculations.

In any case, it is interesting to keep in mind an absolute number for the SR. According to Dimson, Marsh, and Staunton (2006), the global equity risk premium is on the order of 4.5 percent with respect to the short-term interest rate. The volatility of a global equity portfolio is in the neighborhood of 18 percent annually. This implies an annualized SR of 0.25, or 0.072 on a monthly basis.

***Interpreting Sharpe ratios: what they can tell us.*** Possible benchmarks against which pension system SRs can be compared are, for example, a portfolio of all available securities in a given country (the aggregate "market" portfolio), an equity portfolio, a fixed-income portfolio, and the absolute zero. The last approach will be adopted for practical reasons. Lo (2002) develops a methodology to determine whether SRs are significantly different from zero. When they are not, it implies that the returns offered by the pension system correspond essentially to the low-risk asset's return. On the other hand, if they are significantly positive, it means that the pension systems have delivered a positive risk premium per unit of volatility, which should imply higher welfare than having invested the same funds in short-term low-risk assets. However, a significantly positive SR does not necessarily mean that

fund managers have added value because a passive or naive investment strategy in a well-diversified risky portfolio is also expected to
deliver a significantly positive risk premium per unit of risk (for
example, see note 2).

As explained, the SR is a valid measure for comparing alternative risky
portfolios that will be combined with "*the* riskless asset." This seemingly
simple concept has the practical complication of requiring the selection
of a reasonable riskless asset.

In practice, a truly riskless asset may not exist, so instead we can use a
low-risk asset in the country. Here it is important to keep in mind that
investors are assumed to consume in their home countries, so the basis
currency is local and inflation indexed. To calculate the SR, instead of
assuming that the local riskless asset has no volatility, we can take this
explicitly into account by measuring the SR as

$$SR = \frac{\overline{r_{Pt} - r_{ft}}}{SD(r_{Pt} - r_{ft})}.$$

(1)

The numerator is the excess return with respect to the low-risk asset,
and the denominator corresponds to the standard deviation of the excess
returns. This is similar to the information ratio (see table 3.1), if we use
the low-risk asset as the benchmark. We just need to worry that portfolio
returns and the riskless asset are measured in the same unit. To determine
if this ratio is significantly different from zero, the result in Lo (2002) is
used. Assuming *independent and identically distributed (i.i.d.)* excess
returns, the standard error of the SR is

$$SE = \sqrt{\left(1 + \frac{1}{2}(S_p)^2\right)/T}.$$

(2)

A 95% confidence interval is SR ± 1.96 SE.[2]

A second consideration is the investment horizon. If we assume that the
investment horizon is not short term (as should be the case for pension
funds), then equation (1) can be adapted to consider this. The intuition is
that, for example, if we have a 20-year planning horizon, the riskless asset
would be closer (but not exactly equal) to a zero-coupon bond maturing
in 20 years. If marked to market, however, this 20-year zero-coupon bond
will have significant volatility. It follows that short-term volatility is not
necessarily a good risk measure. Indeed, if we find a portfolio that is highly
correlated with the short-term return on the 20-year bond, then it has good
hedging properties or low risk from the long-term horizon perspective.

**Table 3.1  Performance Measures**

### A: Classics

| Type | Statistic | Authors | Observations | Information required |
|---|---|---|---|---|
| Selectivity | $T_p = \dfrac{\overline{r}_p}{\beta_p}$<br><br>Excess return per unit of systematic risk | Treynor and Mazuy (1966): Treynor ratio | Purpose: rank portfolio managers and combine them into a single portfolio. Needs at least a benchmark for comparison purposes.<br>Problems: statistical power; market timing; changes in risk levels; oversimplification | Nonoverlapping synchronized portfolio, benchmark, and risk-free returns |
| Selectivity | $S_p = \dfrac{\overline{r}_p}{\sigma_p}$<br><br>Excess return per unit of total risk | Sharpe (1966): Sharpe ratio | Purpose: rank portfolio managers and choose a single one, combined with a riskless asset. Needs at least a benchmark for comparison purposes.<br>Problems: statistical power; market timing; changes in risk levels; oversimplification | Nonoverlapping synchronized portfolio and risk-free returns (HPRs) |
| Selectivity | Annualized Sharpe and standard errors;<br>i.i.d. case:<br>$SE = \sqrt{\left(1 + \frac{1}{2}(S_P)^2\right)/T}$ | Lo (2002) | Provides statistical significance tests for the Sharpe ratio and corrects for serial dependence | Nonoverlapping return series |
| Selectivity | $\alpha_p = \overline{r}_p - \beta_p \overline{r}_m$ | Jensen's alpha (1968) | Purpose: detect value added by portfolio manager via selectivity<br>Problems: statistical power; market timing; changes in risk levels; oversimplification; benchmark efficiency | Nonoverlapping synchronized portfolio, benchmark, and risk-free returns |

| Category | Measure | Equation | Purpose/Problems | Data requirements |
|---|---|---|---|---|
| Selectivity | Treynor and Black (1973): appraisal ratio | $\dfrac{\alpha_p}{\sigma_{ep}}$ | Purpose: measure value created by selectivity per unit of diversifiable risk. Implies an optimal way of forming portfolios. Problems: same as Jensen's alpha | Nonoverlapping synchronized portfolio, benchmark, and risk-free returns |
| Selectivity | Goodwin (1998): information ratio | $IR = \dfrac{ER}{\sigma_{ER}}$ $ER = R_{Pt} - R_{Rt}$ | Purpose: measure value created by selectivity ignoring beta Problems: same as Jensen's alpha | Nonoverlapping synchronized portfolio and benchmark returns |
| Market timing | Treynor and Mazuy (1966) | $r_p = \alpha_p + b_{op} r_m + b'_{1p} r_m^2 + \varepsilon'_p$ | Purpose: detect value added by portfolio manager via selectivity and market timing Problems: statistical power; changes in risk levels; oversimplification; benchmark efficiency; other functional forms for changes in risk levels | Nonoverlapping synchronized portfolio, benchmark, and risk-free returns |
| Market timing | Henriksson and Merton (1981) | $r_p = d'_p + b'_{op} r_m + b'_{1p} r_m^+ + \varepsilon'$ $r_m^+ = \max(0; r_m)$ | Problems: statistical power; changes in risk levels; oversimplification; benchmark efficiency; other functional forms for changes in risk levels | Nonoverlapping synchronized portfolio, benchmark, and risk-free returns |

*(continued)*

45

**Table 3.1  Performance Measures** *(Continued)*

*B: Multiple Indices*

| Type | Statistic | Authors | Observations | Information required |
|---|---|---|---|---|
| Selectivity | $\bar{r}_p = \alpha_p + \sum_k \beta_{pk}\bar{r}_k$ | Elton et al. (1996) and Sharpe (1992): asset class indices; Lehmann and Modest (1987), Connor and Korajczyk (1986), Grinblatt and Titman (1989), Brown and Goetzman (1997): empirical indices; Carhart (1997) | Purpose: detect value added by portfolio manager via selectivity Problems: inefficient indices; incomplete specification; timing | Nonoverlapping synchronized portfolio, multiple benchmarks, and risk-free returns |
| Combines selectivity and market timing | $\bar{r}_{pt} = \alpha_{pt} + \sum_k \beta_{pk(t-q)}\bar{r}_k$ Rolling regression for estimating weights | Sharpe (1992) | Purpose: detect value added by portfolio manager via selectivity and market timing Problems: incomplete specification; in principle it represents a feasible strategy for the investor; assumes that changes in portfolio composition add value, even if they are based in public information, for example. | Nonoverlapping synchronized portfolio, multiple benchmarks, and risk-free returns |

## C: Conditional Performance

| Type | Statistic | Authors | Observations | Information required |
|---|---|---|---|---|
| Selectivity corrected for seeming market timing based on public information | $\beta_p(Z) = b_{0p} + B'_p z$ $r_p = \alpha_p + b_{0p} r_m + B'_p (z r_m) + u_p$ | Ferson-Schadt (1996) | Purpose: detect value added via selectivity, correcting for seeming market timing based on public information. Advantage: adjusts benchmarks on a timely basis. Disadvantages: asset-pricing model assumed; market efficiency; functional form of the portfolio adjustment. | Nonoverlapping synchronized portfolio, multiple benchmarks, and risk-free returns and conditioning information |

## D: Other Performance Measures

| Type | Statistic | Authors | Observations | Information required |
|---|---|---|---|---|
| Selectivity | $\alpha = \sum w_t r_{pt}$ subject to $0 = \sum w_t r_{ft}$ (what proportions are needed over time to make the second equation true) | Grinblatt-Titman (1989): positive period weighting measure | Purpose: measure welfare-enhancing portfolio decisions. Weights are interpreted as marginal utility of wealth for power utility. | Nonoverlapping synchronized portfolio, benchmark, and risk-free returns |

*(continued)*

**Table 3.1  Performance Measures** *(Continued)*

**D: Other Performance Measures**

| Type | Statistic | Authors | Observations | Information required |
|---|---|---|---|---|
| Timing | $$PCM = \frac{1}{T}\sum_{i}\sum_{\tau}\Delta w_{j,t}r_{t+1} = \sum_{t} \text{COV}(\Delta w_j, r_j)$$ | Grinblatt-Titman (1993): portfolio change measure | Purpose: measure whether portfolio changes add value<br>Uses actual portfolio holdings<br>Possible behavior involving taking increasing risks, combined with traditional measures | Actual portfolio holdings |
| Conditional timing measure | $$CWM_j =$$ $$E\left[\sum_{j=1}^{N}\left(\tilde{W}_{j,t-1} - E\left[\tilde{W}_{j,t-1}\right]\right)\left(\tilde{R}_{j,t} - E\left[\tilde{R}_{j,t}\mid Z_t\right]\right)Z_{t-1}\right]$$ | Ferson and Khang (2003) | Purpose: decompose the Grinblatt-Titman PCM measure into components attributable to the manager and to public information | Actual portfolio holdings and conditioning information |

*Source:* The authors.

*Note:* HPR = holding period return; PCM = portfolio change measure

Therefore, in equation (1) we can use the short-term return of a long-term bond as the riskless asset, and in this way the SR is adapted to the planning horizon. The necessary assumption for this measure to be valid is that excess returns are uncorrelated through time because this allows us to rank, period by period, the different investment alternatives according to this indicator.[3]

A third question is whether we may consider a foreign currency asset as a "riskless" asset, such as a U.S. Treasury bill (T-bill) or Treasury bond (T-bond). Even though these assets may be riskless in terms of default probability, they are not so when measured in local currency because of currency risk. However, to compare results against different risk-free benchmarks, and to understand performance, we may still want to consider a T-bill or a T-bond as the minimum risk asset, but all returns have to be measured in local currency (or in the same currency as the portfolio whose performance is being evaluated).

Therefore, based on the different measures for the SR, we can meaningfully ask whether the different pension systems have delivered significant risk premia per unit of risk with respect to the low-risk benchmarks considered.

***What Sharpe ratios don't tell us.*** *Limitations of Comparing across Asset Classes and Different Time Periods:* For illustration purposes, figure 3.2 compares monthly five-year rolling SRs of the Standard & Poor's total return index and a 10-year-term U.S. government bond index, considering a short-term U.S. government bond index as the risk-free rate.[4]

Figure 3.2 illustrates that until the early 1990s, SRs for U.S. stocks and bonds evolved quite similarly, but that from that point on these two asset classes show very different behavior. Therefore, SRs can be expected to vary widely over time (at least considering five-year periods) and across asset classes. This implies that comparing pension funds that have invested differently or comparing different time frames may not always be meaninful, just as we cannot meaningfully say ex ante that investing in stocks is better or worse than investing in bonds. It depends on risk aversion and the investment horizon, among other things.

*Limitations of Comparing across Countries:* The assumptions required for the SR to be a valid ranking instrument are particularly unwarranted when comparing across countries. First, it is not the same investor who is considering the different alternatives. Therefore, because we cannot compare welfare across countries, we cannot effectively compare SRs either. Second, foreign exchange risk and real interest rate risk are

**Figure 3.2    Sharpe Ratios of U.S. Stocks and Bonds, Five-Year Rolling Estimates**

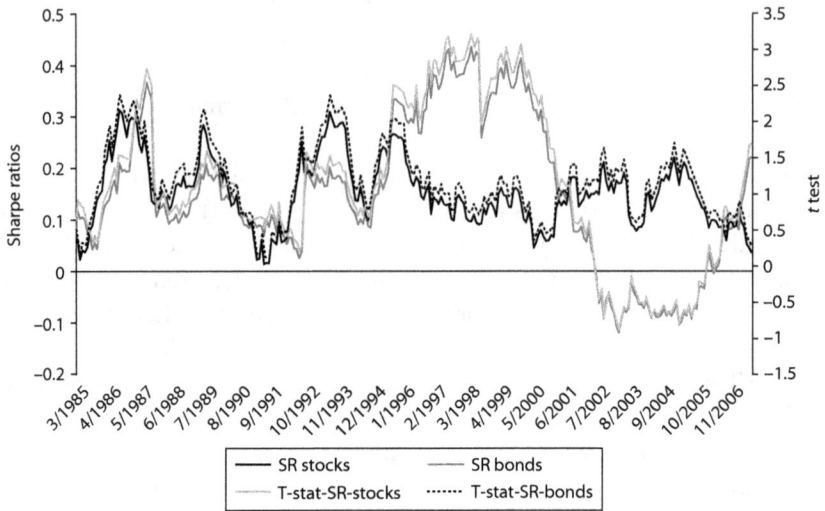

*Source:* Elaborated by the authors based on data from the Global Financial Database.

viewed differently in different countries (see, for example, Walker 2006, 2008). Third, the very meaning of the SR is unclear when a riskless rate does not exist or when proxies for it are used. Even if riskless rates exist, comparability across countries is questionable. This was partially addressed above, when the assumptions behind choosing different proxies for the riskless asset were discussed.

The numerator of the SR conceptually corresponds to a risk premium with respect to a low-risk or riskless asset. This premium should depend on the macroeconomic and financial risks faced by a country and the asset class considered. On the other hand, the volatility measure in the denominator should capture risk, and it may be argued that it constitutes an adjustment for risk and therefore SRs should be comparable across countries. This is wrong, in the authors' opinion. Volatility may not be a comprehensive measure of risk. Intuitively, as a country becomes developed, SRs may be expected to fall for a given asset class, especially because certain kinds of risks are not well measured with volatilities or covariances (such as "peso problem" risks).

Therefore, all these considerations have to be kept in mind when comparing SRs across countries and time periods.

### Other Performance Measures

Table 3.1 provides a detailed summary of the other most important portfolio performance evaluation measures and techniques. In all cases the four parts of the table seek to determine if the portfolio manager adds value via either security selection or market timing. The reference point is always a passive investment strategy of similar risk. Most of the measures require the existence of a (set of) benchmark(s) against which the value added is measured. In other words, to apply these measures, a benchmark that is relevant to the portfolio under consideration is required.

It would be useful to estimate Grinblatt and Titman's (1993) portfolio change measure, taking as a reference the initial portfolio compositions of the pension fund systems and measuring whether there is value added. The methodology in this case consists of selecting indices representative of the different asset classes held by the pension funds, weighing the asset class returns by the fraction that they represent in each pension fund's portfolio and then comparing this benchmark return with the observed returns. Unfortunately, in most cases the official databases lump together government bonds, independently of the country that issues such bonds (local versus foreign), and the same is done with stocks. Therefore, if local and foreign asset classes cannot be disentangled, it is impossible to come up with a combined benchmark to judge performance. This naturally suggests revising the way in which pension fund portfolio composition is summarized and presented.

***Sharpe's style (or empirical attribution) analysis.*** Because it seems particularly useful in this case, the complementary methodology chosen here also belongs to Sharpe (1992). Its purpose is to detect the value added by a portfolio manager via selectivity, market timing, or both. It may use several benchmarks or indices. A typical implementation that is used here considers six asset classes: local T-bills or deposits and local T-bonds, both in local currency, local equity, U.S. T-bills, U.S. T-bonds, and global equity. The annex specifies precisely what indices were used for each country.

The methodology searches for non-negative portfolio (index) weights that minimize the variance of $r_{pt} - r_{Bt}$, where $r_{pt}$ represents the pension fund return and $r_{Bt}$ is the return of the weighted average of index returns. This methodology is similar to a least squares regression, subject to non-negativity constraints on the coefficients. The weights are represented by the $\beta$'s in equation (3). In Sharpe's words, $r_{Bt}$ is the *Style* return, and thus this methodology is sometimes called *Style Analysis*. An interesting application, as suggested by Sharpe, is to estimate the portfolio weights with information until time $t$, and then use them out of sample to weigh the index returns in $t + 1$, and then repeat the estimation until $t + 1$ to apply it to index returns in $t + 2$. These are rolling estimates. In both cases (for the in- and out-of sample or rolling estimates), the value added is estimated as the return difference, called *Selection* return, represented by the alpha in equation (3):[5]

$$\overline{r_{pt}} = \alpha_p + \sum_k \beta_{pk(t-q)} \overline{r_{kt}} \equiv \alpha_p + \overline{r_{Bt}} \equiv \text{ Selection} + \text{Style.} \qquad (3)$$

This methodology has several advantages: it considers endogenous benchmarks of similar "style" to the evaluated portfolio, the rolling approach allows portfolio weights to change over time, and because these are in principle observable, the benchmark can be replicated. The use of several benchmarks in this manner is more likely to yield "mean-variance efficient" combined benchmarks.[6] Notice that if a portfolio invests in an asset class not considered among the benchmarks (local corporate bonds, for example), the approach assumes that a combination of the included benchmarks (government bonds plus local stocks, for example) should yield similar results. This is an application of the "replicating portfolio" idea, in which asset classes should have similar expected returns as their replicating portfolios.

***Attribution: what it does and does not tell us.*** It is important to keep in mind that attribution or style analysis takes as given the asset classes in which pension funds have invested and their (estimated) composition. So the question it answers is if there has been value added with respect to a portfolio of the same *style* (for example, which considers the same asset classes and the proportions assigned to each). A very different question is whether the portfolios chosen by the managers (or imposed by the legal investment restrictions) are "optimal" or "efficient" from the perspective of a future pensioner. This is a complex issue that cannot be answered by this analysis and one that is addressed in the subsequent chapters of this volume. However, we should be able to say at least that from a future pensioner's perspective, long-term local indexed bonds should dominate short-term ones, so if the estimated portfolio composition is heavily tilted toward short-term instruments, these portfolios are likely to be inefficient from a long-term asset allocation perspective. However, if long-term indexed bonds do not exist, the best protection against unexpected changes in inflation rates may indeed be to invest in short-term bonds.

## Required Data

In addition to riskless asset proxies and benchmarks, we need the pension portfolio return data in a format not always available from pension fund regulatory authorities (as collected by the OECD).

To illustrate the main points regarding data requirements, an example is provided. Assume that there are two pension funds whose (monthly) returns and other characteristics are as described in table 3.2. We want to obtain the pension system's aggregate rate of return. The correct way of calculating the aggregate or average should yield a return equivalent to the rate of growth in total wealth after investing in the funds in proportion to the relative importance of each at the beginning of each period. All subsequent inflows and outflows should be proportional to those received or paid by each pension fund in the system. To accomplish this we should determine first the return at the individual pension fund level for whatever period it is reported, and then calculate a weighted average using the relative importance of each fund at the *beginning* of each return calculation period. In practice, this calculation assumes that all additions and withdrawals to the funds happen at the end of each period. This method is usually called time-weighted returns, which differs from the internal rate of return because the latter explicitly considers inflows and outflows and the relative importance of each.

In the example the system's rate of return in period 1 should be calculated as

$$\frac{-1.29\% \times \$9,000,000 - 3.86\% \times \$10,000,000}{\$9,000,000 + \$10,000,000} = -2.64\%.$$

### Lagged Aggregate Weights

To obtain the pension system's return, it is necessary to calculate the weighted average of each pension fund return, but the weights must correspond to the proportion that each fund represented at the beginning of each return period. Otherwise we systematically overweight the funds with the highest returns and underweight the funds with the lowest returns. This bias is more important in the case of more volatile funds and it accumulates over time. In the present example, the difference is unimportant, but these errors are likely to accumulate over time.

### Weighted Average of Share (Quota) Values

Certain pension fund authorities estimate aggregate pension systems' returns as the growth rate in the size-weighted average of individual

**Table 3.2  Example of Proper Calculations of Pension System Returns**

| | Fund A | | | | | Fund B | | | | System | System |
|---|---|---|---|---|---|---|---|---|---|---|---|
| Period | Return (%) | Size ($) | No. shares | Price per share ($) | Return (%) | Size ($) | No. shares | Price per share ($) | | return (%) | return index |
| 0 |  | 9,000,000 | 1000 | 9,000.00 |  | 10,000,000 | 800 | 12,500.00 | | | 1000.0 |
| 1 | −1.29 | 9,180,000 | 1033 | 8,883.64 | −3.86 | 10,188,125 | 848 | 12,017.05 | | −2.65 | 973.5 |
| 2 | 3.17 | 9,363,600 | 1022 | 9,164.92 | −0.37 | 10,377,541 | 867 | 11,972.47 | | 1.31 | 986.3 |
| 3 | −0.09 | 9,550,872 | 1043 | 9,156.59 | 0.22 | 10,589,120 | 882 | 11,999.08 | | 0.07 | 987.0 |
| 4 | −2.00 | 9,741,889 | 1086 | 8,973.06 | 0.96 | 10,795,474 | 891 | 12,114.04 | | −0.45 | 982.6 |
| 5 | 0.63 | 9,936,727 | 1100 | 9,029.42 | 0.32 | 11,009,687 | 906 | 12,153.26 | | 0.47 | 987.2 |
| 6 | 1.14 | 10,135,462 | 1110 | 9,131.95 | −0.98 | 11,212,043 | 932 | 12,034.74 | | 0.03 | 987.4 |
| 7 | −0.19 | 10,338,171 | 1134 | 9,114.58 | 1.55 | 11,456,022 | 937 | 12,220.83 | | 0.72 | 994.6 |
| 8 | 2.22 | 10,544,934 | 1132 | 9,317.07 | 3.34 | 11,704,870 | 927 | 12,628.74 | | 2.81 | 1022.5 |
| 9 | 0.46 | 10,755,833 | 1149 | 9,360.02 | 1.67 | 11,919,991 | 928 | 12,840.12 | | 1.10 | 1033.7 |
| 10 | 3.84 | 10,970,950 | 1129 | 9,719.41 | 2.87 | 12,127,267 | 918 | 13,209.26 | | 3.33 | 1068.2 |
| 11 | 1.59 | 11,190,369 | 1133 | 9,873.56 | −1.63 | 12,418,041 | 956 | 12,994.37 | | −0.10 | 1067.1 |
| 12 | 0.49 | 11,414,176 | 1150 | 9,921.47 | 1.10 | 12,702,160 | 967 | 13,137.71 | | 0.81 | 1075.7 |

Source: Authors.

pension fund shares (or *quotas*). Defining $p_{kt}$ as the share value of fund $k$ at time $t$ and $F_{kt}$ as the corresponding size of the fund, then the average *quota* return is estimated as

$$r_{AVGQt} = \frac{\frac{\sum_{k=1}^{N} F_{kt} P_{kt}}{\sum_{k=1}^{N} F_{kt}}}{\frac{\sum_{k=1}^{N} F_{kt-1} P_{kt-1}}{\sum_{k=1}^{N} F_{kt-1}}} - 1.$$

For example, using the data from table 3.2, for month 12 the return would be estimated as

$$\frac{\frac{(\$11,414,176 \times \$9,921.47 + \$12,702,160 \times \$13,137.71)}{(\$11,414,176 + \$12,702,160)}}{\frac{(\$11,190,369 \times \$9,873.56 + \$12,418,041 \times \$12,994.37)}{(\$11,190,369 + \$12,418,041)}} - 1.$$

In general, this way of calculating returns is incorrect because it depends on the arbitrary absolute value assigned to one share by each pension fund at one point in time. In the present example this results in a cumulative return of 7.13 percent instead of the correct number, which is 7.57 percent. Even if initial share values were all equal, the estimated system's return may be wrong if different funds have different returns.

### Nonoverlapping Synchronized Portfolio, Benchmark, and Risk-Free Returns

Unlike certain macroeconomic or statistical time series, in the case of asset prices or portfolios, the value that contains the most information is not the average, but the last one. This follows from the idea that asset prices follow processes similar to random walks. Furthermore, to calculate variances or covariances with other financial series, it is also necessary for the data to be "synchronized," meaning that they should coincide as closely as possible in terms of the observation dates. Of course, a measurement problem may appear when securities are traded infrequently, but this does not justify the use of averages because this worsens the asynchronicity problem. On the contrary, using overlapping data tends to reduce the observed volatility, and thus it artificially increases SRs. In the present example, assume a riskless rate of zero, and the SR using nonoverlapping data is 0.41. Using bimonthly overlapping data, for example, reduces volatility by 11 percent, increasing the SR correspondingly.

## *Clear Portfolio Composition Separation between Asset Classes*

As argued above, to assess the performance of pension fund systems it is best to group the assets in which pension funds invest into meaningful categories that are representative of relatively homogeneous asset classes. At a minimum, a separation between local and foreign, short- and long-term government bonds, short- and long-term corporate bonds, and equity is suggested. If other asset classes, such as "alternative" investments, become important, they should also be considered separately. This allows the implementation of other performance evaluation procedures, such as Grinblatt and Titman (1993), which may help understand the effects of investment restrictions, for example.

## The Pension Fund Database

The pension fund database gathered by the OECD is summarized in table 3.3. In the annex, where each of the countries studied is presented, there are additional details regarding assumptions and calculations. Of the universe of countries that could have been analyzed (22), 11 had to be discarded because they have an insufficient number of observations to make valid inferences. Other countries were not included in the analysis because of overlapping returns (Colombia, Costa Rica, and El Salvador). Overlapping returns appear too smooth (reflected in low variance and covariance estimates), and, as explained, the SRs (as well as other risk-adjusted measures) end up being artificially high. Eliminating the countries for which the data could not support the analysis left 11 countries. In addition, for the countries with more than one pension fund type, the results are presented separately.

Regarding the effects of using returns calculated based on the systems' average quota or share values, comparisons could be performed in the cases of Argentina, Mexico, and Peru because in these cases and for some subperiods data were available for individual pension fund sizes and returns. In the case of Argentina, the "correct" calculation for the period 1994–2005 yields an additional annualized average return of 79 basis points and a higher annualized volatility of 25 basis points. In the case of Mexico, for the period for which both sources of return estimates (1997–2004) were available, the "correct" average annualized return is 15 basis points lower, and the annualized volatility is only 4 basis points lower. These orders of magnitude sometimes seem low, but keep in mind

**Table 3.3    General Description of the OECD Pension Fund Database**

| Country | Data date | Comments | Analyzed |
|---|---|---|---|
| Argentina | Monthly average quota return Sept. 1994–May 2007; daily returns Jan. 1994–Dec. 2005 | Likely errors in average quota returns | Yes |
| Australia | Annual 1990–2005 | Insufficient data points | No |
| Bolivia | Daily June 1997 | | Yes |
| Canada | Annual 1990–2005 | Insufficient data points | No |
| Chile | Monthly since 1981 | | Yes |
| Colombia | Monthly June 1995–Dec. 2001 | Overlapping three-year returns | No |
| Costa Rica | Monthly July 2002–Dec. 2004 | Overlapping annual returns | No |
| Czech Republic | Annual 1995–2004 | Insufficient data points | No |
| El Salvador | Monthly June 1999–Dec. 2004 | Overlapping annual returns | No |
| Estonia | Monthly June 2002–Dec. 2005 average quota returns | Likely errors in returns | Yes |
| Hong Kong, China economy | Annual 2002–2005 | Insufficient data points | No |
| Hungary | Quarterly calculated returns | | Yes |
| Japan | Annual 1990–2005 | Insufficient data points | No |
| Kazakhstan | Annual 1999–2004 | Insufficient data points | No |
| Mexico | Monthly | | Yes |
| Netherlands | Annual 1986–2006 | | Yes |
| Peru | Monthly average quota return since 1993; daily returns since 2001 | Likely errors in returns before 2001 | Yes |
| Poland | Daily May 1999–Dec. 2005 | | Yes |
| Sweden | Annual 1990–2005 | Insufficient data points | No |
| United Kingdom | Quarterly calculated returns Mar. 1992–Dec. 2006 | | Yes |
| United States | Annual 1998–2004 | Insufficient data points | No |
| Uruguay | Monthly Aug. 1996–Dec. 2005 | | Yes |

*Source:* Authors.

that returns compound over time as will the error. Finally, for Peru, the error in the average returns is about –30 basis points (bp) per year, but the difference in annualized volatilities is about 182 bp. This probably happens because the average quota was also smoothed by calculating monthly averages. The point is that variances and covariances will be incorrectly estimated if the system's average monthly quota value is used. In these three cases, performance measures are presented using the reestimated return series and also using the ones reported by the pension authorities despite the difficulties, because the official series tend to be longer.

## Legal and Administrative Considerations

Three important issues have to be considered to make the calculations comparable: valuation methodologies, expenses charged to the funds, and legal investment restrictions.

### Valuation

Regarding valuation, if instruments are not marked to market or if they seldom trade, they will appear to have artificially low volatility. An extreme example would be a bond portfolio whose components are not traded and thus accrue the interest rate of the moment of purchase. Most countries reviewed in table 3.4 claim to use valuation at market prices, with the exception of fixed income in Mexico, for which the country has a special valuation agency. In many cases this agency uses criteria not fully consistent with market valuation. However, it is possible to assume that in most developing nations financial securities do not trade frequently and thus prices will be too smooth. Lo (2002) suggests a way of adjusting SRs when there is serial correlation, which is likely to appear if securities are infrequently traded. This adjustment, however, is not considered in this analysis.

### Expenses

Table 3.4 indicates that in three of the Latin American countries expenses are charged to the fund. In Chile this happens only indirectly, via the expenses charged by foreign mutual funds. For OECD countries and Eastern Europe, information on the treatment of expenses is not available. The importance of this issue is evident because countries that charge expenses to the funds will appear to have lower returns.

### Legal Restrictions

Table 3.4 also shows that legal investment restrictions are dissimilar between countries. Some countries face more severe investment restrictions. These should be considered when building benchmarks to evaluate performance, but even in the case of SRs certain asset classes may have significantly different values for this parameter, not necessarily implying better or worse performance. This issue is addressed by using Sharpe's (1992) empirical attribution methodology, which allows the estimation of the actual relative importance of each asset class in pension fund portfolios.

**Table 3.4     Summary of Investment Regulations**

| | Latin American Countries | | | | | |
|---|---|---|---|---|---|---|
| | Asset valuation[a] | | Minimum return | Investment expenses charged to the PF | Investment limits (%) | |
| | Stock | Fixed income[b] | | | Equity | Foreign |
| Argentina | M/LP | M/LP | Yes | No | 50 | 20 |
| Bolivia | M/LP | M/LP | No | Yes | 40 | 12 |
| Colombia | M/LP | M/LP | Yes | Yes | 30 | 20 |
| Costa Rica | M/LP | M/LP | No | Yes | 10 | 50 |
| Chile | M/LP | M/LP | Yes | Yes[c] | Multifunds | 30 |
| Dominican Republic | NA | NA | Yes | No | NA | NA |
| El Salvador | M/AP$_{10}$ | M/LP | Yes | No | 5 | 0 |
| Mexico | M/LP | E | No | No | 15 | 20 |
| Peru | M/LP | M/LP | Yes | No | 35 | 10 |
| Uruguay | M/LP | M/LP$_{10}$ | Yes | No | 0 | 0 |

| | OECD and Eastern European Economies | | | | | |
|---|---|---|---|---|---|---|
| | Asset valuation[a] | | Minimum return | Investment expenses charged to the PF | Investment limits | |
| | Stock | Fixed income[b] | | | Equity | Foreign |
| Australia | M | M | NA | NA | No limit | No limit |
| Canada | M | M | NA | NA | 50 | No limit |
| Czech Republic | M | M | NA | NA | No limit | No limit (OECD) |
| Estonia | M | M | NA | NA | NA | NA |
| Hong Kong, China economy | M | M | NA | NA | NA | NA |
| Hungary | M | M | NA | NA | 50 | No limit |
| Ireland | NA | NA | NA | NA | No limit | No limit |
| Japan | M | M | NA | NA | No limit | No limit |
| Kazakhstan | M | M | NA | NA | NA | NA |
| Poland | M/LP | M | NA | NA | 40 | 5 |
| Sweden | M | M | NA | NA | NA | NA |
| Switzerland | NA | NA | NA | NA | 50 | 30 |
| United Kingdom | M | M | NA | NA | No limit | No limit |
| United States | M | M | NA | NA | No limit | No limit |

*Source:* Authors.
*Note:* AP$_{10}$ = average 10-day prices; E = estimated; LP = last price; M = market, NA = not available.
a. There are different rules for liquid and illiquid assets.
b. There are different rules for long- and short-term debt instruments.
c. Part of expenses for foreign investments are charged to the pension fund.

## Results

As explained, four alternative specifications are used for the risk-free asset to estimate the SRs. These are, if available, a short-term local rate (STL), a long-term local bond return (LTL), a short-term U.S. rate (T-bill) (STU), and a long-term U.S. bond return (T-bond) (LTU).[7] In all cases monthly (or quarterly) holding period returns are first estimated and then subtracted from pension fund portfolio returns to obtain excess returns. Standard deviations are also estimated using excess returns.

The other set of estimated statistics corresponds to the Selection return based on Sharpe's (1992) methodology. Single (in-sample) average portfolio weights were estimated (ATT-AVG) when enough data were available (at least three years, which leaves us with 30 degrees of freedom). Out-of-sample or rolling estimates (ATT-ROLL) require more data availability. It is important to keep in mind that Attribution or Style analysis does not judge what the optimal portfolios may be. It takes the actual or estimated portfolio composition (Style) as reference and checks whether there is value added.

When possible, the asset classes considered in this estimation process are the following: (1) local currency short-term government fixed income (or deposits), (2) local currency long-term government fixed income, (3) local stock market returns, (4) unhedged U.S. T-bills, measured in local currency, (5) unhedged U.S. T-bonds, measured in local currency, and (6) global equity, measured in local currency. It is interesting to notice that hedging is equivalent to shorting U.S. dollar deposits and buying local currency deposits with the proceeds, so it is implicitly considered in the analysis via a reduction in the estimated investment in U.S. T-bills and an increase in local bills. However, non-negativity restrictions are imposed, so the effects of hedging may not be completely captured.

The results of this exercise are presented below. The annex provides a detailed explanation for each country of the data used for each of these estimations. It also presents the estimation details and the results that are discussed next.

### Results by Country

*Argentina.* Argentina's performance history is marked by its recent debt crisis. Exhibit A.1.3 (annex) shows its performance indicators. A meaningful local long-term bond index for this country was not found, so the SR could not be estimated with respect to this reference (LTL), but the overall picture that appears is that on average this pension system has had a performance statistically indistinguishable from investing in short-term local deposits. Perhaps because of the large devaluation, SR against short and long foreign bonds are not significantly positive either. Looking at exhibit A.1.1, the Attribution analysis detects an average combination of about 80 percent in short-term instruments, 16 percent in local stocks, and 4 percent in global equity. Exhibit A.1.2, however, shows a significant composition change near the devaluation date. Before that, because of high co-linearity between local and foreign bills, the Attribution analysis estimates unstable weights. Significant value added is not detected either with average (ATT AVG) or rolling weights (ATT ROLL) using the entire sample period. However, portfolio weights seem to stabilize after the devaluation. Considering only the last three years of data, the out-of-sample or rolling approach indeed finds significant value added of 66 basis points per month.

**Bolivia.** As observed in exhibit A.2.1, Bolivia's pension fund system shows significantly positive SRs with respect to local short-term bonds and U.S. T-bills. However, SRs are not significantly positive against long-term U.S. bonds, which in this period offered significant capital gains. Given the relatively low levels of autocorrelation, at least in the latter two cases, these results do not seem to be a consequence of smoothing or to valuation practices. This result is likely to be explained by a long period with high local interest rates (starting at levels of 18 percent and ending in 6 percent). The point seems to be that Bolivia's pension system may have captured the local risk premium despite the bias toward short-term securities.

**Chile.** Chile has a multifund system. The oldest fund corresponds to fund C today. Since 2000, a second low-risk fund has been introduced (which corresponds to fund E today). Since 2002, Chile has had five funds (A, B, C, D, and E) ranked from "aggressive" to "conservative," respectively.

Exhibit A.3.1 first shows the average weight estimates for the aggregate pension fund portfolio in Chile. The second row shows the average weights for fund C. There are no differences between the two, partly because fund C is the oldest. It is noticeable that a large fraction appears invested, on average, in short-term local fixed income. The relative importance of long-term local fixed income appears to significantly substitute short-term local fixed income in the middle of the sample period. In any case, the relatively large average fraction invested in short-term local income (which is in part a consequence of the evolution of the pension system) explains why LTL and LTU appear not to be significant in exhibit A.3.3. This is partly explained by the systematic drop in long-term interest rates during the sample period. However, looking at the attribution indicators in the same exhibit, there is significant evidence of out-of-sample selectivity, meaning that the average portfolio was adjusted through time and/or securities chosen in such a way that generated significant Selection returns.

Turning to the younger funds, A, B, and D, in all cases *all* performance indicators are significant. However, the $R^2$'s are not large (in the neighborhood of 0.5), which may indicate that important asset classes to evaluate performance may have been omitted. In particular, it is known that Chilean pension fund portfolios have invested significantly in emerging markets, and this has been a high-return period for this asset class. Whether this is luck or systematic choice is open to question.

Finally, regarding fund E, the third graph of exhibit A.3.2 indicates that its composition has been quite stable, with about 40 percent invested in short-term local bonds and 60 percent long-term local ones. This explains why in a period of falling long-term interest rates the LTL ratio is significantly negative. The in-sample selectivity statistic is significantly positive, but the out-of sample one is not, so changes in portfolio composition in this case have not added value.

**Estonia.** The average style of the three funds of the Estonian pension system is presented in exhibit A.4.1, with about 73 percent invested in short-term fixed income, 4 in local stocks, 9 percent in foreign bonds, and 14 percent in global equity. The estimated average weights in exhibit A.4.1 are broadly consistent the fund profiles. The $R^2$'s however, are relatively low. This may be due to valuation issues and smoothing, given that the conservative fund, which invests mainly short-term local fixed income, has the lowest $R^2$. On the contrary, the Progressive fund has the highest. The performance indicators in exhibit A.4.2 show significant results with respect to the short-term fixed-income alternatives, but not with respect to the long-term ones. The selection returns using the average portfolio weights are significant for the system's average, and for the balanced and progressive funds. A familiar story appears in the case of the conservative fund: the SR using long-term local fixed income is marginally significantly negative, which is explained by the recent worldwide drop in interest rates.

*Hungary.* The Hungarian pension system appears to have invested on average 82 percent in local long-term bonds and 18 percent in global equity (exhibit A.5.1). All of its performance measures are significant (exhibit A.5.2) because local long-term interest rates were very high at the beginning of the sample period (around 16 percent) and dropped to about 7 percent during the period. The pension funds appear to have been invested primarily in long-term local bonds, realizing significant capital gains.

*Mexico.* As in other countries, Mexico's pension fund portfolio appears heavily tilted toward short-term local fixed income. This is observed both in the average estimated weights (exhibit A.6.1) and in the rolling weights (exhibit A.6.2). This explains why although the STL and STU indicators are significantly positive, the LTL and LTU are not. The attribution indicators (especially those estimated using the system's return weighted average [RWA] alternative, which the authors believe to be the correct return measure) also are significant. This means that the evolution of the portfolio composition (and perhaps also security selection) appear to have added value, but starting from a very conservative initial point. The relatively low $R^2$'s, however, may indicate that, as in the case of Chile, an asset class may be missing in the portfolio performance evaluation process. Still, portfolio performance is significantly better than the estimated composite benchmarks'.

*Netherlands.* For the Netherlands we have 20 annual data points. Statistical inference with only 20 data points is questionable, but it must be recognized that using annual data is more meaningful that using shorter-term returns. However, perhaps because of the 20 data points, the SR with respect to the local risk-free rate is only marginally significant. With respect to the U.S. short-term rate, the ratio is significant, but it is not so with respect to local and U.S. long-term rates. The average style analysis indicates about 36 percent in equities (local and foreign), 30 percent in short-term bills, and 33 percent in bonds. The annual (in-sample) Selection return (or alpha) is a sizable 1.3 percent, which turns out to be significantly positive. Unfortunately, this analysis has only 14 degrees of freedom, implying that it has important limitations regarding the statistical power of the present inferences.

*Peru.* In the case of Peru, a relevant local long-term bond index or interest rate series was not found, so this asset class is excluded from the analysis.

Here very significant differences are observed between using average quota returns and the more appropriate RWA returns. Considering the latter, the estimated average portfolio composition is presented in the first row of exhibit A.8.1. Roughly one-third is invested in local short-term fixed income, another one-third in short-term U.S.-dollar-denominated bonds, 20 percent in local stocks and the rest abroad, 3 percent in bonds, and 7 percent in global equity. It is interesting to notice the portfolio rebalancing toward short-term U.S. dollars that appears toward the end of the sample period (exhibit A.8.2). Considering RWA returns, all indicators are significantly positive, even the out-of-sample selection return, with an out-of-sample $R^2$ of 70 percent.

**Poland.** Judging by exhibit A.9.2 the Polish pension fund portfolio composition has been fairly stable, with about 50 percent in local bills, 20 percent in local bonds, and 30 percent in local equity. This portfolio has a significant SR only when judged against short-term U.S. dollar T-bills. The portfolio also shows a significant in-sample excess return with respect to the estimated composite benchmark, adding about 17 bp per month, but when the portfolio proportions are allowed to change, the excess return is no longer significant. These results may be affected by valuation practices, such that if long-term bond returns are smoothed, they will be counted as short term.

**United Kingdom.** For the United Kingdom quarterly data are available since 1992. This study works with the median fund. Because the median fund may change its identity from year to year, it is not clear that we are following a homogeneous series. Notice that this is not equivalent to analyzing the average fund. Further details of the data utilized are presented in the annex. Applying the chosen methodologies to the median pension fund implies the following results. First, the only significant SR is found against the short-term U.S. rate. The average style analysis yields 80 percent in equity (local and global), 16 percent in local bonds, and 4 percent in short-term dollar-based short-term instruments. Rolling weights tell a similar story. The in- and out-of-sample selection returns are significantly positive. Excess returns are 1.2 and 2.4 percent, respectively, although the latter has only 24 degrees of freedom. This possibly reflects that U.K. funds have chosen alternative asset classes with significant excess returns, but it may also reflect the unknown effects of using the median, or that managers have added value.

*Uruguay.* Uruguay appears to have invested principally in local currency short-term instruments. The only significant SR is obtained against the short-term U.S. T-bill benchmark. This result is obtained because of the high local short-term interest rates whose higher returns were not compensated on average by the recent debt and neighborhood crisis. In other words, the results presumably reflect that the Uruguayan pension fund delivered a good part of the local risk premium.

## Overview

Figures 3.3–3.6 present a graphical overview of the results. It is necessary to keep in mind that using different periodicities affects the results. In the case of SRs, monthly data were multiplied by $12^{0.5}$ and quarterly data by $4^{0.5}$ to make them comparable with annual data (used only in the case

**Figure 3.3    Short-Term Local Currency Sharpe Ratios**

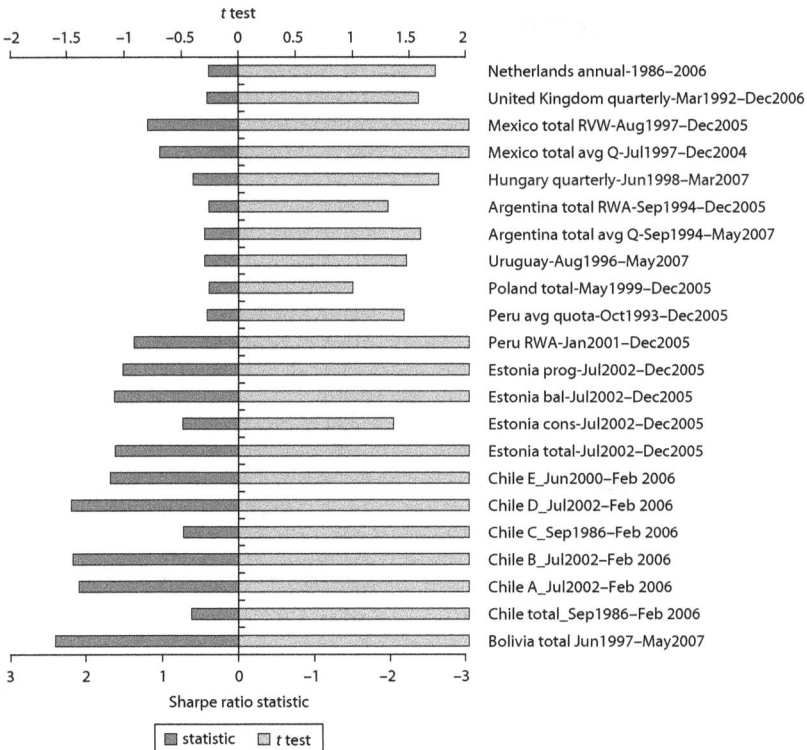

*Source:* Authors' estimates.

**Figure 3.4    Long-Term Local Currency Sharpe Ratios**

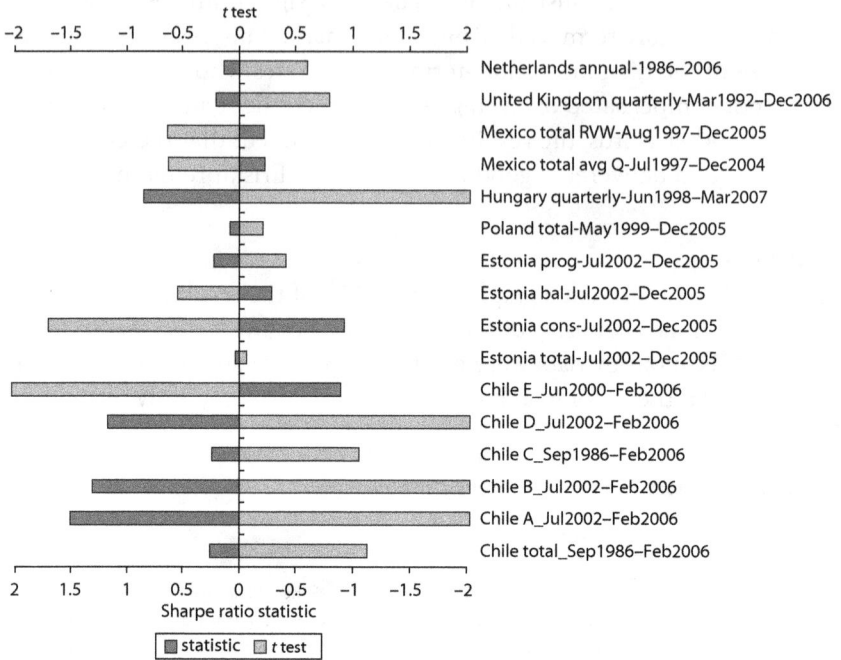

*Source:* Authors' estimates.

of the Netherlands). Regarding Selection returns, monthly returns are multiplied by 12 and quarterly data by 4 to make them comparable with annual data.

A first and likely most important conclusion, which is derived from figure 3.3, is that in all cases the STL ratios are positive and in most cases significantly so, particularly for the reformed systems. This means that pension funds appear to have delivered positive risk-adjusted risk premia, using the short-term interest rate as the risk-free rate.

When considering as a reference the long-term local bond (figure 3.4), in most cases the ratio is also positive. It is significantly negative in two cases, and significantly positive in four. The explanation for the negative and significant LTLs is that local long-term interest rates fell and portfolios were invested in relatively short instruments. Here no clear differences can be seen between the systems in developed and emerging markets.

**Figure 3.5    In-Sample Selection Returns**

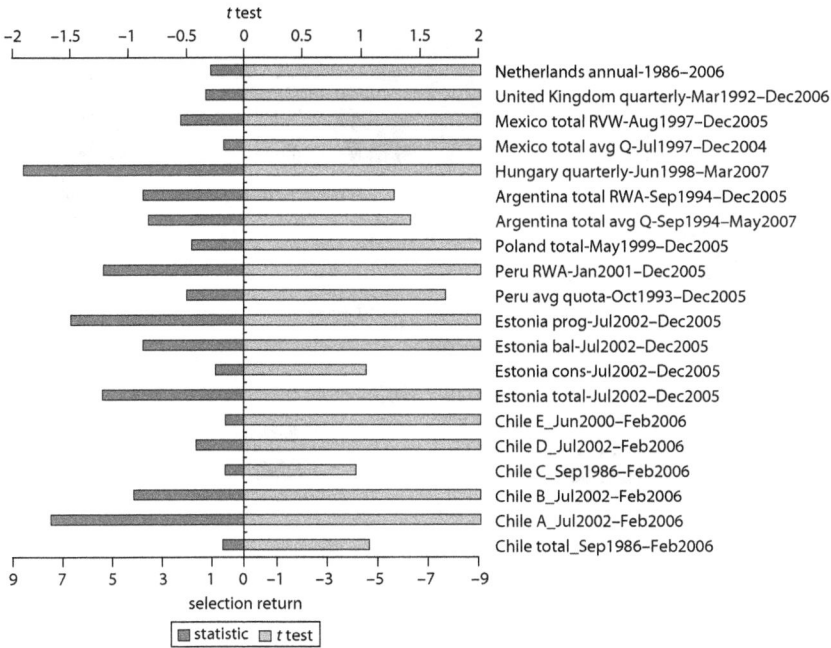

*Source:* Authors' estimates.

Finally, figures 3.5 and 3.6 summarize the in-sample and out-of-sample selection returns. Most selection returns are positive, and in a majority of cases they are significantly so.

The overall picture that arises from this analysis is that in pension systems utilizing these risk-adjusted performance measures, fund performance has tended to be positive. In many cases this arises from taking advantage of the local risk premium, falling local long-term interest rates, or both. Equity portfolio choices also seem to have been beneficial to portfolio performance during this period.

## Conclusions

Using a version of the SR, a portfolio performance analysis of the pension funds of 11 countries (2 of which are considered to be industrialized and 9 considered as emerging economies) was undertaken. The analysis estimated SRs against several alternative specifications for

**Figure 3.6    Out-of-Sample Selection Returns**

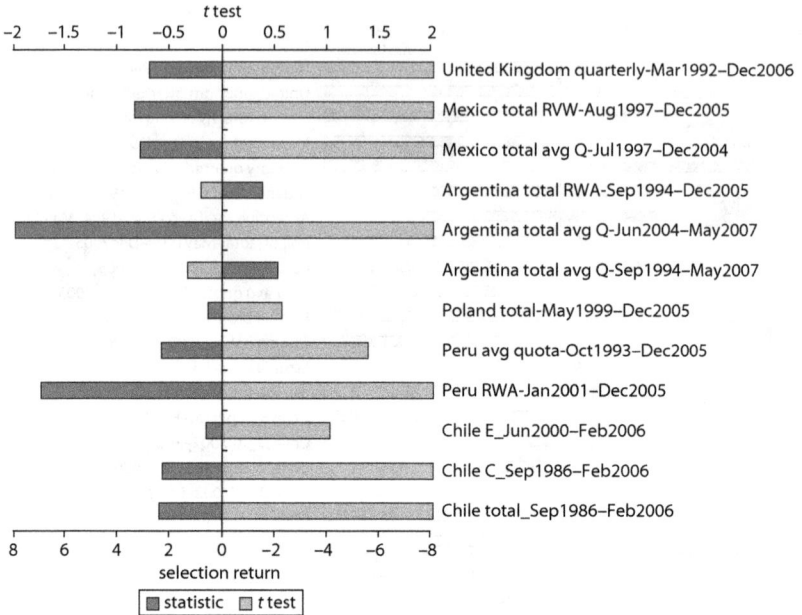

*Source:* Authors' estimates.

low-risk reference assets and by applying Sharpe's (1992) Attribution methodology (or Style Analysis). This is one of the first relatively comprehensive and detailed exploratory studies of the performance of pension funds that is primarily oriented to emerging market pension funds. It is limited by the type and availability of the data, and its principal virtue may be to indicate how to overcome the difficulties that are encountered when performing this kind of analysis in these contexts.

The pension funds analyzed indicate an overall "positive" performance. Based on the measure used, most of them are deemed to have delivered a significantly positive volatility-adjusted risk premium. This does not necessarily mean that there has been value added by portfolio managers, but it does at least mean that the regulations imposed in many countries have not obstructed the delivery of such premia.

Results may be explained by a wise or fortunate evolution of portfolio compositions or of the investment restrictions imposed by regulatory authorities. Although each country has its own story, a few common forces are driving their respective results, such as taking advantage of the local (country and exchange rate) risk premium implicit in local interest rates, in the case of most emerging economies.

Because the analysis takes portfolio compositions as given, it does not allow us to verify whether fund performances have been close to portfolios' that are "optimal" in some sense. However, in the context of long-term portfolio decisions, we know that long-term bonds may dominate short-term ones. Because the results support that in many cases—because of incentives, regulations, or unwise decisions—pension funds have not taken advantage of falling long-term (local and worldwide) interest rates (given a bias toward short-term fixed-income instruments), on the negative side it may be concluded that in general pension fund portfolios may have been distant from optimal ones.

## Annex: Country Performance Fact Sheets

The sources of all tables and figures are the authors' calculations.

### Argentina

***Fund Return Data Available.*** For Argentina we have two sets of data.

The first data set consists of monthly average quota values of the system. The monthly return was calculated as the log of the ratio of the consecutive quota values.

Sample period: September 1994–May 2007

The second set is composed of:

– Daily quota value for each institution
– Total asset value for each institution calculated by the end of each month
– Sample period: September 1994–December 2005

For calculating the return of the system with the second data set we proceeded as follows:

– We eliminated the institutions that were not operating by the end of the sample period. The institutions that were not considered (eliminated) were absorbed by other institutions, and the authors have been informed (OECD) that the final quota values include adjustments to consider the institutions that were absorbed.

 – We calculated the monthly return of each institution as the ratio of consecutive quota values. Then those returns were weighted by the previous month's end-of-period relative weight of the assets of each institution.

We expect to get more accurate results by using the second set of data.

## Benchmarks

| | Description | Source | Series name | Wealth index | Uses |
|---|---|---|---|---|---|
| Short-term local interest rate | Argentina Deposits Total Return Index | Global Financial Database | TRARGBDM | In the database | Sharpe ratio (STL), attribution |
| Long-term local interest rate | — | — | — | — | Sharpe ratio (LTL), attribution |
| Short-term U.S. interest rate | 3-month T-bills in local currency | Global Financial Database | TRUSABIM | In the database | Sharpe ratio (STU), attribution |
| Long-term U.S. interest rate | 10-year T-bonds in local currency | Global Financial Database | TRUSG10M | In the database | Sharpe ratio (LTU), attribution |
| Local stock index | Argentina Total Return Stock Index | Global Financial Database | TRARGSTM | In the database | Attribution |
| Global stock index | MSCI World Free Index in local currency | MSCI.COM | AWIF | In the database | Attribution |
| Exchange rate | Argentine pesos per U.S. dollar | Global Financial Database | _ARS_D | In the database | See above |

*Note:* — = not available.

**Results.** Here we present results that are discussed in the main body of the text.

### A.1.1  Average Attribution Weights (Average Style)

| | Bills (%) | Bonds | Stocks (%) | Bills U.S. (%) | Bonds U.S. (%) | AWIF (%) | $R^2$ |
|---|---|---|---|---|---|---|---|
| Avg. quota Sept. 1994–May 2007 | 79.0 | — | 16.9 | 0.0 | 0.0 | 4.2 | 0.42 |
| RWA Sept. 1994–Dec. 2005 | 80.4 | — | 15.3 | 0.0 | 0.0 | 4.3 | 0.42 |

In the table, "Avg. quota" stands for the official estimate based on the pension system's average share value or quota. "RWA" represents the weighted average of fund returns, following the methodology that we consider appropriate.

### A.1.2   Rolling Attribution Weights

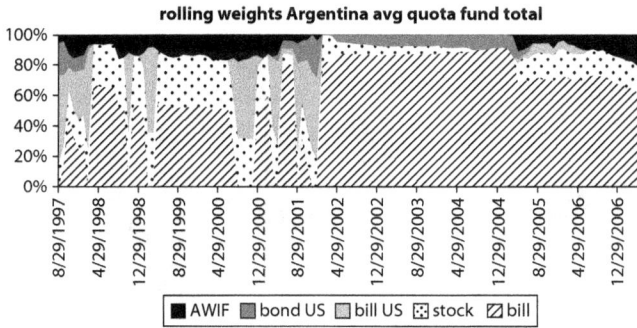

rolling weights Argentina avg quota fund total

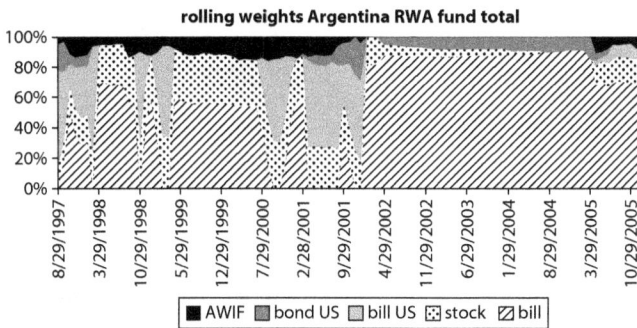

rolling weights Argentina RWA fund total

### A.1.3   Performance Measures: Argentina

| | Sharpe ratios | | | Attribution | |
|---|---|---|---|---|---|
| | A. STL | C. STU | D. LTU | E. ATT AVG | F. ATT ROLL |
| **Argentina Total RWA Sept. 1994–Dec. 2005** | | | | | |
| Statistic | 0.1130 | 0.0144 | −0.0255 | 0.0033 | −0.0013 |
| Std error | 0.0860 | 0.0860 | 0.0858 | 0.0026 | 0.0065 |
| t test | 1.3132 | 0.1681 | −0.2973 | 1.2797 | −0.1988 |

*(continued)*

**A.1.3   Performance Measures: Argentina** (Continued)

| | Sharpe ratios | | | Attribution | |
|---|---|---|---|---|---|
| | A. STL | C. STU | D. LTU | E. ATT AVG | F. ATT ROLL |
| Autocorrelation | 0.0239 | −0.0861 | −0.0627 | 0.0625 | 0.1077 |
| No. observations | 136 | 136 | 136 | 136 | 100 |
| $R^2$ | | | | 0.36 | −1.32[a] |
| **Argentina Total Avg. Quota Sept. 1994–May 2007** | | | | | |
| Statistic | 0.1297 | 0.0279 | −0.0070 | 0.0031 | −0.0018 |
| Std error | 0.0812 | 0.0812 | 0.0808 | 0.0022 | 0.0055 |
| t test | 1.5975 | 0.3454 | −0.0864 | 1.4163 | −0.3231 |
| Autocorrelation | 0.0229 | −0.0650 | −0.0416 | 0.0818 | 0.1121 |
| No. observations | 153 | 153 | 153 | 153 | 117 |
| $R^2$ | | | | 0.42 | −1.27[a] |
| **Argentina Total Avg. Quota June 2004–May 2007** | | | | | |
| Statistic | | | | | 0.0066 |
| Std error | | | | | 0.0023 |
| t test | | | | | 2.8618 |
| Autocorrelation | | | | | 0.0163 |
| No. observations | | | | | 36 |
| $R^2$ | | | | | 0.58[a] |

a. Out of sample.

## Bolivia

*Fund return data available.* For Bolivia we have the following information:

– Daily quota or share value for each pension fund
– Daily total asset value for each pension fund
– Sample period: June 1997–May 2007

For estimating the system's return we proceeded as follows: We calculated the monthly return as the ratio of consecutive month-end quota values for each pension fund. Then those returns were weighted using the previous end-of-month relative importance of each fund in the system.

## Benchmarks

| | Description | Source | Series name | Wealth index | Uses |
|---|---|---|---|---|---|
| Short-term local interest rate | Bolivia 3-month T-bill yield | Global Financial Database | ITBOLM | Constructed here based on interest rate levels[a] | Sharpe ratio (STL), attribution |
| Long-term local interest rate | — | — | — | — | Sharpe ratio (LTL), attribution |
| Short-term U.S. interest rate | 3-month T-bills in local currency | Global Financial Database | TRUSABIM | In the database | Sharpe ratio (STU), attribution |
| Long-term U.S. interest rate | 10-year T-bonds in local currency | Global Financial Database | TRUSG10M | In the database | Sharpe ratio (LTU), attribution |
| Local stock index | — | — | — | — | — |
| Global stock index | MSCI World Free Index in local currency | MSCI.COM | AWIF | In the database | Attribution |
| Exchange rate | Boliviano per U.S. dollar | Global Financial Database | _BOB_D | In the database | See above |

a. It is assumed that the interest rate corresponds to a simple three-month deposit rate, which allows for estimating the price of purchase. The following month the selling market price is estimated based on the corresponding interest rate. The estimated monthly return is the log of the ratio of the selling price to the purchase price.

*Results.* Here we present results that are discussed in the main body of the text.

### A.2.1    Performance Measures: Bolivia

| | Sharpe ratios | | |
|---|---|---|---|
| | A. STL | C. STU | D. LTU |
| **Bolivia Total June 1997–May 2007** | | | |
| Statistic | 0.6918 | 0.9876 | 0.0659 |
| Std error | 0.1016 | 0.1113 | 0.1016 |
| t test | 6.8075 | 8.8701 | 0.7213 |
| Autocorrelation | 0.3588 | −0.0664 | 0.0434 |
| No. observations | 120 | 120 | 120 |

## Chile

*Fund return data available.* For Chile we have the following information:

– Daily quota or share value for each institution and for each fund type
– Daily asset value for each institution and for each fund type
– Sample period:
   • System: July 1981–February 2006
   • Fund A: July 2002–February 2006
   • Fund B: July 2002–February 2006
   • Fund C: July 1981–February 2006
   • Fund D: July 2002–February 2006
   • Fund E: June 2000–February 2006

To calculate the returns of the system and of each fund we followed the following steps:

– We eliminated the institutions that were not operating by the end of the sample period. The institutions that were not considered were absorbed by others, whose quota values consider an adjustment to include the return of the institution that was absorbed (source: Superintendencia de Pensiones).
– We calculated the monthly return as the ratio of the quota value of the end of consecutive months for each institution and of each fund type. Then those returns were weighted by the proportion of assets at the end of the previous month.

*Benchmarks.* Before 1986 no data are available for long-term local interest rates. Therefore results are presented for the system and Fund C from August 1986.

| | Description | Source | Series name | Wealth index | Uses |
|---|---|---|---|---|---|
| Short-term local interest rate | Chile Bill Total Return Index | Global Financial Database | TRCHLBIM | In the database | Sharpe ratio (STL), attribution |
| Long-term local interest rate | From 1986 to 2000, 10-year bond yield From 2001 to 2007, LVA Government UF Index | Bolsa de comercio until December 2000; LVA Indices | — | Constructed here based on interest rate levels[a] until 2000; afterward, LVA database | Sharpe ratio (LTL), attribution |

*(continued)*

| | Description | Source | Series name | Wealth index | Uses |
|---|---|---|---|---|---|
| Short-term U.S. interest rate | 3-month T-bills in local currency | Global Financial Database | TRUSABIM | In the database | Sharpe ratio (STU), attribution |
| Long-term U.S. interest rate | 10-year T-bonds in local currency | Global Financial Database | TRUSG10M | In the database | Sharpe ratio (LTU), attribution |
| Local stock index | Santiago SE Return Index | Global Financial Database | TRCHLSTM | In the database | Attribution |
| Global stock index | GFD World Return Index (1986–1988) | Global Financial Database | TRWLDM, AWIF | In the database | Attribution |
| | MSCI World Free Index in local currency (1988–2006) | MSCI.COM | | In the database | |
| Exchange rate | Peso per U.S. dollar | Global Financial Database | _CLP_D | In the database | See above |

*Note:* — = not available.

a. It is assumed that the interest rate corresponds to a compounded 10-year annuity rate, which allows for estimating the price of purchase. The following month the selling market price is estimated based on the corresponding interest rate for a five-year annuity whose payments are one month closer. The estimated monthly return is the log of the ratio of the selling price to the purchase price.

**Results.** Here we present results that are discussed in the main body of the text.

### A.3.1  Average Attribution Weights (Average Style)

| | Bills (%) | Bonds (%) | Stocks (%) | Bills U.S. (%) | Bonds U.S. (%) | AWIF (%) | $R^2$ |
|---|---|---|---|---|---|---|---|
| Weights total | 43 | 41 | 17 | 0 | 0 | 0 | 0.67 |
| Weights fund C | 43 | 41 | 17 | 0 | 0 | 0 | 0.68 |
| Weights fund A | 30 | 19 | 28 | 0 | 0 | 23 | 0.47 |
| Weights fund B | 38 | 30 | 21 | 0 | 0 | 12 | 0.57 |
| Weights fund D | 42 | 42 | 10 | 0 | 1 | 5 | 0.81 |
| Weights fund E | 37 | 59 | 1 | 0 | 2 | 2 | 0.89 |

## A.3.2    Rolling Attribution Weights

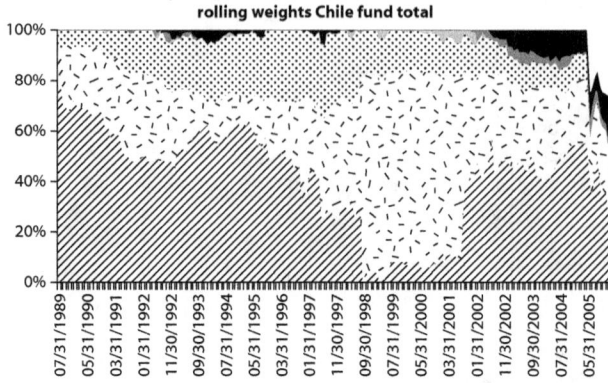

rolling weights Chile fund total

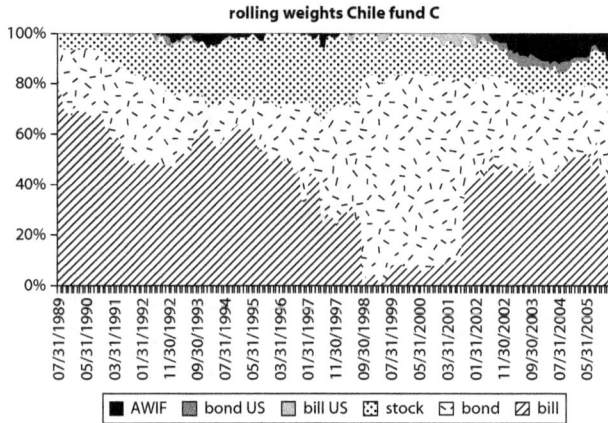

rolling weights Chile fund C

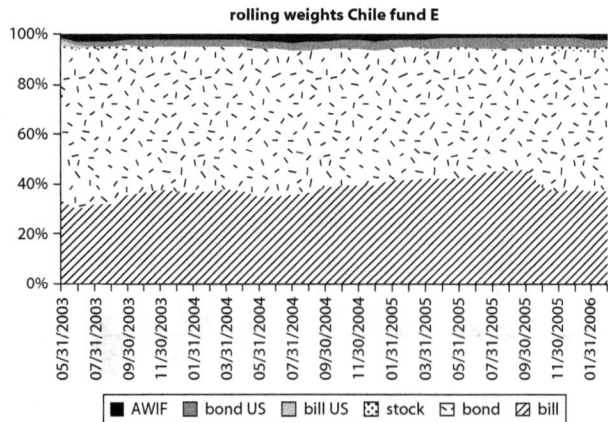

rolling weights Chile fund E

### A.3.3    Performance Measures: Chile

| | Sharpe ratios | | | | Attribution | |
|---|---|---|---|---|---|---|
| | A. STL | B. LTL | C. STU | D. LTU | E. ATT AVG | F. ATT ROLL |
| **Chile A July 2002–Feb. 2006** | | | | | | |
| Statistic | 0.6027 | 0.4345 | 0.5721 | 0.4983 | 0.0063 | |
| Std error | 0.1698 | 0.1634 | 0.1685 | 0.1656 | 0.0024 | |
| t test | 3.5503 | 2.6595 | 3.3957 | 3.0095 | 2.5569 | |
| Autocorrelation | −0.1477 | −0.0580 | −0.0088 | −0.1347 | −0.1510 | |
| No. observations | 41 | 41 | 41 | 41 | 41 | |
| $R^2$ | | | | | 0.47 | |
| **Chile B July 2002–Feb. 2006** | | | | | | |
| Statistic | 0.6259 | 0.3779 | 0.5525 | 0.4648 | 0.0036 | |
| Std error | 0.1708 | 0.1617 | 0.1677 | 0.1644 | 0.0015 | |
| t test | 3.6646 | 2.3378 | 3.2954 | 2.8272 | 2.4470 | |
| Autocorrelation | −0.1877 | −0.1317 | −0.0171 | −0.1615 | −0.1747 | |
| No. observations | 41 | 41 | 41 | 41 | 41 | |
| $R^2$ | | | | | 0.57 | |
| **Chile C Sept. 1986–Feb. 2006** | | | | | | |
| Statistic | 0.2100 | 0.0689 | 0.1101 | 0.0015 | 0.0006 | 0.0019 |
| Std error | 0.0588 | 0.0653 | 0.0583 | 0.0581 | 0.0006 | 0.0007 |
| t test | 3.5733 | 1.0548 | 1.8890 | 0.0264 | 0.9557 | 2.6036 |
| Autocorrelation | 0.2729 | 0.1612 | 0.0708 | 0.1807 | −0.0157 | −0.0816 |
| No. observations | 296 | 235 | 296 | 296 | 235 | 199 |
| $R^2$ | | | | | 0.68 | 0.70[a] |
| **Chile D July 2002–Feb. 2006** | | | | | | |
| Statistic | 0.6322 | 0.3381 | 0.5185 | 0.4615 | 0.0016 | |
| Std error | 0.1711 | 0.1606 | 0.1711 | 0.1606 | 0.0005 | |
| t test | 3.6954 | 2.1058 | 3.1169 | 2.8092 | 3.1142 | |
| Autocorrelation | 0.0599 | 0.1686 | 0.0291 | 0.0101 | −0.1553 | |
| No. observations | 41 | 41 | 41 | 41 | 41 | |
| $R^2$ | | | | | 0.81 | |
| **Chile E: June 2000–Feb. 2006** | | | | | | |
| Statistic | 0.4846 | −0.2580 | 0.1919 | 0.0445 | 0.0006 | 0.0005 |
| Std error | 0.1273 | 0.1224 | 0.1273 | 0.1224 | 0.0003 | 0.0005 |
| t test | 3.8083 | −2.1084 | 1.5799 | 0.3698 | 2.0789 | 1.0344 |
| Autocorrelation | 0.1476 | −0.0504 | 0.1241 | 0.0571 | −0.2547 | −0.0576 |
| No. observations | 69 | 69 | 69 | 69 | 69 | 33 |
| $R^2$ | | | | | 0.89 | 0.86[a] |
| **Chile Total Sept. 1986–Feb. 2006** | | | | | | |
| Statistic | 0.1788 | 0.0736 | 0.2187 | 0.1004 | 0.0007 | 0.0020 |
| Std error | 0.0658 | 0.0653 | 0.0658 | 0.0653 | 0.0007 | 0.0007 |

*(continued)*

**A.3.3    Performance Measures: Chile** *(Continued)*

|  | Sharpe ratios | | | | Attribution | |
|---|---|---|---|---|---|---|
|  | *A. STL* | *B. LTL* | *C. STU* | *D. LTU* | *E. ATT AVG* | *F. ATT ROLL* |
| *t* test | 2.7200 | 1.1262 | 3.3136 | 1.5355 | 1.0662 | 2.6981 |
| Autocorrelation | 0.2219 | 0.1585 | 0.1936 | 0.1581 | −0.0153 | −0.0826 |
| No. observations | 235 | 235 | 235 | 235 | 235 | 199 |
| $R^2$ |  |  |  |  | 0.67 | 0.70[a] |

a. Out of sample.

## Estonia

Estonia has a multifund system, which is composed of three funds: Conservative, Balanced, and Progressive. They differ in the proportion invested in fixed-rate instruments.

***Fund return data available.*** For Estonia we have the following information:

- Monthly average quota value for the system calculated at the end of each month.
- Monthly average quota value for each fund type (Conservative, Balanced, and Progressive)
- Sample period: June 2002–December 2005

According to the OECD database description, quota average values are calculated by using the relative importance of each fund at the end of each month. To measure the system's monthly return, we calculated the log of the ratio of consecutive monthly quota values of the system. The same methodology was applied to each fund type.

### Benchmarks

|  | Description | Source | Series name | Wealth index | Uses |
|---|---|---|---|---|---|
| Short-term local interest rate | Estonia current account deposit rate | Global Financial Database | ICESTDM | Constructed here based on interest rate levels[a] | Sharpe ratio (STL), attribution |
| Long-term local interest rate | Estonia long-term bond yield | Global Financial Database | IGESTM | Constructed here based on interest rate levels[b] | Sharpe ratio (LTL), attribution |

*(continued)*

| | Description | Source | Series name | Wealth index | Uses |
|---|---|---|---|---|---|
| Short-term U.S. interest rate | 3-month T-bills in local currency | Global Financial Database | TRUSABIM | In the database | Sharpe ratio (STU), attribution |
| Long-term U.S. interest rate | 10-year T-bonds in local currency | Global Financial Database | TRUSG10M | In the database | Sharpe ratio (LTU), attribution |
| Local stock index | Omx Talinn SE Total Return Index | Global Financial Database | _OMXTGID | In the database | Attribution |
| Global stock index | MSCI World Free Index in local currency | MSCI.COM | AWIF | In the database | Attribution |
| Exchange rate | Kroons per U.S. dollar | Global Financial Database | _EEK_D | In the database | See above |

a. It is assumed that the interest rate corresponds to a simple three-month deposit rate, which allows for estimating the price of purchase. The following month the selling market price is estimated based on the corresponding interest rate. The estimated monthly return is the log of the ratio of the selling price to the purchase price.

b. It is assumed that the interest rate corresponds to a compounded five-year annuity rate, which allows for estimating the price of purchase. The following month the selling market price is estimated based on the corresponding interest rate for a five-year annuity whose payments are one month closer. The estimated monthly return is the log of the ratio of the selling price to the purchase price.

***Results.*** Here we present results that are discussed in the main body of the text.

### A.4.1   Average Attribution Weights (Average Style)

| | Bills (%) | Bonds (%) | Stocks (%) | Bills U.S. (%) | Bonds U.S. (%) | AWIF (%) | $R^2$ |
|---|---|---|---|---|---|---|---|
| Estonia total | 73 | 0 | 4 | 0 | 9 | 14 | 0.36 |
| Estonia Conservative | 91 | 2 | 2 | 0 | 5 | 0 | 0.04 |
| Estonia Balanced | 79 | 0 | 3 | 0 | 8 | 9 | 0.37 |
| Estonia Progressive | 64 | 0 | 5 | 0 | 10 | 21 | 0.45 |

### A.4.2   Performance Measures: Estonia

| | Sharpe ratios | | | Attribution | |
|---|---|---|---|---|---|
| | A. STL | B. LTL | C. STU | D. LTU | E. ATT AVG |
| **Estonia Balanced July 2002–Dec. 2005** | | | | | |
| Statistic | 0.4692 | –0.0836 | 0.3253 | 0.2022 | 0.0033 |
| Std error | 0.1626 | 0.1546 | 0.1583 | 0.1559 | 0.0010 |
| t test | 2.8861 | –0.5411 | 2.0546 | 1.2971 | 3.3240 |
| Autocorrelation | 0.0386 | 0.0332 | 0.1658 | 0.1787 | 0.0647 |

(continued)

**A.4.2    Performance Measures: Estonia** *(Continued)*

| | Sharpe ratios | | | Attribution | |
|---|---|---|---|---|---|
| | *A. STL* | *B. LTL* | *C. STU* | *D. LTU* | *E. ATT AVG* |
| No. observations | 42 | 42 | 42 | 42 | 42 |
| $R^2$ | | | | | 0.37 |
| **Estonia Conservative July 2002–Dec. 2005** | | | | | |
| Statistic | 0.2120 | −0.2674 | 0.2083 | 0.1123 | 0.0009 |
| Std error | 0.1560 | 0.1570 | 0.1560 | 0.1548 | 0.0009 |
| *t* test | 1.3588 | −1.7026 | 1.3353 | 0.7255 | 1.0432 |
| Autocorrelation | 0.0701 | −0.1068 | 0.1019 | 0.1648 | 0.0684 |
| No. observations | 42 | 42 | 42 | 42 | 42 |
| $R^2$ | | | | | 0.04 |
| **Estonia Progressive July 2002–Dec. 2005** | | | | | |
| Statistic | 0.4383 | 0.0641 | 0.4146 | 0.2738 | 0.0056 |
| Std error | 0.1615 | 0.1545 | 0.1608 | 0.1572 | 0.0017 |
| *t* test | 2.7132 | 0.4152 | 2.5782 | 1.7418 | 3.3175 |
| Autocorrelation | −0.1278 | −0.0141 | 0.1699 | 0.1594 | −0.1084 |
| No. observations | 42 | 42 | 42 | 42 | 42 |
| $R^2$ | | | | | 0.45 |
| **Estonia Total July 2002–Dec. 2005** | | | | | |
| Statistic | 0.4678 | 0.0102 | 0.3770 | 0.2481 | 0.0046 |
| Std error | 0.1625 | 0.1543 | 0.1625 | 0.1543 | 0.0014 |
| *t* test | 2.8782 | 0.0662 | 2.3607 | 1.5836 | 3.2799 |
| Autocorrelation | −0.1197 | −0.0221 | 0.1629 | 0.1736 | −0.0863 |
| No. observations | 42 | 42 | 42 | 42 | 42 |
| $R^2$ | | | | | 0.36 |

## Hungary

*Fund return data available.* In the case of Hungary, the return data are the following:

– Quarterly returns for each individual pension fund
– Lagged quarterly total assets for each individual pension fund used to weigh each quarter's returns
– Sample period: June 1998–March 2007

For calculating the system's quarterly return we weighted the given returns of each institution by using the initial weight of the assets of the institution of the total assets of the system at the beginning of the quarter.

## Benchmarks

| | Description | Source | Series name | Wealth index | Uses |
|---|---|---|---|---|---|
| Short-term local interest rate | Hungary 3-month T-bill yield | Global Financial Database | ITHUN3D | Constructed here based on interest rate levels[a] | Sharpe ratio (STL), attribution |
| Long-term local interest rate | Hungary 5-year government note yield | Global Financial Database | IGHUN5D | Constructed here based on interest rate levels[b] | Sharpe ratio (LTL), attribution |
| Short-term U.S. interest rate | 3 month T-bills in local currency | Global Financial Database | TRUSABIM | In the database | Sharpe ratio (STU), attribution |
| Long-term U.S. interest rate | 10-year T-bonds in local currency | Global Financial Database | TRUSG10M | In the database | Sharpe ratio (LTU), attribution |
| Local stock index | Budapest Stock Exchange Index | Global Financial Database | _BUDX | In the database | Attribution |
| Global stock index | MSCI World Free Index in local currency | MSCI.COM | AWIF | In the database | Attribution |
| Exchange rate | Forint per U.S. dollar | Global Financial Database | _HUF_D | In the database | See above |

a. It is assumed that the interest rate corresponds to a simple three-month deposit rate, which corresponds to the return of the following quarter.

b. It is assumed that the interest rate corresponds to a compounded five-year annuity rate, which allows for estimating the price of purchase. The following quarter the selling market price is estimated based on the corresponding interest rate for a five-year annuity whose payments are one quarter closer. The estimated quarterly return is the log of the ratio of the selling price to the purchase price.

**Results.** Here we present results that are discussed in the main body of the text.

### A.5.1   Average Attribution Weights (Style)

| | Bills (%) | Bonds (%) | Stocks (%) | Bills U.S. (%) | Bonds U.S. (%) | AWIF (%) | $R^2$ |
|---|---|---|---|---|---|---|---|
| Hungary total | 0.0 | 82.0 | 0.0 | 0.0 | 0.0 | 18.0 | 0.60 |

**A.5.2    Performance Measures: Hungary**

| | Sharpe ratios | | | Attribution | |
|---|---|---|---|---|---|
| | A. STL | B. LTL | C. STU | D. LTU | E. ATT AVG |
| **Hungary Quarterly June 1998–Mar. 2007** | | | | | |
| Statistic | 0.2998 | 0.4246 | 0.5038 | 0.3710 | 0.0214 |
| Std error | 0.1704 | 0.1765 | 0.1704 | 0.1765 | 0.0068 |
| *t* test | 1.7595 | 2.4059 | 2.8075 | 2.1232 | 3.1583 |
| Autocorrelation | −0.0117 | 0.2199 | −0.2701 | −0.3212 | 0.2736 |
| No. observations | 36 | 36 | 36 | 36 | 36 |
| $R^2$ | | | | | 0.60 |

## Mexico

Mexico has a multifund pension system, which is composed of two funds (Siefore Básica 1 and 2). The SB2 fund started in 2005.

*Fund return data available.* For Mexico we have two sets of data. The first set of data consists of monthly average quota values of the system. The monthly return was calculated as the log of the ratio of the consecutive quota values.

The second set of data is composed by daily values of:

– Quota value for each institution and each fund type
– Total asset value for each institution and each fund type

For calculating the return of the system and of each fund, we did the following:

– Eliminated the institutions that were not operating by the end of the period in study. Those institutions that were not considered (eliminated) were absorbed by other institutions, whose quota value includes an adjustment to include the return of the institution that was absorbed.
– Calculated the monthly return of each institution and each fund type as the ratio of the consecutive end-of-the-month quota values. Then those returns were weighted by using the initial weight of the assets of the institution and fund type on total assets of the system at the beginning of the month.

We expect the estimates to be more accurate based on the latter data set.

## Benchmarks

|  | Description | Source | Series name | Wealth index | Uses |
|---|---|---|---|---|---|
| Short-term local interest rate | Mexico Bills Total Return Index | Global Financial Database | _MXFR1D | In the database | Sharpe ratio (STL), attribution |
| Long-term local interest rate | Mexico 5-year Government Bonds Total Return Index | Global Financial Database | TRMEXGVM | In the database | Sharpe ratio (LTL), attribution |
| Short-term U.S. interest rate | 3-month T-bills in local currency | Global Financial Database | TRUSABIM | In the database | Sharpe ratio (STU), attribution |
| Long-term U.S. interest rate | 10-year T-bonds in local currency | Global Financial Database | TRUSG10M | In the database | Sharpe ratio (LTU), attribution |
| Local stock index | Mexico SE Return Index | Global Financial Database | _IRTD | In the database | Attribution |
| Global stock index | MSCI World Free Index in local currency | MSCI.COM | AWIF | In the database | Attribution |
| Exchange rate | New peso per U.S. dollar | Global Financial Database | _MXN_D | In the database | See above |

**Results.** Here we present results that are discussed in the main body of the text.

### A.6.1    Average Attribution Weights (Average Style)

|  | Bills (%) | Bonds (%) | Stocks (%) | Bills U.S. (%) | Bonds U.S. (%) | AWIF (%) | $R^2$ |
|---|---|---|---|---|---|---|---|
| Weights avg. quota | 93.2 | 3.3 | 3.5 | 0.0 | 0.0 | 0.0 | 0.47 |
| Weights using RWA | 93.0 | 3.4 | 3.6 | 0.0 | 0.0 | 0.0 | 0.47 |

In the table, "Avg. quota" stands for the official estimate based on the pension system's average share value or quota. "RWA" represents the weighted average of fund returns, following the methodology that we considered appropriate.

### A.6.2   Rolling Attribution Weights

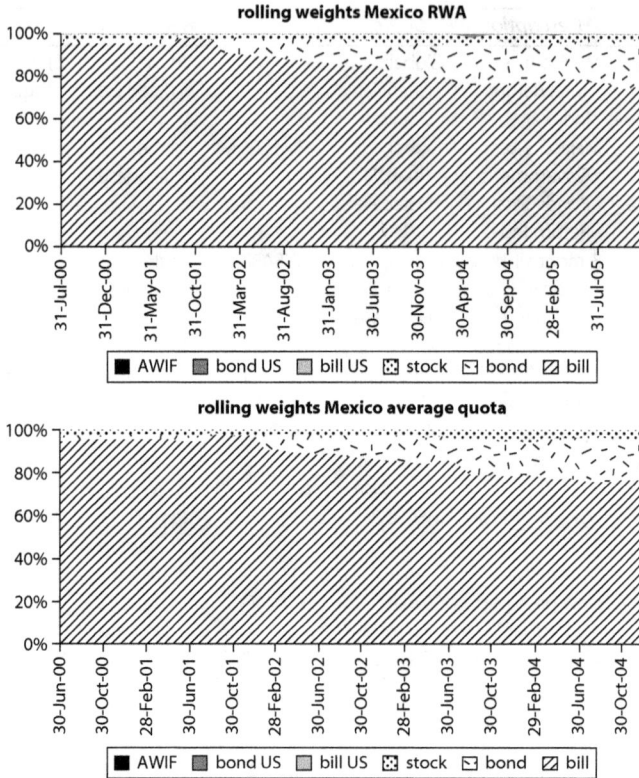

rolling weights Mexico RWA

rolling weights Mexico average quota

### A.6.3   Performance Measures: Mexico

| | Sharpe ratios | | | | Attribution | |
|---|---|---|---|---|---|---|
| | A. STL | B. LTL | C. STU | D. LTU | E. ATT AVG | F. ATT ROLL |
| **Mexico Total Avg. Quota July 1997–Dec. 2004** | | | | | | |
| Statistic | 0.2994 | −0.0659 | 0.2107 | 0.0767 | 0.0007 | 0.0026 |
| Std error | 0.1077 | 0.1055 | 0.1077 | 0.1055 | 0.0007 | 0.0010 |
| t test | 2.7788 | −0.6247 | 1.9772 | 0.7264 | 2.8098 | 2.5416 |
| Autocorrelation | 0.2007 | 0.0155 | 0.0588 | 0.0903 | −0.0463 | −0.0801 |
| No. observations | 90 | 90 | 90 | 90 | 90 | 54 |
| $R^2$ | | | | | 0.47 | 0.03[a] |
| **Mexico Total RVW Aug. 1997–Dec. 2005** | | | | | | |
| Statistic | 0.3450 | −0.0632 | 0.2261 | 0.1020 | 0.0021 | 0.0028 |
| Std error | 0.1024 | 0.0996 | 0.1024 | 0.0996 | 0.0006 | 0.0006 |
| t test | 3.3689 | −0.6347 | 2.2433 | 1.0229 | 3.4130 | 4.6598 |
| Autocorrelation | 0.2327 | 0.0177 | 0.0546 | 0.0793 | −0.0463 | 0.0948 |
| No. observations | 101 | 101 | 101 | 101 | 101 | 65 |
| $R^2$ | | | | | 0.47 | 0.50[a] |

a. Out of sample.

## Netherlands

*Fund return data available.* In the case of the Netherlands, the return data are the following:

- Annual returns for the total system. These returns are calculated using the return of each type of asset and the weight of each asset in the system's portfolio. The original data source is WM Company and DNB.
- Sample period: 1986–2006.

### Benchmarks

| | Description | Source | Series name | Wealth index | Uses |
|---|---|---|---|---|---|
| Short-term local interest rate | Netherlands Total Return Bills Index | Global Financial Database | TRNLDBIM | In the database | Sharpe ratio (STL), attribution |
| Long-term local interest rate | Netherlands government Bond Return Index | Global Financial Database | TRNLDGVM | In the database | Sharpe ratio (LTL), attribution |
| Short-term U.S. interest rate | 3-month T-bills in local currency | Global Financial Database | TRUSABIM | In the database | Sharpe ratio (STU), attribution |
| Long-term U.S. interest rate | 10-year T-bonds in local currency | Global Financial Database | TRUSG10M | In the database | Sharpe ratio (LTU), attribution |
| Local stock index | Netherlands Total Return Stock Index | Global Financial Database | TRNLDSTM | In the database | Attribution |
| Global stock index | GFD World Return Index (1986–1988) | Global Financial Database | TRWLDM | In the database | Attribution |
| | MSCI World Free Index in local currency (1988–2006) | MSCI.COM | | In the database | |
| Exchange rate | Guilder per U.S. dollar | Global Financial Database | _NLG_D | In the database | See above |

*Results.* Here we present results that are discussed in the main body of the text.

### A.7.1   Average Attribution Weights (Average Style)

| | Bills (%) | Bonds (%) | Stocks (%) | Bills U.S. (%) | Bonds U.S. (%) | AWIF (%) | $R^2$ |
|---|---|---|---|---|---|---|---|
| Avg. weights | 9 | 21 | 14 | 21 | 13 | 22 | 0.8992 |

### A.7.2   Performance Measures: The Netherlands

| | Sharpe ratios | | | Attribution | |
|---|---|---|---|---|---|
| | A. STL | B. LTL | C. STU | D. LTU | E. ATT AVG |
| **Netherlands Annual 1986–2006** | | | | | |
| Statistic | 0.3920 | 0.1353 | 0.4502 | 0.1550 | 0.0130 |
| Std error | 0.2264 | 0.2246 | 0.2264 | 0.2246 | 0.0051 |
| *t* test | 1.7313 | 0.6024 | 1.9186 | 0.6891 | 2.5659 |
| Autocorrelation | 0.1497 | −0.0253 | 0.1712 | 0.0691 | 0.0799 |
| No. observations | 21 | 21 | 21 | 21 | 21 |
| $R^2$ | | | | | 0.8993 |

## Peru

Peru has a multifund system. Because of data availability in the sample period, we considered only fund 2.

*Fund return data available.* For Peru we have two sets of data:

- Monthly quota value for the system, which, according to the OECD database description, is a weighted average of monthly quota values for the overall system, using as weights the relative importance of each fund at the end of each month.
- Sample period for monthly data: October 2003–December 2005.
- Daily quota value for each pension fund, and total value assets for each pension fund. According to the OECD, there are no daily data before 2001.
- Sample period for daily data: January 2001–December 2005 (RWA).

This represents a problem because the calculations that we obtained are not comparable within the two sets of data. By using daily values of assets and quota we can obtain more accurate results. Calculations were made by using separately each data set. For the first set of data (monthly data), we calculated the monthly return as the log of the ratio of consecutive monthly average quota values. For the second set of data (daily data), we calculated the system's monthly return as the ratio using quota values for the end of consecutive months for each pension fund. Then those returns were weighted by the relative weight of the fund's assets at the end of the previous month.

## Benchmarks

| | Description | Source | Series name | Wealth index | Uses |
|---|---|---|---|---|---|
| Short-term local interest rate | Peru Time Deposit Rate (CD del BCRP) | Global Financial Database | | Constructed here based on interest rate levels[a] | Sharpe ratio (STL), attribution |
| Long-term local interest rate | — | — | — | — | Sharpe ratio (LTL), attribution |
| Short-term U.S. interest rate | 3-month T-bills in local currency | Global Financial Database | TRUSABIM | In the database | Sharpe ratio (STU), attribution |
| Long-term U.S. interest rate | 10-year T-bonds in local currency | Global Financial Database | TRUSG10M | In the database | Sharpe ratio (LTU), attribution |
| Local stock index | Peru Stock Return Index | Global Financial Database | TRPERSTM | In the database | Attribution |
| Global stock index | MSCI World Free Index in local currency | MSCI.COM | AWIF | In the database | Attribution |
| Exchange rate | Nuevo sol per U.S. dollar | Global Financial Database | _PEN_D | In the database | See above |

*Note:* — = not available.

a. It is assumed that the interest rate corresponds to a simple three-month deposit rate, which allows for estimating the price of purchase. The following month the selling market price is estimated based on the corresponding interest rate. The estimated monthly return is the log of the ratio of the selling price to the purchase price.

*Results.* Here we present results that are discussed in the main body of the text.

### A.8.1    Average Attribution Weights (Average Style)

| | Bills (%) | Bonds (%) | Stocks (%) | Bills U.S. (%) | Bonds U.S. (%) | AWIF (%) | $R^2$ |
|---|---|---|---|---|---|---|---|
| Peru fund RWA | 33.9 | | 21.4 | 34.7 | 2.8 | 7.2 | 0.79 |
| Peru fund avg. quota | 78 | | 9 | 13 | 0 | 0 | 0.23 |

The first row represents the estimated portfolio weights based on what we consider to be the better return estimates, corresponding to the RWA. The second row uses average quota returns that are subject to significant measurement error, explaining the low $R^2$ and the other results.

### A.8.2    Rolling Attribution Weights

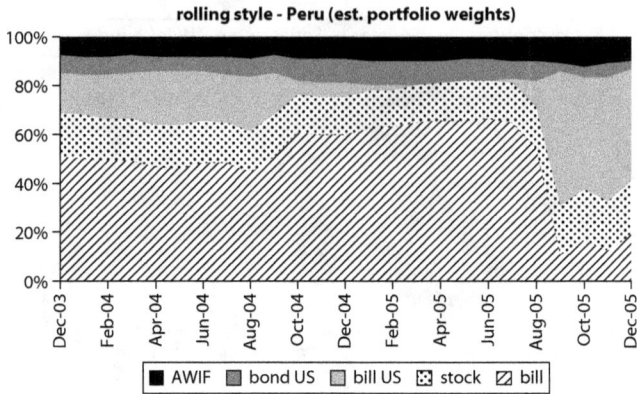

rolling style - Peru (est. portfolio weights)

■ AWIF   ▨ bond US   ▨ bill US   ▨ stock   ▨ bill

### A.8.3    Performance Measures: Peru

|  | Sharpe ratios | | | Attribution | |
|---|---|---|---|---|---|
|  | A. STL | C. STU | D. LTU | E. ATT AVG | F. ATT ROLL |
| **Peru Avg Quota Oct. 1993–Dec. 2005** | | | | | |
| Statistic | 0.1202 | 0.2686 | 0.1039 | 0.0019 | 0.0019 |
| Std error | 0.0828 | 0.0840 | 0.0828 | 0.0011 | 0.0014 |
| t test | 1.4520 | 3.1998 | 1.2561 | 1.7150 | 1.4012 |
| Autocorrelation | 0.4397 | 0.3870 | 0.2702 | 0.1410 | 0.0450 |
| No. observations | 147 | 147 | 147 | 147 | 111 |
| $R^2$ |  |  |  | 0.23 | 0.15 |
| **Peru RWA Jan. 2001–Dec. 2005** | | | | | |
| Statistic | 0.3966 | 0.5350 | 0.2433 | 0.0045 | 0.0057 |
| Std error | 0.1341 | 0.1380 | 0.1341 | 0.0011 | 0.0027 |
| t test | 2.9582 | 3.8763 | 1.8570 | 4.3063 | 2.1133 |
| Autocorrelation | −0.0875 | −0.0552 | −0.0147 | −0.0641 | −0.0228 |
| No. observations | 60 | 60 | 60 | 60 | 24 |
| $R^2$ |  |  |  | 0.79 | 0.70[a] |

a. Out of sample.

## Poland
*Fund return data available.* For Poland we have the following information:

- Daily quota value for each pension fund
- Daily total asset value for each pension fund
- Sample period: May 1999–December 2005

For estimating the system's return:

- We did not consider the institutions that were not operating at the end of the sample period. Those institutions were absorbed by other institutions, and we were informed by the OECD that the quota value of the remaining institutions includes an adjustment.
- We calculated the monthly return of each institution as ratio of consecutive end-of-month quota values. Then weighted average return was estimated using the initial relative importance of each pension fund at the end of the previous month.

## Benchmarks

|  | Description | Source | Series name | Wealth index | Uses |
|---|---|---|---|---|---|
| Short-term local interest rate | Poland T-bill Total Return Index | Global Financial Database | TRPOLBIM | In the database | Sharpe ratio (STL), attribution |
| Long-term local interest rate | Poland 10-year Government Bond Return Index | Global Financial Database | TRPOLGVM | In the database | Sharpe ratio (LTL), attribution |
| Short-term U.S. interest rate | 3-month T-bills in local currency | Global Financial Database | TRUSABIM | In the database | Sharpe ratio (STU), attribution |
| Long-term U.S. interest rate | 10-year T-bonds in local currency | Global Financial Database | TRUSG10M | In the database | Sharpe ratio (LTU), attribution |
| Local stock index | Warsaw SE General Index | Global Financial Database | _WIGD | In the database | Attribution |
| Global stock index | MSCI World Free Index in local currency | MSCI.COM | AWIF | In the database | Attribution |
| Exchange rate | Zloty per U.S. dollar | Global Financial Database | _PLN_D | In the database | See above |

## Results

Here we present results that are discussed in the main body of the text.

### A.9.1   Average Attribution Weights (Average Style)

|  | Bills (%) | Bonds (%) | Stocks (%) | Bills U.S. (%) | Bonds U.S. (%) | AWIF (%) | $R^2$ |
|---|---|---|---|---|---|---|---|
| Poland total | 51.6 | 18.6 | 29.0 | 0.0 | 0.0 | 0.9 | 0.88 |

### A.9.2   Rolling Attribution Weights

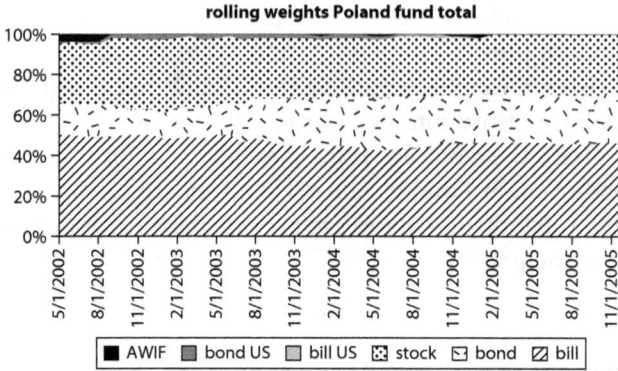

rolling weights Poland fund total

### A.9.3   Performance Measures: Poland

| | Sharpe ratios | | | | Attribution | |
|---|---|---|---|---|---|---|
| | A. STL | B. LTL | C. STU | D. LTU | E. ATT AVG | F. ATT ROLL |
| **Poland Total May 1999–Dec. 2005** | | | | | | |
| Statistic | 0.1125 | 0.0239 | 0.2344 | 0.1589 | 0.0017 | 0.0004 |
| Std error | 0.1129 | 0.1125 | 0.1129 | 0.1125 | 0.0008 | 0.0008 |
| t test | 0.9972 | 0.2122 | 2.0553 | 1.4039 | 2.0929 | 0.5726 |
| Autocorrelation | 0.1001 | 0.1371 | 0.0838 | 0.1268 | −0.0188 | 0.3742 |
| No. observations | 79 | 79 | 79 | 79 | 79 | 43 |
| $R^2$ | | | | | 0.88 | 0.94 |

## United Kingdom

***Fund return data available.*** For the United Kingdom we have the following available return data:

– Quarterly returns for the system. The original source of those data is Combined Actuarial Performance Services Limited median returns for all pension funds participating in the CAPS Trustee Service (Watson-Wyatt).
– Sample Period: quarterly, March 1992–December 2006.

## *Benchmarks*

| | Description | Source | Series name | Wealth index | Uses |
|---|---|---|---|---|---|
| Short-term local interest rate | U.K. Bills Total Return Index | Global Financial Database | TRGBRBIM | In the database | Sharpe ratio (STL), attribution |
| Long-term local interest rate | U.K. 10-year Government Bonds Total Return Index | Global Financial Database | TRGBRGVM | In the database | Sharpe ratio (LTL), attribution |
| Short-term U.S. interest rate | 3-month T-bills in local currency | Global Financial Database | TRUSABIM | In the database | Sharpe ratio (STU), attribution |
| Long-term U.S. interest rate | 10-year T-bonds in local currency | Global Financial Database | TRUSG10M | In the database | Sharpe ratio (LTU), attribution |
| Local stock index | FTSE-100 Total Return Index | Global Financial Database | _TFTSED | In the database | Attribution |
| Global stock index | MSCI World Free Index in local currency | MSCI.COM | — | In the database | Attribution |
| Exchange rate | Pound daily | Global Financial Database | _GBP_D | In the database | See above |

*Note:* — = not available.

***Results.*** Here we present results that are discussed in the main body of the text.

### A.10.1    Average Attribution Weights (Average Style)

| | Bills (%) | Bonds (%) | Stocks (%) | Bills U.S. (%) | Bonds U.S. (%) | AWIF (%) | $R^2$ |
|---|---|---|---|---|---|---|---|
| United Kingdom | 0 | 16 | 62 | 4 | 0 | 18 | 0.9787 |

### A.10.2    Rolling Attribution Weights

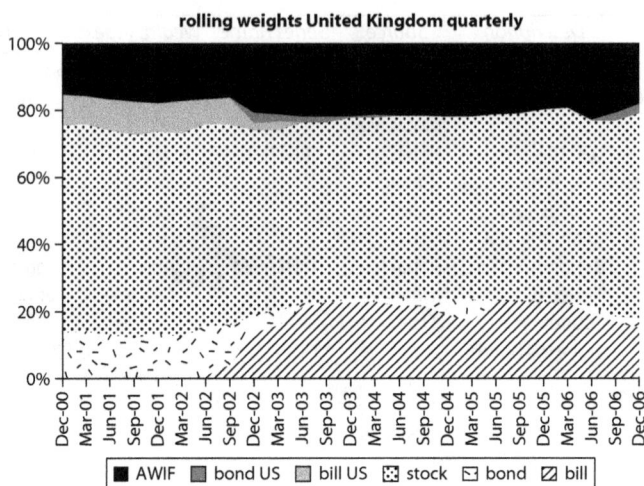

rolling weights United Kingdom quarterly

### A.10.3    Performance Measures: United Kingdom

| | Sharpe ratios | | | | Attribution | |
|---|---|---|---|---|---|---|
| | A. STL | B. LTL | C. STU | D. LTU | E. ATT AVG | F. ATT ROLL |
| **United Kingdom Quarterly Mar. 1992–Dec. 2005** | | | | | | |
| Statistic | 0.2064 | 0.1030 | 0.2760 | 0.1292 | 0.0037 | 0.0068 |
| Std error | 0.1305 | 0.1294 | 0.1305 | 0.1294 | 0.0011 | 0.0017 |
| t test | 1.5821 | 0.7960 | 2.0983 | 0.9968 | 3.4328 | 4.1189 |
| Autocorrelation | −0.0347 | −0.0613 | −0.1421 | −0.0762 | 0.3718 | 0.0425 |
| No. observations | 60 | 60 | 60 | 60 | 60 | 24 |
| $R^2$ | | | | | 0.9787 | 0.9867 |

## Uruguay

**Fund return data available.** For Uruguay, we have the following pension fund return data:

– Monthly quota value for each institution
– Monthly asset value for each institution
– Sample period: August 1996–May 2007

To measure the system's monthly return, we calculated the monthly returns as the ratio of consecutive monthly quota values for each pension fund and weighted them by the relative weight of each fund's assets at the end of the previous month.

## Benchmarks

| | Description | Source | Series name | Wealth index | Uses |
|---|---|---|---|---|---|
| Short-term local interest rate | Uruguay Savings Deposit Rate | Global Financial Database | ICURYSM | Constructed here based on interest rate levels[a] | Sharpe ratio (STL), attribution |
| Long-term local interest rate | — | — | — | — | Sharpe ratio (LTL), attribution |
| Short-term U.S. interest rate | 3-month T-bills in local currency | Global Financial Database | TRUSABIM | In the database | Sharpe ratio (STU), attribution |
| Long-term U.S. interest rate | 10-year T-bonds in local currency | Global Financial Database | TRUSG10M | In the database | Sharpe ratio (LTU), attribution |
| Local stock index | — | Global Financial Database | — | — | Attribution |
| Global stock index | MSCI World Free Index in local currency | MSCI.COM | AWIF | In the database | Attribution |
| Exchange rate | Peso per U.S. dollar | Global Financial Database | _UYU_D | In the database | See above |

Note: — = not available.
a. It is assumed that the interest rate corresponds to a simple three-month deposit rate, which allows for estimating the price of purchase. The following month the selling market price is estimated based on the corresponding interest rate. The estimated monthly return is the log of the ratio of the selling price to the purchase price.

*Results.* Here we present results that are discussed in the main body of the text.

### A.11.1   Performance Measures: Uruguay

| | Sharpe ratios | | |
|---|---|---|---|
| | A. STL | C. STU | D. LTU |
| **Uruguay Aug. 1996–May 2007** | | | |
| Statistic | 0.1299 | 0.1763 | 0.0884 |
| Std error | 0.0881 | 0.0884 | 0.0879 |
| t test | 1.4746 | 1.9946 | 1.0059 |
| Autocorrelation | 0.4085 | 0.1643 | 0.1851 |
| No. observations | 130 | 130 | 130 |

## Notes

1. For instance, the CAPM assumes that the market portfolio maximizes the Sharpe ratio, and from that condition the CAPM equation is a direct consequence.

2. For example, applying this to the global equity portfolio (using Dimson, Marsh, and Staunton's [2006] estimates) gives us a range of $0.25 \pm 0.10$ (so it is significantly different from zero at a 5 percent significance level).

3. The monthly returns of long-term bonds are obtained from bond wealth indices, which assume that all cash flows are reinvested in the portfolio of bonds considered in the index. Bond returns are caused by changes in interest rates (capital gains and losses) and by the effect of the passage of time, which implies that cash flows get closer (interest accrual), thus implying a positive trend. If only a series of interest rates is available, we transform interest rates into bond prices, and with bond prices we can obtain short-term returns and create a similar wealth index.

4. Data source: Global Financial Database.

5. This methodology yields as a special case Jensen's Alpha, described in table 3.1.A, if only a short-term fixed income and a stocks benchmark are considered.

6. A large body of literature has worried about benchmark efficiency for portfolio evaluation purposes since Roll's (1978) critique. If portfolio performance is measured against an inefficient benchmark, we are likely to find positive performance even though it does not exist in reality.

7. See note 2.

## References

Carhart, M. 1997. "Persistence in Mutual Fund Performance." *Journal of Finance* 52: 57– 82.

Brown, Stephen J., and William N. Goetzmann. 1997. "Mutual Fund Styles." *Journal of Financial Economics* 43 (3): 373–99.

Connor, Gregory, and Robert A. Korajczyk. 1986. "Performance Measurement with the Arbitrage Pricing Theory: A New Framework for Analysis." *Journal of Financial Economics* 15 (3): 373–94.

Dimson, E., P. Marsh, and M. Staunton. 2006. "The Worldwide Equity Premium: A Smaller Puzzle." Draft, London School of Economics.

Elton, Edwin J., M. J. Gruber, and C. R. Blake. 1996. "The Persistence of Risk-Adjusted Mutual Fund Performance." *Journal of Business* 69 (2): 133–57.

Ferson, W., and K. Khang. 2002. "Conditional Performance Measurement Using Portfolio Weights: Evidence for Pension Funds." *Journal of Financial Economics* 65 (2): 249–82.

Ferson, Wayne E., and Rudi W. Schadt. 1996. "Measuring Fund Strategy and Performance in Changing Economic Conditions." *Journal of Finance* 51 (2): 425–61.

Goodwin, T. 1998. "The Information Ratio." *Financial Analyst Journal* 54 (4): 34–43.

Grinblatt, Mark, and Sheridan Titman. 1993. "Performance Measurement without Benchmarks: An Examination of Mutual Fund Returns." *Journal of Business* 6 (1): 47–68.

Henriksson, R., and R. Merton. 1981. "On Market Timing and Investment Performance II. Statistical Procedures for Evaluation Forecasting Skills." *Journal of Business* 54 (4): 513–33.

Jensen, Michael. 1968. "The Performance of Mutual Funds in the Period 1945–1964." *Journal of Finance* 23 (2): 389–416.

Lehmann, Bruce N., and David M. Modest. 1987. "Mutual Fund Performance Evaluation: A Comparison of Benchmarks and Benchmark Comparisons." *Journal of Finance* 42 (2): 233–65.

Lo, Andrew. 2002. "The Statistics of Sharpe Ratios." *Financial Analysts Journal* 58 (4): 36–52.

Roll, Richard. 1978. "Ambiguity When the Performance Is Measured with the Security Market Line." *Journal of Finance* 33 (4): 1051–69.

Sharpe, William F. 1966. "Mutual Fund Performance." *Journal of Business* 39 (1): 119–38.

———. 1992. "Asset Allocation: Management and Performance Measurement." *Journal of Portfolio Management* 18 (winter): 7–19.

Treynor, Jack. 1965. "How to Rate Management of Investment Funds." *Harvard Business Review* 43 (1): 63–75.

Treynor, Jack, and K. Mazuy. 1966. "Can Mutual Funds Outguess the Market?" *Harvard Business Review* 44 (4): 131–36.

Treynor, Jack L., and Fischer Black. 1973. "How to Use Security Analysis to Improve Portfolio Selection." *Journal of Business* 46 (1): 66–86.

Walker, E. 2006. "Cobertura cambiaria e inversión internacional de portafolio: una perspectiva local." *Economía Chilena* 9 (2): 41–59.

———. 2008. "Strategic Currency Hedging and Global Portfolio Investments Upside Down." *Journal of Business Research* 61 (6): 657–68.

CHAPTER 4

# Portfolio Choice, Minimum Return Guarantees, and Competition in Defined Contribution Pension Systems

## Pablo Castañeda and Heinz P. Rudolph

Demographic change has triggered a wave of pension reform around the world. Several of the countries that have undergone this trend have moved from pay-as-you-go (PAYGO) to defined contribution (DC) pension systems based on individual savings accounts. Regulation in these younger pension systems typically includes minimum return guarantee provisions to prevent the risk of financial downturns,[1] yet the consequences of these regulations over the asset allocation of the pension system remain to be fully understood.[2]

This chapter studies the portfolio choice problem of pension fund managers who operate in a competitive setting and that are subject to

We thank Zvi Bodie, Esteban Jadresic, Olivia Mitchell, Theo Nijman, Felipe Zurita, Salvador Valdés-Prieto, and Félix Villatoro, participants in the OECD–World Bank Research Workshop on the Performance of Privately Managed Pension Funds (Ciudad de México), and seminar participants at Universidad Adolfo Ibáñez (School of Management) and PUC-Chile (Instituto de Economía) for helpful comments and suggestions. The views expressed in this chapter are the authors' only and do not necessarily represent those of the World Bank, its executive directors, or the countries that they represent.

minimum return guarantees (MRGs), such as those in Latin America and Central Europe pension systems. In particular, the chapter takes a standard dynamic portfolio choice problem (for example, Merton 1969, 1971) and studies the effects of MRGs in a setting in which fund managers have relative performance concerns and dynamic portfolio selection is subject to strategic considerations, along the lines of Basak and Makarov (2008, hereafter BM).

For the case of the Black and Scholes (1973) setting, this chapter is able to derive the (pure strategy Nash) equilibrium portfolio policies in closed form. Two special cases are addressed: one in which the MRG is based on a peer-group benchmark portfolio, and another in which the benchmark portfolio is index based.[3] The results show that in both cases the equilibrium portfolios take a simple form: they are the weighted sum of investment rules that are themselves optimal for scenarios that may be realized once the uncertainty is fully revealed. In the case in which only two managers populate the economy, the scenarios correspond to the cases in which both, neither, or at least one manager ends up restricted by the MRG constraint at the end of the investment horizon.

As shown by BM, equilibrium investment rules become *myopic* when relative performance concerns among portfolio managers reach their peak.[4] It is shown that this is also the case when the investment opportunity set is stochastic (for example, time-varying stock returns, interest rates, volatility, and correlations). Because long-term investors are expected to take the changes in the opportunity set into account (for example, Samuelson 1979; Campbell and Viceira 1999, 2001, 2002; Campbell, Viceira, and White 2003), this result suggests that the MRG type of regulation should be careful when the intensity of competition among fund managers—proxied by relative performance concerns—is relatively high. In this sense, the results suggest that the use of index-based benchmark portfolios may help to mitigate this problem when the myopic investment rule is suboptimal.

This chapter is related to several strands of the literature. On the issue of portfolio selection, it follows the classical literature of Samuelson (1969) and Merton (1969, 1971), using the martingale approach developed by Cox and Huang (1989, 1991) and Karatzas, Lehoczky, and Shreve (1987). On the issue of performance constraints, the chapter is related to the literature on portfolio insurance (for example, Basak 1995, 2002; Jensen and Sørensen 2001; Teplá 2001; Deelstra, Grasselli, and Koehl 2003) and capital guarantees (for example, El Karoui, Jeanblanc, and Lacoste 2005). On the issue of portfolio choice and benchmarking, it is related to the papers by Basak, Shapiro, and Teplá (2006) and Basak, Pavlova, and Shapiro (2007, 2008). Finally, on the issue of portfolio choice and relative performance concerns, it is related to the seminal work of BM, from which this chapter borrows extensively.

The chapter is organized as follows. The next section presents the model and the main results. The discussion section summarizes the main findings and briefly concludes. All derivations are collected in an annex at the end of the document.

## A Model Economy

The starting point of the analysis is the model developed by BM, which includes strategic considerations in an otherwise standard dynamic portfolio choice problem, on top of which is introduced a minimum return guarantee, and the consequences are studied over the resulting (pure strategy Nash) equilibrium portfolios.

### The Economic Setting

Consider a continuous-time finite horizon economy with a frictionless financial market made up of two financial assets: a (locally) riskless bond or money market account ($B$) and a risky stock ($S$). The dynamics of the prices of these assets is governed by the following laws of motion:

$$\frac{dB_t}{B_t} = r_t dt \text{ and } \frac{dS_t}{S_t} + \delta_t dt = \mu_t dt + \sigma_t dW_t,$$

where $\{(r_t, \delta_t, \mu_t, \sigma_t) \in R \times R_+ \times R_+ \times R/\{0\}\}_{0 \leq t \leq T}$ corresponds to the (instantaneous) interest rate, the dividend rate, expected return, and the volatility of the stock, respectively, and $W_t \in R$ is a standard Brownian motion process. All stochastic processes are assumed to be well defined, in the sense that $B$ and $S$ have a strong solution, and the (Novikov) condition,

$$E\left[\frac{1}{2}\int_0^T \theta_t^z dt\right] < \infty,$$

is assumed to be satisfied, where $\theta \equiv \sigma^{-1}(\mu - r)$ is the market price of risk.

The economy is populated by asset managers in charge of managing the savings of a mandatory DC pension system. For the sake of simplicity this study looks at an economy populated by two asset managers.[5] Each asset manager has to chose an investment policy, $\pi_i \equiv \{\pi_{it}: \Omega \times [0, T] \to R\}_{0 \leq t \leq T}$, where $\pi_i$ denotes the fraction invested in the risky asset over time by pension fund, given a fund with initial value of $x_i > 0$ at time zero. Formally, the dynamics of the pension fund of manager is governed by the following law of motion:

$$\begin{cases} \dfrac{dX_{it}^{\pi}}{X_{it}^{\pi}} = \left(1 - \pi_{it}\right)r_t dt + \pi_{it}\left(\dfrac{dS_t}{S_t} + \delta_t dt\right); \\ X_{i0} = x_i; X_{it}^{\pi} \geq 0, \forall t \in [0,T]; X_{iT}^{\pi} \equiv X_{iT}. \end{cases}$$

(1)

Let us consider an economy in which asset managers have absolute and relative performance concerns: that is, they care about the terminal value of the fund under management, but also about their performance relative to that of their peers. In particular, this discussion adopts the *envy* interpretation advanced by BM and defines the preferences of each asset manager as a function of final wealth and its relative performance:[6]

$$v_i\left(X_{iT}, \hat{R}_{iT}\right) \equiv \frac{1}{1-\gamma_i}\left(X_{iT}^{1-\beta_i} \hat{R}_{iT}^{\beta_i}\right)^{1-\gamma_i}, i \in \{1,2\},$$

(2)

where $\hat{R}_{iT} \equiv (X_{iT}/x_i) \div (X_{jT}/x_j)$ is the relative return between fund $i$ and $j$, $\gamma_i > 0$ is the parameter of relative risk aversion, and $\beta_i \in [0,1]$ is a parameter capturing the *relative performing bias*, that is, the extent to which relative performance concerns alter the investment decisions of a normal manager.[7] In particular, when $\beta_i = 0$, we are back in the traditional case without strategic interaction, whereas the case $\beta_i = 1$ implies that the only concern of manager $i$ is to beat manager $j \neq i$ in terms of $\hat{R}_{iT}$.

Next introduced is the MRG concerns of the asset manager as a benchmarking restriction to the portfolio problem (Basak, Shapiro, and Teplá 2006; Basak, Pavlova, and Shapiro 2008) of the form

$$R_{iT} \geq R_T e^{-\varepsilon_i}, i \in \{1,2\},$$

(3)

where $R_{iT} \equiv (X_{iT}/x_i)$, $R_T \equiv (X_{1T} + X_{2T})/(x_1 + x_2)$ is the peer-group average return, and $\varepsilon_i > 0$ is the allowed shortfall: that is, $\varepsilon_i = \infty$ implies that the manager is unrestricted (as in BM), and $\varepsilon_i = 1$ percent means that the maximum log-return shortfall allowed is 1 percent relative to the peer-group benchmark.

The reasoning behind this modeling choice is to think that the board of the asset management company deals with the MRG concern by imposing a relative performance or benchmarking constraint to the portfolio manager (for example, Basak, Shapiro, and Teplá 2006; Basak, Pavlova, and Shapiro 2007, 2008).

Remark 1 *Notice that in the current setting $R_T$ is influenced by the relative size of each pension fund. In particular, the relative performance constraint in equation (3) is less stringent for the portfolio manager in charge of the bigger pension fund.*

## Strategic Interaction

Following BM, this discussion introduces strategic interaction among asset managers by relying on the martingale approach of Cox and Huang (1989, 1991) and Karatzas, Lehoczky, and Shreve (1987). In particular, this can be accomplished by taking $(X_{1T}, X_{2T})$ as the relevant *strategy space* and restricting the analysis to the pure strategy Nash equilibrium concept solution.

Consider the case in which managers decide over $(X_{1T}, X_{2T})$ simultaneously, similar to what happens in the classical Cournot duopoly game.

Definition 1 *Given manager $j$'s selection of $X_{jT}$, manager $i$'s Cournot best response function is the solution to the following maximization problem:*

$$\max_{X_{iT} \in A} v_i\left(X_{iT}, R_{iT}\right) s.t. \begin{cases} E[\xi_T X_{iT}] \le x_i \\ R_{iT} \ge R_T e^{-\epsilon_i} \end{cases}, \tag{P.0}$$

*for $i, j \in \{1,2\}$ $i \ne i$, where $A \equiv \{X_{iT} \ge 0 : v_i < \infty\}$, and*

$$\xi_T = exp\left(-\int_0^T \left(r_t + \frac{1}{2}\theta_t^2\right)dt - \int_0^T \theta_t dW_t\right)$$

*is the unique stochastic discount factor (SDF) that is compatible with the absence of arbitrage opportunities.*

Proposition 1 *Manager $i$'s Cournot best response function is given by*

$$X_{iT} = \begin{cases} \left(v_i \xi_T\right)^{-\frac{1}{\gamma_i}} X_{jT}^{\frac{\beta_i(\gamma_i - 1)}{\gamma_i}} & if \ \xi_T \le y_i^{-1} K_i^{-\gamma_i} X_{jT}^{-\overline{\gamma}_i} \\ K_i X_{jT} & if \ \xi_T > y_i^{-1} K_i^{-\gamma_i} X_{jT}^{-\overline{\gamma}_i} \end{cases}, \tag{4}$$

*for $i, j \in (1,2)$ $i \ne j$, where, $\overline{\gamma}_i = \gamma_i (1 - \beta_i) + \beta_i$, $K_i = x_i / (e^{\epsilon_i}(x_i + x_j) - x_i)$, and $y_i > 0$ is defined in Proposition 2.*

Proposition 1 shows that the Cournot best response function for manager $i$, $\hat{X}_{iT}$, has two parts: one that captures the behavior of the asset manager when unconstrained (that is, the segment for low values of $\xi_T$, equivalent to equations (15) and (16) in BM), and a second one that captures the behavior when the asset manager is constrained by the benchmarking restriction (that is, the segment for high values of $\xi_T$).

> Corollary 1 *Notice that not only is an unrestricted log utility manager myopic in the classical sense (that is, not considering the fluctuations in the investment opportunity set), but also it is myopic in the sense of not reacting to its rival's actions.*

Corollary 1 records an additional form of myopia for the case of the log investor (that is, $\gamma_i = 1$), which, in addition to not acting in response to changes in the investment opportunity set, it also does not act in reaction to the opponent's strategy.

Note that the expression in equation (4) has a similar structure to that in Proposition 2 in BM. In the present case, however, the specific form of the best response function arises because of the benchmarking constraint, as opposed to the preferences under analysis. In this sense the problem here is closer to the literature on portfolio insurance and European capital guarantees; see, for example, Basak (1995, 2002), Karatzas and Shreve (1998), and El Karoui, Jeanblanc, and Lacoste (2005).

> Corollary 2 *Suppose that the economy is as in the economic setting discussed so far. Then, when both managers are unrestricted ($\varepsilon_1 = \varepsilon_2 = \infty$) and the relative performing bias of both managers is maximum ($\beta_1 = \beta_2 = 1$), the optimal investment policy of each manager converges to the myopic solution $\pi_{it}^* = (\mu_t - r_t)/(\sigma_t^2), i \in \{1,2\}$.*

Corollary 2 extends the findings in BM for the case of a stochastic investment opportunity set. The result implies that the limiting behavior of the relative performance bias is the myopic portfolio, which should not come as a surprise because the myopic portfolio is known to be the one that maximizes the expected growth of terminal wealth (for example, Merton 1990; Bajeux-Besnainou and Portait 1997; Platen 2005). Still, what is a bit surprising is the fact that the limiting behavior of relative performing concerns— easily associated with a more competitive environment—may result in equilibrium portfolios that are likely to be suboptimal for long-term investors, such as pension funds (for example, Samuelson 1979; Campbell and Viceira 1999, 2001, 2002; Campbell, Viceira, and White 2003). This allows a new foundation for optimal contracting (principal-agent) problems within asset management activities because the framework in which the trade-off is between effort and output seems to be less appropriate to the task.

## Equilibrium Portfolios under Benchmarking Constraints

Similar to the case with asymmetric relative performance concerns studied in section 4 of BM, the presence of a benchmarking constraint may also prevent equilibrium from existing. Equilibrium is shown to take the form of a weighted sum,

$$X^*_{iT} 1_{\{\xi_T \in \Xi_{uu}\}} + X^*_{uT} 1_{\{\xi_T \in \Xi_{ux}\}} + X^*_{xT} 1_{\{\xi_T \in \Xi_{xu}\}}, \tag{5}$$

where $X^*_{1T}$ stands for the optimal wealth of manager $i \in \{1, 2\}$ when neither manager ends up restricted by the benchmarking constraint at time $T$, $X^*_{uT}$, and $X^*_{xT}$ stands for the optimal wealth when either manager $j \neq i$ or manager $i$ is restricted by the benchmarking constraint, respectively. The sets $\Xi_{uu}$, $\Xi_{ux}$, and $\Xi_{xu}$ denote the domain of $\xi_T$ for which each of the previous cases is valid. Existence, uniqueness, and multiplicity of equilibria in this context requires the union, union and intersection, and intersection of these sets to be, respectively, nonempty, the positive real line and the empty set, and nonempty. Further details are provided in Proposition A.1 and Corollary A.1 in the annex for an economy like the one described in the economic setting under consideration.

### Peer-Group Benchmarking

This discussion now moves to the characterization of the equilibrium portfolios. To this end, it records first a well-known result that connects the present problem with the one studied by BM and helps develop the necessary notation before stating the main result.

Corollary 3 *When manager $i \in \{1, 2\}$ is unrestricted ($\varepsilon_i = \infty$) and the relative performing bias is absent ($\beta_i = 0$), the optimal investment policy is given by*

$$\pi^M_{it} = \frac{\mu_t - r_t}{\gamma_i \sigma^2_t} + \pi^H_{it},$$

*where $\pi^H_{it}$ is the hedging component of the optimal portfolio identified in the proof. Moreover, when $(\mu, \gamma, \sigma)$ are constant, $\pi^M_{iT} = 0$ and $\pi^M_{it} = \pi^M_i$.*

Proposition 2 *Suppose that $(\mu, \gamma, \sigma)$ are constant and that the parameters of the model are such that*

$$1 - \frac{\bar{\gamma}_1 (\beta_2 (\gamma_2 - 1) + \gamma_1)}{\Gamma} < 0, \ 1 - \frac{\bar{\gamma}_2 (\beta_1 (\gamma_1 - 1) + \gamma_2)}{\Gamma} > 0, \ 1 - \bar{\gamma}_1 \bar{\gamma}_2 < 0,$$

*where $\bar{\gamma}_i = \gamma_i (1 - \beta_i) + \beta_i$ and $\Gamma = \gamma_1 \gamma_2 (1 - \beta_1 \beta_2) + \beta_1 \beta_2 (\gamma_1 \gamma_2 - 1)$. Then the equilibrium portfolio policy of manager $i, j \in \{1, 2\}, i \neq j,$ is given by*

$$\pi_{it}^* = f_{i1t}^* \left\{ \frac{\gamma_i}{\gamma\left(\beta_i,\beta_j\right)} \pi_i^M + \Psi_{i1t}^* \right\} + f_{i2t}^* \left\{ \frac{\gamma_i}{\gamma_i} \pi_i^M + \Psi_{i2t}^* \right\}$$

$$+ f_{i3t}^* \left\{ \frac{\gamma_j}{\gamma_j} \pi_j^M + \Psi_{i3t}^* \right\},$$

(6)

*where $\gamma(\beta_i, \beta_j) = (\gamma_i \gamma_j (1-\beta_i\beta_j) + \beta_i\beta_j (\gamma_i + \gamma_j -1))/(\gamma_j + \beta_i (\gamma_i - 1))$, $\phi(.)$ and $\phi(.)$ stand for the cumulative distribution function and probability density function of the standard normal distribution, and $\{f_{ikt}^*, \Psi_{ikt}^*\}_{k \in \{1,2,3\}}$ are defined in the proof found in the annex.*

Proposition 2 characterizes the optimal investment rule for the case in which the MRG is based on a peer-group benchmark portfolio. The resulting expression corresponds to a weighted sum (as $f_{ikt}^* \in [0, 1]$ and $f_{i1t}^* + f_{i2t}^* + f_{i3t}^* = 1$) of portfolio policies that are themselves optimal for different scenarios that can occur at time $T$. The quantities attached to each weighting factor involve two components: the equilibrium portfolio policy that finances the equilibrium terminal wealth that is optimal in the corresponding scenario (see equation (5)), and the marginal change in its conditional probability of occurrence, $\Psi_{ikt}^*$. For instance, in the case of the term attached to the first weight $\left(f_{i1t}^*\right)$,

$$\frac{\gamma_i}{\gamma\left(\beta_i,\beta_j\right)} \pi_i^M + \Psi_{i1t}^*,$$

the term on the left-hand side stands for the optimal investment rule in the scenario in which neither of the two portfolio managers is restricted by the MRG constraint at time $T$, whereas the term on the right-hand side corresponds to the marginal change at time $t$ in the conditional probability that the respective scenario turns out to be optimal at time $T$. The term on the right-hand side is also present in cases of incentive schemes rendering local convexities in preferences (for example, Castañeda 2006; Basak, Pavlova, and Shapiro 2007, 2008). The statement in Corollary 2 also applies in this case because $\gamma(1,1) = 1$, and hence the term on the left-hand side reduces to the myopic portfolio.

The quantities attached to the other weighing factors follow a similar structure. In particular, the term on the left-hand side attached to the second and third factors corresponds to the optimal investment policy in the scenario in which either manager $j$ or $i$ is restricted by the MRG constraint, respectively. In the case of the second term, the equilibrium portfolio shows the effects of the relative performance bias. When the bias is completely absent (that is, $\beta_i = 0$ and hence $\bar{\gamma}_i = \gamma_i$), the equilibrium portfolio turns out to be the unconstraint optimal policy $\pi_i^M$. On the other hand, when the bias reaches its peak (that is, $\beta_i = 1$ and hence $\bar{\gamma}_i = 1$), the equilibrium portfolio corresponds to the myopic portfolio. The third term—associated with the case in which manager $i$ is restricted—follows the same logic. This time, however, it is the intensity of manager's $j$ bias that matters. When the bias is completely absent (that is, $\beta_j = 0$ and hence $\bar{\gamma}_j = \gamma_j$), manager $i$ sticks to manager $j$'s unconstraint portfolio policy $\pi_j^M$. On the other hand, when the relative performing bias of manager $j$ is at its maximum (that is, $\beta_j = 1$ and hence $\bar{\gamma}_j = 1$), manager $i$ adopts the optimal growth portfolio.

It is also worth noticing that the fraction invested in equity, in the cases in which at least one manager is constrained, is affected by the value of the risk aversion parameter and the relative performing bias. In particular, when $\gamma_i > 1$, it follows that $\bar{\gamma}_i (\beta_i):[0,1] \rightarrow [\gamma_i, 1]$ and hence $(\gamma_i/\bar{\gamma}_i)\pi_i^M \geq \pi_i^M$, whereas the opposite is true when $\gamma_i < 1$.

### Index-Based Benchmarking

To contrast the previous results, consider the case in which the benchmarking constraint is index based. To this end, the index-based analog of the performance constraint (4) is introduced, that is,

$$R_{iT} \geq R_{iT}^Y e^{-\varepsilon_i}, \ i \in \{1,2\}, \tag{7}$$

where $R_{iT}^Y \equiv Y_{iT}/Y_{i0}$ and $Y_{iT}$ are the terminal value of the dynamics embedded in the following system:

$$\begin{cases} \dfrac{dY_{it}^\pi}{Y_{it}^\pi} = \left(1-\pi_t^Y\right)rdt + \pi_t^Y\left(\dfrac{dS_t}{S_t}+\delta dt\right); \\ Y_{i0} = x_i; Y_{it}^\pi \geq 0, \forall t \in [0,T]; Y_{it}^\pi \equiv Y_{iT}, \end{cases} \tag{8}$$

where $\pi^Y \equiv \{\pi_{it}^Y \in R\}_{\{0 \leq t \leq T\}}$ is the investment policy of the benchmark portfolio relevant to manager $i \in \{1,2\}$, which is given by the fraction invested by the benchmark portfolio in the risky asset. For simplicity, it will be assumed that $\pi_t^Y = \pi^Y, \forall t \in [0,T]$.

Remark 2 *Notice that the only difference between $Y_{1t}^\pi$ and $Y_{2t}^\pi$ is the initial value of the benchmark portfolio, which is set equal to the value of the fund managed by each manager at time zero. Both managers hence face an identical performance constraint, that is $(Y_{1T}/Y_{10}) = (Y_{2T}/T_{20})$, $\forall t \in [0,T]$.*

Proposition 3 *Suppose that the parameters of the model are as in Proposition 2. Then the equilibrium portfolio under an index-based benchmark portfolio for manager $i \in \{1,2\}$, $i \neq j$ is given by the following expression:*

$$\pi_{it}^{**} = f_{i1t}^{**} \left\{ \frac{\gamma_i}{\gamma(\beta_i, \beta_j)} \pi_i^M + \Psi_{i1t}^{**} \right\} + f_{i2t}^{**} \left\{ \pi_i^M + \pi^Y \beta_i \left( 1 - \frac{1}{\gamma_i} \right) + \Psi_{i2t}^{**} \right\}$$
$$+ f_{i3t}^{**} \left\{ \pi^Y + \Psi_{i3t}^{**} \right\} + f_{i4t}^{**} \left\{ \pi^Y + \Psi_{i4t}^{**} \right\},$$

*where $\left\{ f_{ikt}^{**}, \Psi_{ikt}^{**} \right\}_{k \in \{1,2,3,4\}}$ are defined in the annex.*

Proposition 3 characterizes the optimal investment rule of fund manager $i$ when the MRG restriction is index based (that is, the solution to the problem of maximizing equation (2), subject to equations (8) and (7)). Similar to the previous case, the resulting equilibrium portfolio corresponds to a weighted sum of portfolio policies that are themselves optimal for different possible scenarios. In this case the scenarios correspond to the cases in which neither manager (first term of $\pi_{it}^{**}$), either manager $i$ or manager $j$ (second and third terms of $\pi_{it}^{**}$), or both managers (fourth term of $\pi_{it}^{**}$) are restricted by the benchmarking restriction at time $T$.

Compared to the peer-group benchmarking case, the index-based case has some particular features. In particular, the optimal portfolio in the scenario in which manager $i$ is the only one unrestricted by the benchmarking constraint,

$$\pi_i^M + \pi^Y \beta_i \left( 1 - \frac{1}{\gamma_i} \right),$$

is a combination of two investment motives: one given by the adoption of the unconstrained optimal policy ($\pi_i^M$), and the other given by the optimal response to the strategy of his opponent (set equal to $\pi^Y$ because the restriction is binding), where the latter depends on the strength of the relative performance bias ($\beta_i$) and the degree of relative risk aversion of manager ($\gamma_i$).

## Discussion

Our results show that the combination of relative performance concerns and MRGs affect asset allocation in important ways. First, MRG regulation alone gives rise to time-varying investment policies because the stochastic weights in $\pi^*$ and $\pi^{**}$ vary over time. This may be seen as openly favoring an active trading strategy as opposed to a passive one.

Second, when the benchmark portfolio is peer group based, MRGs favor the investment of the whole system to be driven by the least restricted manager (simply suppose that $f_{i3t}^{**}$ is relatively bigger than $f_{i3t}^{**}$). Although this may not have been a conscious decision, it is relevant for policy-making purposes to ask whether this is something that is indeed desired, especially when managers interested in relative performance may drive the asset allocation of the whole pension system to a suboptimal position.

Third, it is important to note that the present model does not give any useful purpose for the MRGs and hence leaves open the motivation for its existence. In this sense, if MRGs are thought of as a way to limit the risks of financial downturns, the present results show that a MRG based on a peer-group benchmark may not be best way to achieve this because it leaves the asset allocation completely driven by the risk preferences and relative performance concerns of asset managers. In fact, the only case in which the institutional design makes perfect sense is in the case in which it is socially desirable for asset managers to adopt myopic portfolios because competition may help to achieve higher values of $\beta$. It is the authors' opinion that the pension system's own goals, and the increasing evidence of the time-varying coefficient of the model, discard this alternative. Overall, an index-based MRG seems to be preferred because it restricts investment policies in a clear way.

Fourth, one of the main drawbacks of MRGs, such as those in equations (3) and (7), is that they motivate herding among portfolio managers, as can be deduced from the equilibrium portfolio policies subject to both index-based and peer-group–based benchmark portfolios. In this context the question naturally emerges of the relevance of regulation and relative performance concerns as contributors to the observed herding behavior in DC pension systems. The present characterization of the equilibrium portfolio policy helps to shed light on the issue. In particular, unless $\gamma_1 = \gamma_2 = 1$, when the relative performance bias is nearly absent, the equilibrium portfolio should tend to a linear combination of the unconstrained equilibrium portfolios, which, if different from the myopic portfolio, can provide a testable implication to take the model to the data.

## Annex

### On the Existence and Uniqueness of Equilibrium

The Nash equilibrium corresponds to mutually consistent best responses, $\left(\hat{X}_{1T}, \hat{X}_{2T}\right)$. In this regard we have the following result:

Proposition A.1 *Let the economy be as in the economic setting described in the main text. Then there are two candidate Nash equilibria:*

1. *One in which both managers are unconstrained by the benchmarking restriction (3), given by (for $i,j \in \{1,2\}$, $j \neq i$)*

$$X_{iT}^{*} = y_i^{-\frac{1}{\Gamma \gamma_i}} y_j^{-\frac{\beta_i(\gamma_i-1)}{\Gamma}} \xi_T^{-\frac{\beta_i(\gamma_i-1)+\gamma_j}{\Gamma}}, \; for \; \xi_T \in \Xi_{uu},$$

*where*

$$\Xi_{uu} \equiv \left\{ \xi_T : \xi_T^{\Psi_i} \leq A_i \; and \; \xi_T^{\Psi_j} \leq A_j \right\},$$

$$\Psi_i \equiv 1 - \frac{\left(\gamma_i(1-\beta_i)+\beta_i\right)\left(\beta_j(\gamma_j-1)+\gamma_i\right)}{\Gamma},$$

$$A_i \equiv K_i^{-\gamma_i} y_j^{\frac{\gamma_i(1-\beta_i)+\beta_i}{\Gamma \gamma_j}} y_i^{\frac{(\gamma_i(1-\beta_i)+\beta_i)\beta_j(\gamma_j-1)}{\Gamma}-1}$$

*and*

2. *One in which at least one of the managers is restricted by (5), given by*

$$\begin{cases} X_{uT}^{*} = \left(y_u \xi_T\right)^{-\frac{1}{\gamma_u}} K_x^{\frac{\beta_u(\gamma_u-1)}{\gamma_u}} \\ X_{uT}^{*} = \left(y_u \xi_T\right)^{-\frac{1}{\gamma_u}} K_x^{\frac{\gamma_u}{\gamma_u}} \end{cases}$$

*for $\xi_T \in \Xi_{ux}$, where $(u,x)$ stand for the "unrestricted" and "restricted" manager, respectively, and*

$$\Xi_{ux} \equiv \left\{ \xi_T : \xi_T^{1-\frac{\bar{\gamma}_x}{\gamma_u}} \geq B_u^{(u,x)} \right\},$$

*where $B_u^{(u,x)} \equiv y_x^{-1} y_u^{\frac{\bar{\gamma}_x}{\gamma_u}} K_x^{\frac{\bar{\gamma}_x \beta_u(1-\gamma_u)}{\gamma_u}-\gamma_x}$. In both cases $y_i > 0$ and $y_j > 0$ are such that*

$$E\left[ \xi_T \left( X_{iT}^{*} 1_{\{\xi_T \in \Xi_{uu}\}} + X_{uT}^{*} 1_{\{\xi_T \in \Xi_{ux}\}} + X_{xT}^{*} 1_{\{\xi_T \in \Xi_{xu}\}} \right) \right] = x_i, \forall i, u, x \in \{1,2\}, i \neq j$$

Regarding the existence and uniqueness of equilibrium, the following result is obtained, which parallels the discussion in BM.

Corollary A.1 *Suppose that the parameters of the model are as in Proposition 2. The following then follow:*

*A unique Nash equilibrium exists if*

$$\{\xi_a \leq \xi_T \leq \xi_b\} \cup \{\xi_T < \xi_c\} \cup \{\xi_T > \xi_d\} = R_{++}$$

and

$$\{\xi_a \leq \xi_T \leq \xi_b\} \cap \{\xi_T < \xi_c\} \cap \{\xi_T > \xi_d\} = ?;$$

*Multiple equilibria may exist if*

$$\{\xi_a \leq \xi_T \leq \xi_b\} \cup \{\xi_T < \xi_c\} \cup \{\xi_T > \xi_d\} = R_{++}$$

and

$$\{\xi_a \leq \xi_T \leq \xi_b\} \cap \{\xi_T < \xi_c\} \cap \{\xi_T > \xi_d\} \neq ?;$$

and

*No equilibrium may exist if*

$$\{\xi_a \leq \xi_T \leq \xi_b\} \cup \{\xi_T < \xi_c\} \cup \{\xi_T > \xi_d\} \subset R_{++}$$

or

$$\{\xi_a \leq \xi_T \leq \xi_b\} \cap \{\xi_T < \xi_c\} \cap \{\xi_T > \xi_d\} \neq ?,$$

*where*

$$\xi_a = K_1^{-\gamma_1/\Psi_1} y_2^{\bar{\gamma}_1/\Gamma\Psi_1\gamma_2} y_1^{\bar{\gamma}_1\beta_2(\gamma_2-1)/\Gamma\Psi_1-\Psi_1},$$

$$\xi_b = K_2^{-\gamma_2/\Psi_2} y_1^{\bar{\gamma}_2/\Gamma\Psi_2\gamma_1} y_2^{\bar{\gamma}_2\beta_1(\gamma_1-1)/\Gamma\Psi_2-\Psi_2},$$

$$\xi_c = y_2^{-\bar{\gamma}_1/(\bar{\gamma}_1-\bar{\gamma}_2)} y_1^{\bar{\gamma}_2/(\bar{\gamma}_1-\bar{\gamma}_2)} K_2^{(\bar{\gamma}_2\beta_1(1-\gamma_1)-\bar{\gamma}_1\gamma_2)/(\bar{\gamma}_1-\bar{\gamma}_2)},$$

$$\xi_d = y_1^{-\bar{\gamma}_2/(\bar{\gamma}_2-\bar{\gamma}_1)} y_2^{\bar{\gamma}_1/(\bar{\gamma}_2-\bar{\gamma}_1)} K_1^{(\bar{\gamma}_1\beta_2(1-\gamma_2)-\bar{\gamma}_2\gamma_1)/(\bar{\gamma}_2-\bar{\gamma}_1)}.$$

## Proofs

**Proof of Proposition 1** First, notice that $vi \, (.,.)$ can be written as

$$v_i = \frac{\left(X_{iT}X_{jT}^{-\beta_i}\right)^{1-\gamma_i}}{1-\gamma_i}, \text{ for } i,j \in \{1,2\}, i \neq j.$$

Next, for the benchmarking constraint the following set equality is obtained: $\{R_{iT} \geq R_T e^{-\varepsilon_i}\} \equiv \{X_{iT} \geq K_i X_{jT}\}$, where $K_i = x_i / \left( e^{\varepsilon_i} \left( x_i + x_j \right) - x_i \right)$. Then the first-order-conditions (FOC) from manager's $i$ portfolio problem is given by $\partial v_i(\cdot,\cdot) / \partial X_{iT} = y_i \xi_T$, where $y_i > 0$ is the Lagrange multiplier attached to the static budget constraint. In the absence of the benchmarking restriction, the Cournot best response function of manager $i$ would have been simply $\hat{X}_{iT} = (y_i \xi_T)^{-1/\gamma_i} X_{jT}^{\beta_i(\gamma_i - 1)/\gamma_i}$ as in BM. Instead, taking the benchmarking restriction into account, we obtain

$$\hat{X}_{iT} = \begin{cases} (y_i \xi_T)^{-1/\gamma_i} X_{jT}^{\beta_i(\gamma_i-1)/\gamma_i} & \text{if } \xi_T \leq y_i^{-1} K_i^{-\gamma_i} X_{jT}^{-\bar{\gamma}_i} \\ K_i X_{jT} & \text{if } \xi_T > y_i^{-1} K_i^{-\gamma_i} X_{jT}^{-\bar{\gamma}_i} \end{cases},$$

where $\bar{\gamma}_i = \gamma_i (1 - \beta_i) + \beta_i$.

**Proof of Corollary 2** Because $\varepsilon_1 = \varepsilon_2 = \infty$, we are back in the case studied by BM, except that now $(r, \mu, \sigma)$ are not constant. Hence, the Cournot best response functions are given by $\hat{X}_{iT} = (y_i \xi_T)^{-1/\gamma_i} X_{jT}^{\beta_i(\gamma_i-1)/\gamma_i}$, for $i \in \{1, 2\}$, $i \neq j$. Plugging $\hat{X}_{jT}$ into the expression for $\hat{X}_{jT}$, the (pure strategy Nash) equilibrium value is obtained for

$$X_{iT}^* = y_i^{-\gamma_j/\Gamma} y_j^{\beta_i(1-\gamma_i)/\Gamma} \xi_T^{(\beta_i(1-\gamma_i)-\gamma_j)/\Gamma},$$

where $\Gamma = \gamma_i \gamma_j \left( 1 - \beta_i \beta_j \right) + \beta_i \beta_j \left( \gamma_i + \gamma_j - 1 \right)$, and $y_i$ and $y_j$ are strictly positive constants that satisfy

$$E\left[ \xi_T X_{iT}^* \right] = x_i \text{ and } E\left[ \xi_T X_{jT}^* \right] = x_j.$$

Finally, $\pi_{it}^* = D_t(X_{it}^*)/X_{it}^* \sigma_t$ (see, for example, Detemple, Garcia, and Rindisbacher 2003), where $D_t (.)$ is the Malliavin derivative operator[8] and $X_{it}^* = E_t\left[ \xi_{t,T} X_{it}^* \right]$, from which is obtained

$$\pi_{it}^* = \sigma_t^{-1} \theta_t + \left( \xi_t X_t^* \right)^{-1} \sigma_t^{-1} E_t \left[ D_t \left( \xi_T X_{iT}^* \right) \right]$$

$$= \frac{1}{\gamma(\beta_i,\beta_j)} \frac{\mu_t - r_t}{\sigma_t^2} + \frac{1}{\xi_t X_t^* \sigma_t} E_t \left[ \left( \frac{1}{\gamma(\beta_i,\beta_j)} - 1 \right) H_{t,T} \xi_T X_{iT}^* \right],$$

where $\gamma(\beta_i,\beta_j) \equiv (\gamma_i \gamma_j (1 - \beta_i \beta_j) + \beta_i \beta_j (\gamma_j + \gamma_i - 1)) / (\gamma_j + \beta_i(\gamma_i - 1))$

and $H_{t,T} \equiv \int_t^T (D_t r_s + \theta_s D_t \theta_s) ds + \int_t^T D_t \theta_s dW_s.$

The result follows directly from the fact that $\gamma(1,1) = 1$.

**Proof of Corollary 3** The assertion follows directly from Corollary 2 and the fact that $\gamma(0,\beta_j) = \gamma_i$.

**Proof of Proposition A.1** To find a Nash equilibrium, one must look for mutually consistent best responses for both managers. In this setting there are four possible combinations, depending on whether each manager is either restricted or unrestricted by the benchmarking constraint. The set of possible cases is hence given by the pairs (unrestricted, unrestricted), (unrestricted, restricted), (restricted, unrestricted), and (restricted, restricted), where each pair is to be read as (outcome for manager 1, outcome for manager 2). Because both managers cannot be restricted by the benchmarking constraint simultaneously, we are left with only three possible cases.[9] For the (unrestricted, unrestricted) case it follows that the mutually consistent best responses are given, for $i \in \{1,2\}, i \neq j$, by:

$$X_{iT}^* = (y_i \xi_T)^{-1/\gamma_i} \left( \hat{X}_{jT} \right)^{\beta_i (\gamma_i - 1)/\gamma_i}$$
$$= y_i^{-\gamma_j/\Gamma} y_j^{\beta_i (1-\gamma_i)/\Gamma} \xi_T^{(\beta_i (1-\gamma_i) - \gamma_j)/\Gamma},$$

which holds in the interval

$$\xi_T^{\Psi_i} \leq K_i^{-\gamma_i} y_j^{(\gamma_i (1-\beta_i) + \beta_i)/\Gamma \gamma_j} y_i^{(\gamma_i (1-\beta_i) + \beta_i)\beta_j (\gamma_j - 1)/\Gamma - 1}$$

and

$$\xi_T^{\Psi_j} \leq K_j^{-\gamma_j} y_i^{(\gamma_j (1-\beta_j) + \beta_j)/\Gamma \gamma_i} y_j^{(\gamma_j (1-\beta_j) + \beta_j)\beta_i (\gamma_i - 1)/\Gamma - 1},$$

where

$$\Psi_i = 1 - \left( \gamma_i (1-\beta_i) + \beta_i \right) \left( \beta_j (\gamma_j - 1) + \gamma_i \right) / \Gamma$$

and corresponds to the limiting values of the SDF for which $X_{iT}^* = K_i X_{jT}^*$ and $X_{jT}^* = K_j X_{iT}^*$. For the two remaining cases, it follows that the mutually consistent best responses are given by

$$\begin{cases} X_{uT}^* = \left(y_u \xi_T\right)^{-1/\bar{\beta}_u \gamma_u} K_x^{\beta_u (\gamma_u -1)/\bar{\beta}_u \gamma_u} \\ X_{xT}^* = K_x^{1/\bar{\beta}_u} \left(y_u \xi_T\right)^{-1/\bar{\beta}_u \gamma_u} \end{cases} , \text{ for } \xi_T ? B_b^{(u,x)} \text{ as } 1 - \overline{\gamma}_x / \overline{\gamma}_u \gtrless 0,$$

where $u$ and $x$ stand for the "unrestricted" and "restricted" manager, respectively, $\Xi_{ux} \equiv \{\xi_T \ : \ \xi_T^{1-\overline{\gamma}_x/\overline{\gamma}_u} ? B_u^{(u,x)}\}, B_u^{(u,x)} = y_x^{-1} y_u^{\overline{\gamma}_x/\overline{\gamma}_u} K_x^{\overline{\gamma}_x \beta_u (1-\gamma_u)/\overline{\gamma}_u - \gamma_x}.$

**Proof of Proposition 2** The optimal wealth process is given by

$$\begin{aligned}
X_{it}^* &= E_t \left[ \xi_{t,T} \left( X_{iT}^* 1_{\{\dot{\xi}_a \le \xi_T \le \xi_b\}} + X_{uT}^* 1_{\{\xi_T < \dot{\xi}_c\}} + X_{xT}^* 1_{\{\xi_T > \dot{\xi}_d\}} \right) \right] \\
&= E_t \left[ \xi_t^{-1} \left\{ y_i^{-1/\bar{\beta}\gamma_i} y_j^{\beta_i (1-\gamma_i)/\bar{\beta}\gamma_i \gamma_j} \xi_T^{1+(\beta_i(1-\gamma_i)-\gamma_j)/\bar{\beta}\gamma_i \gamma_j} \right\} 1_{\{\xi_T \in [\dot{\xi}_a, \xi_a]\}} \right] \\
&\quad + \left(y_i\right)^{-1/\bar{\beta}_i \gamma_i} K_j^{\beta_i(\gamma_i-1)/\bar{\beta}_i \gamma_i} \xi_t^{-1} E_t \left[ \left\{ \xi_T^{1-1/\bar{\beta}_i \gamma_i} \right\} 1_{\{\dot{\xi}_a \le \xi_T \le \xi_b\}} \right] \\
&\quad + \left(y_j\right)^{-1/\bar{\beta}_j \gamma_j} K_i^{\gamma_i/\bar{\gamma}_j} \xi_t^{-1} E_t \left[ \left( \left\{ \xi_T^{1-1/\bar{\gamma}_j} \right\} 1_{\{\xi_T > \dot{\xi}_d\}} \right) \right] \\
&= B_{i1t} + B_{i2t} + B_{i3t}.
\end{aligned}$$

Similar steps to those in the proof of Proposition 3 can be used in the proof of Proposition 2.

**Proof of Proposition 3** First, notice that the new portfolio choice problem of manager $i$ can be written in a similar way as problem (P.0), simply by replacing $R_T$ with $R_T^Y$. The resulting best response function is hence given by (see the proof of Proposition 1)

$$X_{iT} = \begin{cases} \left(y_i \xi_T\right)^{-1/\gamma_i} X_{jT}^{\beta_i(\gamma_i-1)/\gamma_i} & \text{if } \xi_T \le y_i^{-1} e^{\gamma \varepsilon_i} Y_{iT}^{-\gamma_i} X_{jT}^{\beta_i(\gamma_i-1)} \\ Y_{iT} e^{-\varepsilon_i} & \text{if } \xi_T > y_i^{-1} e^{\gamma_i \varepsilon_i} Y_{iT}^{-\gamma_i} X_{jT}^{\beta_i(\gamma_i-1)} \end{cases},$$
$$\text{for } i, j \in \{1, 2\}, i \ne j.$$

The set of candidate Nash equilibria are hence given by the pairs (unrestricted, unrestricted); (unrestricted, restricted); (restricted, unrestricted); and (restricted, restricted), where each pair is to be read as (outcome for manager 1, outcome for manager 2). Because the value of the benchmark portfolio is independent of the actual investment plan chosen by each manager, it is possible for the (restricted, restricted) case to emerge as a possible equilibrium.

For the (unconstrained, unconstrained) case, the equilibrium is then

$$X_{iT}^{**} = \left(y_i \xi_T\right)^{-1/\gamma_i} \left(\left(y_j \xi_T\right)^{-1/\gamma_j} \left(X_{iT}^{**}\right)^{\beta_j(\gamma_j-1)/\gamma_j}\right)^{\beta_i(\gamma_i-1)/\gamma_i}$$

$$= \left(y_i \xi_T\right)^{-1/\gamma_i} \left(\left(y_j \xi_T\right)^{-\beta_i(\gamma_i-1)/\gamma_j}\right)\left(X_{iT}^{**}\right)^{\beta_i\beta_j(\gamma_j-1)(\gamma_i-1)/\gamma_i\gamma_j}$$

$$= \left(y_i \xi_T\right)^{-\gamma_j/\Gamma} \left(y_j \xi_T\right)^{-\beta_i(\gamma_i-1)/\Gamma},$$

which holds in the interval

$$\xi_T^{1+\beta_i(\gamma_i-1)\left(\beta_j(\gamma_j-1)+\gamma_i\right)/\Gamma+\gamma_i\sigma\psi/\theta}$$

$$\leq e^{\gamma_i\varepsilon_i} \left(Y_{i0}k_0\right)^{-\gamma_i} y_j^{-\gamma_i\beta_i(\gamma_i-1)/\Gamma} y_i^{-\beta_i(\gamma_i-1)\left(\beta_j(\gamma_j-1)+\gamma_i\right)/\Gamma-1}$$

and

$$\xi_T^{1+\beta_j(\gamma_j-1)\left(\beta_i(\gamma_i-1)+\gamma_j\right)/\Gamma+\gamma_j\sigma\psi/\theta}$$

$$\leq e^{\gamma_j\varepsilon_j} \left(Y_{j0}k_0\right)^{-\gamma_j} y_i^{-\gamma_j\beta_j(\gamma_j-1)/\Gamma} y_j^{-\beta_j(\gamma_j-1)\left(\beta_i(\gamma_i-1)+\gamma_j\right)/\Gamma-1}.$$

Notice that

$$Y_{iT} = Y_{i0} \exp\left\{\left(r+\psi(\mu-r)\right)T+\sigma\psi W_T\right\}$$

$$= Y_{i0} \exp\left\{\left(r+\psi(\mu-r)\right)T\right\}\exp\left\{-\theta W_T\right\}^{-\sigma\psi/\theta}$$

$$= Y_{i0} \exp\left\{\left(r+\psi\sigma\theta/2-r\sigma\psi/\theta\right)T\right\}\exp\left\{-\left(r+\theta^2/2\right)T-\theta W_T\right\}^{-\sigma\psi/\theta}$$

$$= Y_{i0}k_0\xi_T^{-\sigma\psi/\theta}.$$

Similarly, for the (restricted, unrestricted) and (unrestricted, restricted) cases,

$$\begin{cases} X_{uT}^{**} = \left(y_u\xi_T\right)^{-1/\gamma_u} \left(X_{xT}^{**}\right)^{\beta_u(\gamma_u-1)/\gamma_u} \\ X_{xT}^{**} = Y_{xT}e^{-\varepsilon_x} \end{cases},$$

which holds in the interval

$$\xi_T^{1-\gamma_u\sigma\psi/\theta+\beta_u(\gamma_u-1)\sigma\psi/\theta}$$

$$\leq y_u^{-1}e^{\gamma_u\varepsilon_u} \left(Y_{u0}k_0\right)^{-\gamma_u} \left(Y_{x0}k_0e^{-\varepsilon_x}\right)^{\beta_u(\gamma_u-1)}$$

and

$$\xi_T^{1+(\beta_x(\gamma_x-1)/\gamma_u)\left(1+\sigma\psi\beta_u(\gamma_u-1)/\theta\right)-\gamma_x\sigma\psi/\theta}$$

$$> y_x^{-1}e^{\gamma_x\varepsilon_x} \left(Y_{x0}k_0\right)^{-\gamma_x} \left(\left(y_u\right)^{-1/\gamma_u} \left(Y_{x0}k_0e^{-\varepsilon_x}\right)^{\beta_u(\gamma_u-1)/\gamma_u}\right)^{\beta_x(\gamma_x-1)}.$$

Finally, for the (restricted, restricted) case,

$$\hat{X}_{iT}^{**} = Y_{iT} e^{-\varepsilon_i} \text{ and } \hat{X}_{jT}^{**} = Y_{jT} e^{-\varepsilon_j},$$

which holds in the interval

$$\xi_T^{1-(\gamma_i(1-\beta_i)+\beta_i)(\sigma\psi/\theta)}$$
$$> y_i^{-1} e^{\gamma_i \varepsilon_i} (Y_{i0}k)^{-\gamma_i} \left(Y_{j0}k_0 \xi_T^{-\sigma\psi/\theta} e^{-\varepsilon_j}\right)^{\beta_i(\gamma_i-1)}$$

and

$$\xi_T^{1-(\gamma_j(1-\beta_j)+\beta_j)(\sigma\psi/\theta)}$$
$$> y_j^{-1} e^{\gamma_j \varepsilon_j} \left(Y_{j0}k_0 \xi_T^{-\sigma\psi/\theta}\right)^{-\gamma_j} \left(Y_{i0}k_0 e^{-\varepsilon_i}\right)^{\beta_j(\gamma_j-1)}.$$

The optimal wealth process is then given by

$$X_{it}^{**} = E_t\left[\xi_{t,T}\left(X_{iT}^{**} 1_{\{\xi_T \in Y_{uu}\}} + X_{uT}^{**} 1_{\{\xi_T \in Y_{ux}\}} + X_{xT}^{**} 1_{\{\xi_T \in Y_{xu}\}} + X_{iT}^{**} 1_{\{\xi_T \in Y_{xx}\}}\right)\right], \quad (A.1)$$

where $Y_{uu}$ is deduced from the context.

Given the assumptions on the parameters,

$$X_{it}^{**} = E_t\left[\xi_{t,T}\left(X_{iT}^{**} 1_{\{\xi_a \leq \xi_T \leq \xi_b\}} + X_{uT}^{**} 1_{\{\xi_T \leq \xi_c\}} + X_{xT}^{**} 1_{\{\xi_T < \xi_d\}} + \hat{X}_{iT}^{**} 1_{\{\xi_T > \max(\xi_e, \xi_f)\}}\right)\right]$$
$$\times C_{1t} + \cdots + C_{4t}.$$

The first term is given by

$$E_t\left[\xi_t^{-1}\left(y_i^{-\gamma_j/\Gamma} y_j^{-\beta_i(\gamma_i-1)/\Gamma} \xi_T^{1-(\gamma_j+\beta_i(\gamma_i-1))/\Gamma}\right) 1_{\{\xi_a \leq \xi_T \leq \xi_b\}}\right]$$
$$= y_i^{-\gamma_j/\Gamma} y_j^{-\beta_i(\gamma_i-1)/\Gamma} \xi_t^{A_{11}-1} e^{-A_{11}(r+\theta^2/2)(T-t)} \left[\int_{z \in Z_1(\xi_t)} \frac{1}{\sqrt{2\pi}} e^{-A_{11}\theta z \sqrt{T-t}-z^2/2} dz\right],$$

where

$$A_{11} = 1 - 1/\gamma_u - (\sigma\psi/\theta)\beta_u(\gamma_u-1)/\gamma_u$$

and

$$\{\xi_a \le \xi_T \le \xi_b\} \Leftrightarrow \left\{ \begin{array}{c} \dfrac{\ln\left(\xi_t / \xi_b\right) - [r + \theta^2 / 2](T - t)}{\theta\sqrt{T - t}} \\ \le z \le \dfrac{\ln\left(\xi_t / \xi_a\right) - [r + \theta^2 / 2](T - t)}{\theta\sqrt{T - t}} \end{array} \right\}$$

$$\Leftrightarrow Z_1(\xi_t) \equiv \left\{ z : \begin{array}{c} \dfrac{\ln\left(\xi_t / \xi_b\right) - [r + \theta^2 / 2](T - t)}{\theta\sqrt{T - t}} \\ \le z \le \dfrac{\ln\left(\xi_t / \xi_a\right) - [r + \theta^2 / 2](T - t)}{\theta\sqrt{T - t}} \end{array} \right\}.$$

The derivation of the other terms follows the same logic and is left as an exercise for the interested reader.

Equilibrium portfolio policy then comes from $\pi_{it}^{**} = D_t(X_{it}^{**}) / X_{it}^{**}\sigma$. In addition, because each of the terms inside the expectation can be written as either $\Phi\left(g(\xi_t)\right)$, $1 - \Phi\left(g(\xi_t)\right)$, or $\Phi\left(g(\xi_t)\right) - \Phi\left(g(\xi_t)\right)$, it follows that

$$D_t(X_{it}^{**}) = C_{i1t}\left[ (1 - A_{11})\theta + \frac{\varphi\left(g_{1i}(\xi_t)\right) - \varphi\left(g_a(\xi_t)\right)}{\Phi\left(g_a(\xi_t)\right) - \Phi\left(g_b(\xi_t)\right)} h \right]$$

$$+ \cdots + C_{i4t}\left[ (1 - A_{14})\theta + \frac{-\varphi\left(g_e(\xi_t)\right)}{\Phi\left(g_e(\xi_t)\right)} h \right],$$

$$\pi_{it}^{**} = f_{i1t}^{**}\left[ \frac{\gamma_i}{\gamma(\beta_i, \beta_j)}\pi_i^M + \frac{\varphi\left(g_b(\xi_t)\right) - \varphi\left(g_a(\xi_t)\right)}{\Phi\left(g_a(\xi_t)\right) - \Phi\left(g_b(\xi_t)\right)} h \right]$$

$$+ \cdots + f_{i4t}^{**}\left[ \pi^Y + \frac{-\varphi\left(g_{ef}(\xi_t)\right)}{\Phi\left(g_{ef}(\xi_t)\right)} h(\xi_t) \right],$$

where $C_{it}$ stands for the optimal wealth of each of the four terms in equation (A.1).

## Notes

1. Minimum return guarantees are common in new DC pension systems, such as those in Latin America and Central Europe; see, for instance, Turner and Rajnes (2001).

2. In particular, previous studies abstract altogether from strategic interaction among pension fund managers; see, for example, Boulier, Huang, and Taillard (2001), Jensen and Sørensen (2001), Teplá (2001); Deelstra, Grasselli, and

Koehl (2003). The paper by Walker (2006) touches on several of the issues addressed in this chapter in an informal way.

3. An index-based benchmark portfolio is composed of financial indexes classified by asset class (for example, S&P 500 index, FTSE 100 index) in a way that reflects the investment objectives and risk preferences of the investor, whereas a peer-group one is set as a combination of the asset allocation selected by the pension fund management industry itself. In the latter case, the implicit performance requirement is dictated as a function of the industry performance; see Blake and Timmermann (2002).

4. A myopic investment rule is one that is optimal for a one-period portfolio problem, and hence it does not take into account future changes in the states variables that describe the state of the economy.

5. The analysis that follows can be extended for $N \geq 2$ along the lines of Remark 1 in BM.

6. BM studied two possible interpretations for the function $\gamma_i$ in equation (1), *envy* and *fund flows*. Under the latter case, the combination of standard CRRA preferences and a specific (smooth) form of fund flows result in equation (1), and the parameters $\beta_i$ and $\gamma_i$ are functionally related. In the case of the envy interpretation, on the other hand, $\beta_i$ and $\gamma_i$ are independent parameters.

7. If the preferences of pension plan members are appropriately represented by $(1-\gamma_i)^{-1}(X_{iT}^{1-\gamma_i})$, $\beta_i \neq 0$ can also be interpreted as a measure of the agency costs because of the activity of delegated portfolio management.

8. The introduction of this operator in portfolio choice problems is due to Ocone and Karatzas (1991). The Malliavin derivative operator is an extension of the classical notion, which extends the concept to functions of the trajectories of $W$. In the same way that the classical derivative measures the local change in the function because of a local change in the underlying variable, the Malliavin derivative measures the change in the function implied by a small change in the trajectory of $W$. See Detemple, Garcia, and Rindisbacher (2003, 2005) for a brief introduction to this operator in the context of a portfolio choice problem and to Nualart (2006) for a comprehensive treatment.

9. In fact, the (restricted, restricted) case is algebraically possible, although it holds only when $X_{1T}^* = X_{2T}^* = \xi_T = 0$, which is a set of measure zero.

## References

Bajeux-Besnainou, Isabelle, and Roland Portait. 1997. "The Nummeraire Portfolio: A New Perspective on Financial Theory." *European Journal of Finance* 3 (4): 291–309.

Basak, Suleyman. 1995. "A General Equilibrium Model of Portfolio Insurance." *Review of Financial Studies* 8 (4): 1059–90.

―――. 2002. "A Comparative Study of Portfolio Insurance." *Journal of Economic Dynamics & Control* 26 (7–8): 1217–41.

Basak, Suleyman, and Dmitry Makarov. 2008. "Strategic Asset Allocation with Relative Performance Concerns." Working Paper, London Business School.

Basak, Suleyman, Anna Pavlova, and Alex Shapiro. 2007. "Optimal Asset Allocation and Risk Shifting in Money Management." *Review of Financial Studies* 20 (5): 1583–1621.

―――. 2008. "Offsetting the Implicit Incentives: Benefits of Benchmarking." *Journal of Banking & Finance* 32: 1883–93.

Basak, Suleyman, Alex Shapiro, and Lucie Teplá. 2006. "Risk Management with Benchmarking." *Management Science* 54 (4): 542–57.

Black, Fisher, and Myron Scholes. 1973. "The Pricing of Options and Corporate Liabilities." *Journal of Political Economy* 81: 637–54.

Blake, David, and Allan Timmerman. 2002. "Performance Benchmarks for Institutional Investors." In *Performance Measurement in Finance*, ed. J. Knight and S. Satchell, 342–64. London: Butterworth-Heinemann.

Boulier, Jean-François, ShaoJuan Huang, and Gregory Taillard. 2001. "Optimal Management under Stochastic Interest Rates: The Case of a Protected Defined Contribution Pension Fund." *Insurance: Mathematics & Economics* 28 (1): 173–89.

Campbell, John Y., and Luis M. Viceira. 1999. "Consumption and Portfolio Decisions When Expected Returns Are Time-Varying." *Quarterly Journal of Economics* 114: 433–96.

―――. 2001. "Who Should Buy Long-Term Bonds?" *American Economic Review* 91 (1): 99–127.

―――. 2002. *Strategic Asset Allocation: Portfolio Choice for Long Term Investors.* Oxford: Oxford University Press.

Campbell, John Y., Luis M. Viceira, and Joshua S. White. 2003. "Foreign Currency for Long-Term Investors." *Economic Journal* 113: C1–C25.

Castañeda, Pablo. 2006. "Portfolio Choice and Benchmarking: The Case of the Unemployment Insurance Fund in Chile." Working Paper 16, Chilean Pensions Supervisor, Santiago, Chile.

Cox, John, and Chi-Fu Huang. 1989. "Optimal Consumption and Portfolio Policies When Asset Prices Follow a Diffusion Process." *Journal of Economic Theory* 49: 33–83.

―――. 1991. "A Variational Problem Arising in Financial Economics." *Journal of Mathematical Economics* 20: 465–87.

Deelstra, Griselda, Martino Grasselli, and Pierre-François Koehl. 2003. "Optimal Investment Strategies in the Presence of a Minimum Guarantee." *Journal of Economic Dynamics & Control* 33: 189–207.

Detemple, Jérôme B., René Garcia, and Marcel Rindisbacher. 2003. "A Monte Carlo Method for Optimal Portfolios." *Journal of Finance* 58 (1): 401–46.

———. 2005. "Intertemporal Asset Allocation: A Comparison of Methods." *Journal of Banking & Finance* 29 (11): 2821–48.

El Karoui, Nicole, Monique Jeanblanc, and Vincent Lacoste. 2005. "Optimal Portfolio Management with American Capital Guarantee." *Journal of Economic Dynamics & Control* 29: 449–68.

Jensen, Bjarne A., and Carsten Sørensen. 2001. "Paying for Minimum Interest Rate Guarantees: Who Should Compensate Who?" *European Financial Management* 7 (2): 183–211.

Karatzas, Ioannis, John Lehoczky, and Steven Shreve. 1987. "Optimal Consumption and Portfolio Decisions for a 'Small Investor' on a Finite Horizon." *SIAM Journal of Control & Optimization* 25: 1557–86.

Karatzas, Ioannis, and Steven Shreve. 1998. *Methods in Mathematical Finance.* New York: Springer.

Merton, Robert C. 1969. "Lifetime Portfolio Selection under Uncertainty: The Continuous-Time Case." *Review of Economics & Statistics* 51 (3): 247–57.

———. 1971. "Optimum Consumption and Portfolio Rules in a Continuous-Time Model." *Journal of Economic Theory* 3: 373–413.

———. 1990. *Continuous Time Finance.* New York: Blackwell.

Nualart, David. 2006. *The Malliavin Calculus and Related Topics.* 2nd ed. New York: Springer.

Ocone, Daniel, and Ioannis Karatzas. 1991. "A Generalized Clark Representation Formula, with Application to Optimal Portfolios." *Stochastics & Stochastics Reports* 34: 187–220.

Platen, Ekhard. 2005. "On the Role of the Optimal Growth Portfolio in Finance." *Australian Economic Papers* 44 (4): 365–88.

Samuelson, Paul A. 1969. "Lifetime Portfolio Selection by Dynamic Stochastic Programming." *Review of Economics & Statistics* 51 (3): 239–46.

———. 1979. "Why We Should Not Make Mean Log of Wealth Big though Years to Act Are Long." *Journal of Banking & Finance* 3 (4): 305–7.

Teplá, Lucie. 2001. "Optimal Investment with Minimum Performance Constraints." *Journal of Economic Dynamics & Control* 25: 1629–45.

Turner, John. A., and David M. Rajnes. 2001. "Rate of Return Guarantees for Mandatory Defined Contribution Plans." *International Social Security Review* 54 (4): 49–66.

Walker, Eduardo. 2006. "Benchmarks, Risks, Returns and Incentives in Defined Contribution Pension Funds: Assessing Alternative Institutional Settings." Draft, Pontificia Universidad Católica de Chile.

# CHAPTER 5

# Labor Market Uncertainty and Pension System Performance

## Olivia S. Mitchell and John A. Turner

As perhaps never before, the financial market crisis is focusing attention on the many ways in which pensions are susceptible to financial market risks. This has brought new interest in monitoring and evaluating the performance of funded pension systems. As discussed in the preceding chapters, performance measurement of pension funds has typically involved a relatively narrow assessment of financial performance derived from the methods applied to mutual funds and other kinds of investment vehicles. Many countries are now approaching the point at which a large proportion of the retirement income of their citizens will be determined by the financial results achieved by privately managed pension funds. Recognizing the importance of this evolution of pension systems, many analysts have been prompted by the recent market collapses to examine how equity risk translates into wealth and benefit payouts under alternative pension regimes.[1]

Extending performance analysis beyond the short-term financial results to the more fundamental question of how to effectively align financial performance objectives (and therefore measurement benchmarks) requires the integration of numerous other parameters beyond simply the risk and return of the invested assets. These include defining a retirement income objective for the funded elements of a system and consideration of variations in life-cycle earnings and how these relate to financial market outcomes. Despite the increasing awareness of the importance of these factors, relatively few analysts to date have explored how human capital risks are incorporated in pension system performance. To contribute to the advancement of this discussion and provide a preface to the following chapters, which consider methodological approaches, a conceptual introduction is given, as well as a review of some of the available evidence related to integrating human capital parameters into pension system performance evaluation.

The specific human capital issues on which this chapter focuses include volatility in labor earnings and uncertainty in hours of work and the length of work life, as well as length of life after retirement. Thus, for instance, wage rates may rise or fall, hours of work may fluctuate, and at the extensive margin, the length of the work life and the retirement period can vary when retirement ages or mortality patterns change. Each of these dimensions of labor market uncertainty involve different ways in which risk influences how workers earn a living—and, in turn, in how this risk is translated into risky retirement income.

This chapter discusses these issues as well as interactions between human capital and capital market risk that must also be accounted for in careful models of pension performance. First, pension structures and how they interact with human capital risk are outlined briefly. The discussion indicates which types of human capital risk have been captured (or ignored) in the literature to date, as well as what kinds of capital market risks are modeled. The chapter then turns to a brief review of existing models and what they can teach us about the relative importance of human capital versus other types of risk. This is followed by a discussion of different ways to judge pension benefit outcomes. The chapter concludes with a discussion of what is needed to better integrate human capital risk when assessing pension performance.

## Pension Structures and Human Capital Uncertainty

To introduce the topic, this section briefly reviews key pension plan types and how different pension systems might interact with uncertainty in human capital resulting from volatility in wage rates and labor earnings, as well as changes in the length of the work life and retirement period.

### Pension Plan Types
**Defined contribution plans.** Defined contribution (DC) pensions are retirement programs in which employer and employee contributions

(in percentage or money terms) are explicitly deferred from workers' paychecks and accumulated in a retirement program. One prominent example is the 401(k) plan in which U.S. workers generally contribute a percentage of their pay, and in which employers may also provide a match based on employee contributions. Similar systems include the Australian Superannuation program, the Chilean-style individual account system, and private accounts under the Swedish-funded DC program (Premium Pension), to name just a few.

In DC plans, pension accruals depend on how much and how often money is contributed to the plans. Because contributions usually depend on labor earnings, the accumulation of retirement assets is directly impacted by workers' earnings and employment patterns, as well as when they work. (Sometimes retirement assets are also made available for hardship withdrawals or loans, in which case benefit adequacy may be influenced by the extent to which the option is exercised.) To dampen the impact of labor market volatility on retirement outcomes, DC plans are sometimes paired with minimum benefit guarantees made available to workers who contribute for a long time—as in the Chilean system before the 2008 reform, in which workers had to contribute for 20 years to earn a right to the minimum pension guarantee (Arenas de Mesa and others 2008). In other cases, governments elect to subsidize contributions for those workers with low or no earnings, as in the case of the German Reister pensions (Maurer and Schlag 2003). In both instances, human capital risk in the form of shocks to employment, labor earnings, and pension contributions will be mitigated by retirees receiving government support (particularly when the minimum benefit is financed with pay-as-you-go transfers outside the DC system). If such safety-net arrangements are not available, DC plans tend to provide relatively little protection for human capital risk: that is, a healthy and highly paid employee who always contributes to his or her plan is likely to end up with a much larger accumulation in the plan compared to a worker whose pay fluctuates, who experiences layoffs, and who may leave the labor force because of medical or other considerations.

DC plans also expose the worker to capital market risk and fiduciary risk: that is, participants often exert some degree of choice over where to invest their contributions, which exposes them to capital market risk arising from directly holding the underlying assets. The recent global financial meltdown illustrates how vulnerable retirement accounts may be to capital market shocks.[2] Fiduciary risk refers to the opportunity for pension assets to be used for purposes other than intended, most recently illustrated by the Argentinian government's takeover of about $30 billion in assets held by investors in the private pension system.[3]

***Defined benefit plans.*** There are many different types of defined benefit
(DB) plans, but for the present purposes, they may be characterized as
retirement plans in which promised benefits are described by formulas
that depend on retiree lifetime labor earnings, years of service, and retirement ages. In many Western nations, DB benefits are typically paid as a life
annuity; in other countries, such as Japan, benefits are traditionally paid as
a lump sum. DB plans treat human capital shocks differently than do DC
plans. In many DB plans, an employee must spend a certain number of
years in the plan before he or she earns a so-called vested right or legal
claim to an eventual retirement payment. Job changes can terminate or
curtail a worker's eventual retirement entitlement, and even when they do
not, the benefit is generally deferred until the plan's normal retirement age
and may not be inflation indexed. For this reason, these types of DB plans
can be quite risky for a mobile workforce: leaving a job with a DB plan or
getting laid off or downsized before retirement can be financially costly to
the affected worker. In this sense the DC structure imposes fewer pension
losses for those in high-turnover jobs and industries, as compared to DB
plans. There are, however, also examples like the Netherlands, where vesting periods are not allowed and where portability of accrued DB rights is
regulated by law and indexing for inflation is the same for deferred pension rights as it is for pensioners. It is also worth noting that DB formulas
can magnify labor market risk, to the extent that the benefit formula is
linked to a worker's final pay. By contrast, DB formulas may use an aver-
aging approach, making the benefit a function of career average pay; this
smoothes labor earnings shocks in the payout levels.

Some analysts argue that DB plans are safer than DC plans because
participants need not bear capital market risk directly. This is thought to
be true because the plan sponsor invests the plan assets and—in theory at
least—boosts contributions if the plan becomes underfunded. Yet the
apparent safety of DB plans is undermined when the plan sponsor fails to
contribute and then goes out of business. As an example, when the
Australian Ansett Airlines filed for bankruptcy in 2002 with an underfunded DB plan, participants experienced large pension losses as a result
(Ferris 2005). In some countries (such as the United Kingdom and the
United States), government agencies have been established to help protect against DB plan underfunding, but it is now clear that these programs
also face a substantial risk of insolvency (Brown 2008). In any event, DB
plans can provide some protection against human capital risk, but they
are far from being clearly "safer" along many dimensions.

*Hybrid plans.* Several variants on the traditional pension models incorporate both DB and DC aspects.[4] Some are DB plans with DC-like features that shift risk traditionally borne by employers to workers by linking payout to market financial indexes. Others are DC plans with rate-of-return guarantees that seek to lower workers' exposure to financial market risks (Turner and Rajnes 2003). Some firms have hybrids that both include a DC plan and promise a DB floor benefit (Cohen and Fitzgerald 2007; McGill and others 2009).

Some pension funds in the Netherlands have their own version of a hybrid pension called the "collective defined contribution" (CDC) system (Bovenberg n.d.). Instead of basing benefits on final average earnings, the Dutch hybrid ties benefits to career average earnings; benefit indexation depends on plan finances. A CDC plan has a benefit formula similar to a DB plan: employers contribute a fixed percentage of wages to these plans and bear no additional liability if plan investments perform poorly. In turn, plan assets are managed by professional money managers, but investment and longevity risks are shifted to employees as a group. When a CDC plan becomes underfunded, the plan-governing body (made up of employer and employee representatives) must determine how to restore full funding. This can be achieved by increasing employee but not employer contributions, or by making benefit accruals and indexing contingent on plan financial performance. If the plan becomes overfunded, the workers generally benefit rather than the employer. Some Dutch companies have added the feature that if the plan becomes overfunded, they can reduce their contribution, but such plans do not qualify as a CDC plan.[5]

## Interactions between Human Capital Uncertainty and Pension Performance

To dig deeper into how human capital uncertainty might affect payouts under different pension plan structures, this section takes up two conceptual issues. First, it discusses how variability in labor earnings might translate into pension payouts under a DB plan, a CDC plan, and a DC plan. Second, it examines the same questions with regard to employment shocks. Table 5.1 summarizes the approach. The discussion is not exhaustive, but instead develops a typology of issues and highlights factors that must be taken into account in policy-relevant models of pension performance.

**Table 5.1    How Human Capital Risks Translate into Pension Outcomes:
A Framework**

| | Pension plan type | | |
| --- | --- | --- | --- |
| Risk | Defined Benefit (DB) | Collective Defined Contribution (CDC) | Defined Contribution (DC) |
| **I. Employee-side labor income shock** | | | |
| Skill obsolescence | Partly smoothed | Like DB | Contributions directly |
| Health shock | (depends on benefit | | affected |
| Disability shock | formula) | | |
| Labor force exit | | | |
| Death | Benefit not bequeathed; survivor benefit possible | | Accumulation may be bequeathed |
| **II. Employer-side employment shock** | | | |
| Hours reduction | Accrual halted; nonvested | Like DB | Accrual protected; |
| Layoff/firing | benefit lost and final | | assets keep earning |
| Retirement | benefit may be very low | | investment returns |

*Source:* Authors' compilation.

## *Wage Shocks*

Payoffs to human capital are reflected in the increment to wages and salaries paid to education, skills and training, and labor market experience. Because wage rates are not fixed over time or over the life cycle, human capital risk involves uncertainty about the returns to these human capital investments. Wage shocks can arise for various reasons, including skill obsolescence, productivity losses due to poor health or disability, or macroeconomic factors that alter the value of worker effort.

Longitudinal administrative records from employers or tax authorities are needed if one is to uncover patterns of pay over workers' lifetimes. Yet microlevel data on wage distributions are difficult to obtain, making it difficult to measure the magnitude and distribution of wage rate shocks and identify their root causes. As a result, most pension models assume a so-called humped-shape earnings profile for life-cycle earnings, taking the form of an inverted U with age. Interestingly, this so-called classic earnings pattern turns out not to be that commonplace, at least in the United States where only 14 percent of U.S. workers fit this profile (Bosworth, Burtless, and Steuerle 2000). In the Bosworth study, approximately the same fraction of workers had real earnings patterns that sagged during their middle work years, another group had flat real earnings profiles, and still another had declining real earnings at a fairly young age. For instance, figure 5.1 shows how the mean earnings varies,

**Figure 5.1    Patterns of Earnings over the Lifetime, with Wage Level Indicator: Excluding and Including Zero Earners**

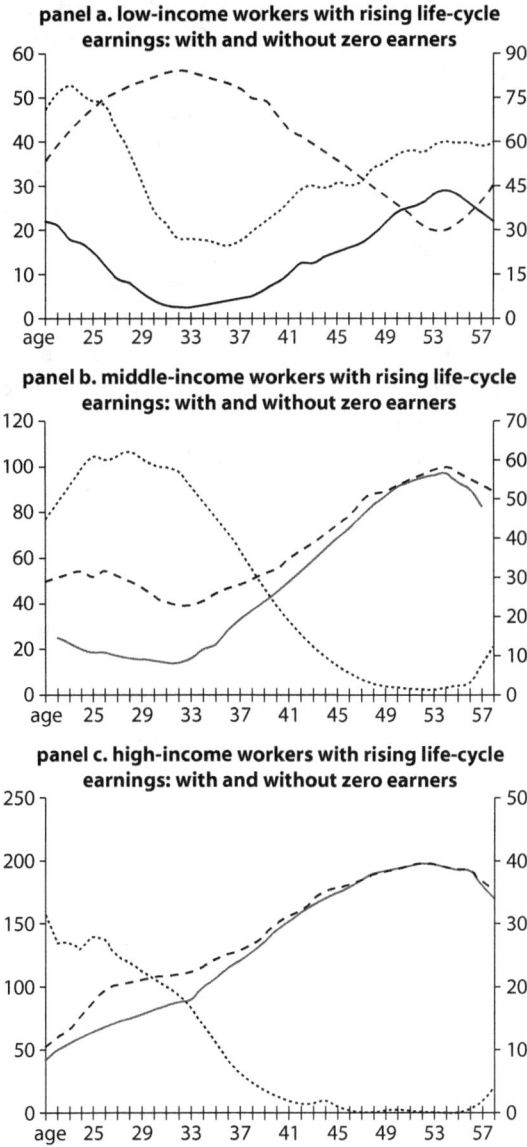

panel a. low-income workers with rising life-cycle earnings: with and without zero earners

panel b. middle-income workers with rising life-cycle earnings: with and without zero earners

panel c. high-income workers with rising life-cycle earnings: with and without zero earners

*Source:* Derived from Bosworth, Burtless, and Steuerle 2000.
*Note:* Average earnings as a percentage of economywide average earnings on left-hand scale; percentage of category with zero earnings in each year measured on right-hand scale. Solid line refers to all workers including unemployed; dashed line refers to workers with positive earnings; and dotted line refers to percentage of workers with zero earnings by age.

depending on whether the average includes or excludes those with zero earnings, and how the percentage with zero earnings varies over the life cycle and by income bracket. This tantalizing evidence, although slim, suggests that the single hump-shaped life-cycle earnings profile is less than relevant for everyone.

Life-cycle earnings profiles also differ considerably by sex and income level. Table 5.2, also taken from Bosworth, Burtless, and Steuerle (2000), underscores this point. The study showed that although one-quarter of U.S. men had hump-shape earnings profiles, only half as many women did. Half of all men had declining life-cycle earnings profiles, and one-third of the women. The data also show that low-earning women were most likely to have declining earnings profiles, but women were—somewhat surprisingly—also more likely to have rising earnings profiles than men. Another notable finding seen in table 5.2 is that including only those with nonzero earnings produces higher and much smoother earnings patterns than would characterize workers as a whole. Including those who are unemployed or laid off thus changes results considerably; as well, the bias due to ignoring zero earnings varies by gender, age, and income level. Whether these patterns are prevalent for other countries and cohorts is unknown, but it is important to find out, so as to determine what "real world" labor patterns mean for "real world" retirement plan outcomes.

Many analysts have worked on the question of why labor earnings differ across workers of different types and over the life cycle. Clearly health shocks and family patterns matter: in the United Kingdom, for instance, women are more likely than men to work part time and to

**Table 5.2    Life-Cycle Earnings Profiles Reported in U.S. Microdata**

| | Earnings level | | |
|---|---|---|---|
| Life-cycle earnings profile | Low | Average | High |
| Hump-shaped (%) | | | |
| Men | 0.5 | 3.4 | 24.1 |
| Women | 4.6 | 5.4 | 2.5 |
| Rising (%) | | | |
| Men | 3.8 | 4.2 | 10.1 |
| Women | 24.1 | 21.8 | 6.2 |
| Declining (%) | | | |
| Men | 10.2 | 18.8 | 24.9 |
| Women | 25.0 | 9.0 | 1.4 |

*Source:* Derived from Bosworth, Burtless, and Steuerle 2000.

interrupt their careers because of care-giving responsibilities; they also tend to retire earlier than men (Hermes 2009). Whether the volatility of labor income shocks also varies across people over the life cycle is less well studied. Mazumder (2001), for instance, uses administrative records to show that the variance in the transitory component of earnings in the United States follows a U-shaped pattern with age, and that such groups as blacks and the less educated have higher lifetime earnings variances than others. Although more remains to be shown along these lines, the patterns imply that projections of pension replacement rates that assume that everyone traces out a smooth earnings profile are inaccurate for many. As an example, Mitchell and Phillips (2006) use U.S. data to show that benefit replacement rates generated for actual workers' career paths tend to be much higher than for simulated hypothetical lifetime earners.[6] This occurs because actual pay profiles are more erratic and lower than commonly used hypothetical profiles; because the benefit formula is more generous to low lifetime earners, benefit replacement rates are therefore higher than usually simulated.

Another factor to note is that shocks to labor earnings may translate differently into retirement incomes, depending on whether the pension regime is DB, DC, or hybrid. Also important are specific plan features, which often include notches or nonlinearities that can dramatically change outcomes with just one more year of work, for instance. As table 5.1 indicates, normally pension benefits depend in some way on lifetime earnings, but in a DC plan, each year of earnings matters for pension outcomes because contributions are deposited annually. Moreover, early years tend to matter the most, when compound interest is earned on assets. By contrast, career-average DB plans tend to weight each year of pay similarly, whereas final-pay formulas count only the last (or last few) years in computing benefit amounts. For this reason, wage shocks occurring late in life tend to have a larger impact on benefit outcomes in DB than in DC plans. Using U.K. parameters, Blake, Cairns, and Dowd (2007) conclude that DC plans are most attractive to workers with the highest career average salaries (relative to final salary), as well as those whose salary peaks early in their careers. Assuming the same constant contribution rate, male personal service workers in that model receive 34 percent higher DC pensions (relative to final salary) than male professionals whose incomes peaked later in their careers. DB plans, by contrast, favor workers with high earnings at the end of their careers, the long-tenured, and persistently high achievers.

## Employment Shocks

This discussion next addresses how pension systems might differ in the
way that they transmit employment shocks into pension outcomes, a
matter of particular concern when labor markets are very fluid or
workers flow in and out of formal sector employment. This is particularly relevant in developing countries with relatively few pension-covered
jobs but many pension-uncovered jobs.[7] In Mexico, for instance, one
finds substantial flows between employment and self-employment; in
the latter case, the worker is unlikely to contribute to the pension
(Bosch and Maloney 2006). In the Chilean individual accounts system,
a large fraction of workers are only intermittently attached to the pension system, in part because their jobs are short term, in part because
they are self-employed and not required to contribute, and in part
because of contribution evasion (figure 5.2; see Arenas de Mesa and
others 2008). In this case, projected replacement rates that assume a
full career of contribution will substantially overestimate retirement
payouts. Moreover, the bias again differs by subgroups; for instance,
Arenas de Mesa and others (2008) show that those with the highest
"density of contributions" (or fraction of the work life during which
positive contributions are made) are the better paid, better educated,
and male employees. Conversely, those least likely to have persistent
pension coverage are women and the less educated. Contribution evasion

Figure 5.2    Pension Contribution Patterns in Chile by Age: Percentage of Available Years in Which Contributions Were Made

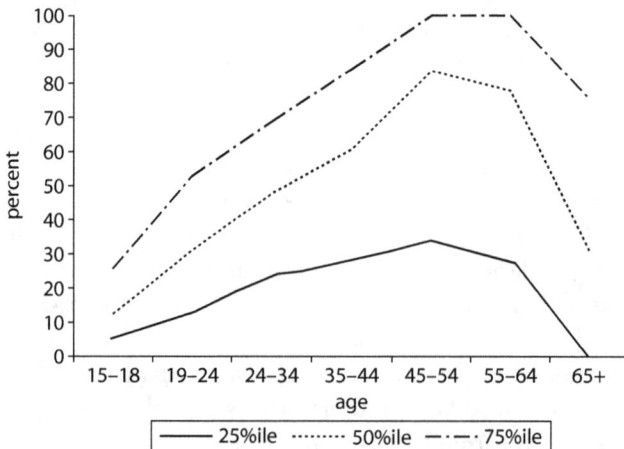

Source: Arenas de Mesa and others 2008.

is also common in developing nations, particularly for small firms and among lower-paid employees (Bailey and Turner 2001).

Pension systems also differ in the way that they handle employment volatility, with few plans offering perfect "pension portability," preserving employee rights to retain pension rights after leaving a job. In the DB context, job changers and those with weak labor market attachment may lose for two reasons. First, they may never gain eligibility for a benefit: for instance, the U.S. Social Security system requires a minimum of 10 years of contributions to receive any retirement pension. In the Netherlands, on the other hand, vesting periods are not allowed. Second, DB backloading rules mean that mobile workers give up the option for rapid benefit accruals just before retirement. In Canada, for instance, a terminated worker's DB benefit is normally fixed in nominal terms, so as soon as the worker leaves his or her firm, the person's deferred pension payment immediately begins to fall in value because of inflation. Job changers may also suffer a DB benefit loss because they give up early retirement subsidies; see McGill and others (2009).[8] The DC model is generally more forgiving of job change, although there can still be problems because of vesting rules.

Another factor that has not much been noted in models of pension performance to date is the role of macroeconomic shocks. Recessions can have an important impact on pension accruals, inasmuch as economic downturns wreak job destruction, erode job creation processes, and generate high levels of involuntary turnover. As an example, in the United States, more than one-fifth of 401(k) participants reduced their contributions and 4 percent stopped contributing in 2008 because of the economic downturn.[9] In Uruguay, Bucheli, Forteza, and Rossi (2007) report an average contribution density of 60 percent over a lifetime, an average that conceals wide extremes, with 28 percent contributing in all months, and another 40 percent contributing less than half the time. For the present purposes, the most interesting finding was that the contribution density was closely linked to the unemployment rate, falling when unemployment was high and rising when it was low. The Uruguay study also reports that contributions for higher-paid employees declined during economic downturns because people lost their jobs, moved to the informal sector, and had greater difficulty finding formal sector jobs; the pattern did not hold for the low paid or for workers in the public sector. In Chile higher national unemployment rates have been found to depress contribution densities for men but have the opposite effect on women, perhaps because women offset labor market changes experienced by their husbands (Berstein, Larraín, and Pino 2005).

### Pension Payouts

The discussion above identified several ways in which human capital risk influences pension accumulations; one should also note how these same factors can influence payouts. This can occur with pre-retirement withdrawals, permitted in such countries as Canada, where, as LeBlanc (2002) shows, people facing substantial reductions in labor income accounted for most of the pre-retirement pension withdrawals.[10] Pension outcomes can also respond to employment via retirement behavior. How long people work and when they retire also shape both pension accumulations and the level of benefits paid during retirement. This is particularly true for DB plans because many countries' national DB systems heavily subsidize early retirement benefits (Gruber and Wise 2007), and these subsidies have induced early retirement. The linkage tends to be exacerbated in recessions, when older workers may view the pension as a subsidized way to leave the labor market rather than remain unemployed.

By contrast, it is sometimes argued that DC plans have no effect on retirement decisions: that is, if payouts are actuarially neutral, there may be no economic benefit or penalty from deferring retirement for an additional year. Several plan design elements, however, can inhibit actuarial neutrality. For instance, a DC plan may sometimes be priced using outdated or unisex mortality tables, making expected benefits for any given individual actuarially unfair (Horneff and others 2009); here the DC plan still can influence retirement patterns. Also if DC accounts earn unexpectedly negative investment returns, wealth effects are likely to induce workers to delay retirement to offset pension losses (Gustman and Steinmeier 2002). This is likely to be important in the current (2009) financial climate. In a related manner, those wishing to annuitize their account balances will tend to delay retirement when interest rates fall because of reduced annuity payments (Soares and Warshawsky 2003).[11]

In sum, this section has shown that DB participants may face the problem of lack of portability when changing jobs, as well as uncertainty about how shocks to labor income will influence benefit payments. They are also exposed to the potential of DB plan termination or bankruptcy, which is discussed further below. In DC plans workers may experience labor or capital market shocks that leave them with periods of low or noncontribution or unexpectedly low benefit amounts.

## Integrating Human Capital Uncertainty into Models of Pension Outcomes

This discussion next turns to an overview of models that have been developed to illustrate the importance of human capital risks for pension outcomes. Our discussion outlines how these models differ according to their structure, inputs, outputs, and solution methods, seeking to illustrate the strengths and weaknesses of different approaches for different purposes. This section first differentiates between deterministic versus stochastic models; it notes that deterministic models can be run using alternative scenarios as a way of exploring the range of outcomes. The discussion then addresses microeconomic optimization models used to study the optimal structure of retirement income systems. It concludes with a discussion of how to integrate human capital and capital market interactions. Table 5.3 summarizes key findings.

### Alternative Modeling Approaches

Models of pension systems can be used to simulate alternative outcomes, often for the purpose of assessing reform options. The building blocks of typical models include labor market patterns—including labor earnings, job change, un- and nonemployment, and retirement patterns—and capital market outcomes—namely, the risk-and-return assumptions pertinent to assets held (in the case of a funded system). In addition, specific pension system behaviors may need to be modeled to determine pension contribution patterns, investment allocations, and, possibly, leakages from these accounts.

*Deterministic versus stochastic models.* To reduce the complexity of the problem, many analysts have taken a deterministic tack, rather than explicitly modeling shocks to human and financial capital. One such approach uses simulation: the World Bank's Prost model is a nonstochastic aggregate approach used by many countries to make aggregate projections of their pension system financial flows.[12] Prost models address pension contributions, entitlements, system revenues, and system expenditures over a long time frame. As another recent example, Munnell, Webb, and Delorme (2006) project DC plan account balances of workers to age 65 (assuming that all retire at that age) based on current age and cohort patterns in the U.S. Survey of Consumer Finances. Thus capital market risk and human capital risk are explicitly ignored, and the authors preserve observed current differences in wealth accumulation over time. They also assume all

**Table 5.3  Examples of Pension Modeling Approaches**

| Model/country | Data/parameter inputs | Outputs/results | Pension framework | Solution methodology | Risk framework |
|---|---|---|---|---|---|
| **I. Aggregate projection model** | | | | | |
| World Bank (2008), Prost | Est, Proj, Agg, NA | Pens, Fund, Ben | SS | Det, Indiv, Agg | NR |
| **II. Micro-projection/description model** | | | | | |
| **1. Deterministic** | | | | | |
| Bosworth, Burtless, and Steuerle (2000), United States | MSim, Hypo, NA | RRi | SS | Det, Indiv | NR |
| Poterba, Venti, and Wise (2007), United States | NU, NA | Adeq | DC | Det, Indiv | NR |
| Munnell, Webb, and Delorme (2006), United States | NU, NA | RRi | DB, DC, SS | Det, Indiv | NR |
| **2. Stochastic** | | | | | |
| Scholz and Seshadri (2008), United States | MSim, Long, Est | Wealth | DB, DC, SS | Opt, Indiv | V, Mort, Health |
| van Rooij, Siegmann, and Vlaar (2005), Netherlands | Agg, Est, NA | Fund | DB | Monte, Agg | R, Bond, Infl |
| Hinz, Homer, and Piacentini (2001), PENSIM, United States | MSim, NA | Pens, Ben | DB, DC, SS | MSim, Indiv | V, R, Bond, Infl, Mort, Health |
| **III. Micro-optimization** | | | | | |
| Horneff and others (2009), United States | MSim, RA, R | Inv | NU | Opt, Monte, Indiv | V, R, Mort, Health, House |
| Kotlikoff (2008), United States | Proj, NA | Consum | DB, DC, SS | Opt, DP, Indiv | NR |
| Hurd and Rohwedder (2008), United States | NU | Consum | NU | Sim, Indiv | Mort |

*Source:* Authors' compilation; see text.

*Note:* Data/parameter inputs:

Labor earnings: Agg = aggregate; Est = estimated; Hypo = hypothetical; Long = longitudinal earnings; MSim = microsimulation; NU = not used in model; Proj = projections

Utility function: NA = none; R = time preference; RA= risk aversion

Outputs/results:

Adeq = adequacy measure; Ben = benefit level; Consum = consumption target; Fund = funding ratio; Inv = investment allocation; Pens = pension assets; RRi = replacement rate for individual(s); Wealth = wealth target

Pension framework:

DB = defined benefit; DC = defined contribution; NU = not used; SS = Social Security

Solution framework:

Agg = aggregate; Coh = cohort; Det = deterministic; DP = dynamic programming; Indiv = individual; Monte = Monte Carlo; MSim = simulation; Opt = optimization; Stoch = stochastic

Risk framework:

NR = no risk included

K market: Bond = bond return; House = housing expenses; Infl = inflation risk; R = equity return

Human capital: Health = health and disability risk; V = longevity risk; V = earnings volatility (including due to unemployment)

Correlation: $\sigma$ = vector of correlations between capital market, human capital, institutional, and political risk

Macrolinks: No feedback loops between macroeconomy and micromodels.

households annuitize their total wealth at retirement (including housing wealth) using an inflation-indexed annuity with a two-thirds survivors benefit. This approach is critiqued by Scholz and Seshadri (2008) as understating retirement replacement rates because it uses a single projected earnings trajectory; it thus overstates future earnings for many people. Other analysts simplify the projection problem in other ways, for instance, by assuming that invested pension assets earn a constant rate of return over time in projecting DC plan accumulations (Mitchell, Moore, and Phillips 2000; Poterba, Venti, and Wise 2007).[13] Researchers have often had to rely on aggregate data and actuarial models to compute benefit replacement rates for hypothetical full-time workers employed over their entire careers (Mitchell 2008). Such a "cell-based" approach uses stylized earnings paths, such as those used in OECD (2007) and Whitehouse (2007) derived from average economywide earnings paths, on the assumption that these hypothetical workers never change their relative position in the earnings distribution and, further, that there is no volatility in earnings profiles. Related work for Peru by Bernal and others (2008) employs aggregate coverage data in an actuarial cell-based model to predict eventual replacement rates; similar simulations for Chile appear in Berstein, Larraín, and Pino (2005) and Favre and others (2006).

An alternative approach for generating pension outcomes employs stochastic simulation to estimate the range of outcomes that might be associated with such factors as longevity, capital market performance, or labor income uncertainty. Following Orcutt (1957), microsimulation models are widely used by policy makers in many nations to project retirement income adequacy with computer models that model individual units, such as people or firms, in a complex system of multiple equations.[14] In such an approach, one or more of the projection factors is assigned a random rather than a fixed value. Each simulation makes random draws for the stochastic variables from their assumed probability distributions and uses those values to produce future pension outcomes. Those outcomes are assumed to represent the distribution of actual outcomes that might be realized in the future. Multiple runs produce an array of results that can then be analyzed statistically, including calculating the probability and size of shortfalls.

A recent criticism of these models is that they usually assume a normal distribution for stock market returns, but it may be that the probability of extreme events is higher than that represented by a normal distribution (this is called the "fat tails" problem; see Laise 2009). Researchers have not yet addressed whether the distribution of human capital risks also are exposed to this sort of nonnormal risk.

The choice of which approach to use depends to some extent on the data inputs available, as well as the questions driving the analysis. For instance, Kotlikoff (2008) treats mortality and stock market rates of return as stochastic and examines the impact of insurance on individuals' retirement saving patterns; his study does not account for human capital risk other than longevity. Other analysts have devoted years to building microsimulation models that do take into account both human capital and capital market risk: models include the Social Security Administration's MINT model (Modeling Income in the Near Term; Sarney 2008), the Urban Institute's DYNASIM model (Dynamic Simulation of Income Model; Butrica, Toder, and Toohey 2008), the Labor Department's PENSIM (Pension Simulation Model; Holmer 2006), the Congressional Budget Office's long-term model (Sabelhaus 2008), the Employee Benefit Research Institute–Investment Company Institute (EBRI-ICI) 401(k) Accumulation Projection model (Holden and VanDerhei 2002a, b), and a new model under development at the Investment Company Institute (Sabelhaus and Brady 2008).[15]

***Microeconomic optimization models.*** An alternative to simulation and projection models is to devise life-cycle economic optimization models that generate desired wealth distributions in retirement. These desirable outcomes can then be compared to actual wealth patterns, to determine whether substantial shortfalls exist. Recent work by Scholz and coauthors arrives at the controversial conclusion that, at least in the United States, much of the population has saved adequately for retirement (Scholz, Seshadri, and Khitatrakun 2006; Scholz and Seshadri 2008). That model necessarily embodies key simplifications: for instance, the authors assume that households face no mortality risk and pay no out-of-pocket health care expenses before retirement, and that workers' pay is subject to a common random shock correlated across time. Uncertainty in retirement arises from post-retirement mortality and health care expenditures, the latter of which are also correlated over time. The authors assume that employees earn a constant real rate of return of 4 percent for both stocks and bonds, so capital market risk is ignored. The paper argues that older couples following an optimal consumption path will reduce consumption by one-third after their children leave home, and by another 30 percent after the death of one spouse. Taking account of household composition changes, they argue that far lower saving rates are needed than are usually recommended by simple projection models and financial advisers. Overall, the authors conclude that most U.S. households have saved optimally for retirement. It must be noted that the simulations take as given current Social Security benefit offerings, which, in fact, may be too optimistic given the system's pending insolvency; they also take mortality patterns as given. To the best of our knowledge, no one has applied this methodology to other countries.

In recent years it has become increasingly feasible to use dynamic optimization to solve microeconomic life-cycle models to determine how sensitive retirement outcomes might be to changes in underlying parameters. Some analysts use an illustrative individual assumed to start working early in life, accumulate retirement assets, and spend these funds to support retirement consumption (Horneff and others 2007, 2009). Such studies generally assume that the equity returns follow a random walk process with log normal returns, given some prespecified mean and standard deviation. These models posit that individuals smooth their expected marginal utilities of consumption by selecting optimal consumption, saving, investment, and decumulation profiles. Early versions of this methodology assumed no uncertainty and adopted set values for future wage growth, returns on pension investments, and life spans.[16] The advent of more computational power has permitted analysts to integrate ever more complexity, including stochastic mortality, risky equity returns, and most recently, risky labor earnings (Horneff and others 2009; Maurer, Mitchell, and Rogala 2009a). This approach generally solves for a household's optimal portfolio mix rather than evaluating what an optimal replacement rate might be because this approach focuses on investment questions and utility maximization rather any particular replacement rate outcome.

As one example, Campbell and others (1999) showed that the riskier is a person's labor income, and the more highly this risk is correlated with capital market volatility, the less he or she will tend to invest in equities. In this framework labor income is cast as a nontradable asset that affects the portfolio allocation of other assets in the worker's optimal portfolio. To the extent that the human capital return profile has bondlike characteristics, this model implies that people with more human capital should favor equity in their pension accounts, particularly early in their careers (Blake, Cairns, and Dowd 2007). Horneff and others (2009) extend the model by showing how human capital and capital market risks influence portfolio choice over the life cycle, particularly focusing on what happens when retirees can purchase payout annuities. Their study shows that investors will optimally hold a high fraction of equities while young, with the fraction in equities falling with age. Further, they will move money from liquid savings into annuities as they approach retirement and continue to do so until their late 70s.[17] Thus models indicate that risky human capital interacts with capital market uncertainty to shape investment decisions in important ways.

The next step in the research arena is to show how interactions between capital market shocks, labor income uncertainty, and retirement outcomes affect portfolios. Some researchers have modeled how work hours over the life cycle might react to volatility in equity returns, but many assume, rather unrealistically, that labor income risk is fully insurable in the capital market (that is, wages are perfectly correlated with traded risky securities).[18] A few authors, most notably Gomes, Kotlikoff, and Viceira (2008), do take the next step by examining how workers might adapt their hours in response to shocks; to simplify the modeling, this study assumes mandatory retirement at a fixed age. In the real world, of course, longer work lives also offer an important way in which older workers can adjust to negative labor and capital market surprises. Chai and others (2009) take the next step by showing that, when both hours of work and retirement ages are endogenous, workers boost their optimal equity holdings, particularly at older ages. Younger people also work more, and introducing annuities prompts earlier retirement and higher participation by the elderly in financial markets.

There is surprisingly little evidence on how correlations between shocks to labor income and capital market returns might drive retirement behavior. Indeed, the most cited study assumes a zero correlation between stock returns and labor income shocks, relying on a U.S. longitudinal study to justify this parameterization (Cocco, Gomes, and Maenhout 2005). More recently, models incorporating human capital risk in pension outcomes are emerging that allow correlations between labor earnings and capital market uncertainty (chapters 6 and 7 of this volume). In general, when labor income uncertainty is correlated with equity return shocks, this will powerfully alter workers' investment portfolios and work patterns. Maurer, Mitchell, and Rogalla (2009a) show that more labor income uncertainty, or reduced old-age benefits, boosts demand for stable income for both the young and retirees. In addition, a declining equity glide path with age is appropriate for workers having little labor income uncertainty; by contrast, for a worker anticipating high income risk, equity exposure starts low and rises to retirement age. In related work, Chai and others (2009) conclude that higher labor income uncertainty spurs demand for stable income among the young as well as the retired, whereas for the middle-aged, there is a trade-off between work hours and retirement ages.

The current coincidence of the equity market meltdown coupled with the prospect of a long global recession underscores the reality that human and financial capital market shocks do occur simultaneously. For instance, Seligman and Wenger (2005) indicate that investment market returns tend to rise during periods of unemployment; to the extent that the stock market is a leading indicator, unemployed workers will miss an opportunity to invest via a pension when equity prices are low and rising. Such unemployment-related losses are larger for low-wage workers because they are more prone to job loss. Behavioral responses can also be important: for instance, Agnew (2004) finds that DC plan participants in the United States have reacted to stock return declines by moving out of equities.

It has not yet been shown what particular format for a DC or DB pension might be better positioned to handle such complex risk interactions. Nevertheless, a few authors have "run the horserace" between plan types, seeking information on which might be superior across a range of financial and human capital risks. For instance, Blake, Cairns, and Dowd (2001) incorporate financial and wage volatility but fix hours and retirement ages; in this framework the authors focus on accumulations only and compare only static and specific preset life-cycle asset allocation strategies. They conclude that using a static asset allocation model may be preferable to a VaR framework when there is uncertainty about the parameters and underlying model driving capital market returns.[19] In another study, Hinz, Holmer, and Piacentini (2001) ask whether human capital risks matter more for DC or DB pension outcomes in the United States; their simulation model takes as input parameters on the timing of various life events factors such as first job start, first job finish, subsequent job starts and finishes, on-the-job promotions, disability, and death. The authors separately estimate hazard functions to predict waiting times between such events, using longitudinal data sets. The paper concludes that DB plans are riskier than DC plans in the U.S. context because of the pension loss experienced by job-changing workers. Their simulations report that DB benefits were 17 percent higher than DC plans on average, but the standard deviation of outcomes was 67 percent higher in DB plans, indicating substantially greater pension risk. Some workers fared better on average in DC plans (see table 5.4). That study did not allow for correlations between labor market uncertainty and shocks to equity returns.

Subsequent research by McCarthy (2003) also used a life-cycle model of consumption and saving to compare DB versus DC plan outcomes, taking

**Table 5.4     Simulated Difference between a DC Account Balance and a DB Lump-Sum Amount: Age 65 Retirees Arrayed by Tenure Quintile (on Longest Job) and Lifetime Earnings Quintile**

| Quintile | Percentage difference between DC lump-sum balance and DB plan lump-sum value at retirement | |
| --- | --- | --- |
| | By job tenure quintile (%) | By lifetime earnings quintile (%) |
| 1 | 4 | 2 |
| 2 | -2 | 3 |
| 3 | -6 | 2 |
| 4 | -8 | -2 |
| 5 | -8 | -24 |

*Source:* Derived from Hinz, Horner, and Piacentini 2001.
*Note:* Values approximate.

into account varying degrees of risk aversion and different wage processes correlated with returns on risky assets. That author found that DC plans provide better risk diversification for workers earlier in life because workers have few financial assets but relatively much human capital. By contrast, he found that DB plans were preferred later in life when they help reduce workers' exposure to financial markets. He also reported that DB plans would be more attractive to individuals with lower risk aversion. Table 5.5 illustrates the calculated sensitivity of the optimal DB replacement rate to human capital risk: the optimal replacement rate falls slightly as productivity growth increases because the absolute benefit level rises. Wage variability has a large effect, however, with the optimal replacement rate rising substantially when wage variability is relatively low. This is because the benefits provided by final average pay DB plans are very sensitive to wage variability at the end of the working life.[20]

In sum, a range of modeling techniques has been used for analyzing pension outcomes in the face of labor income uncertainty. The models differ as to how they deal with human capital risks, and ways remain to integrate labor income uncertainty into models of pension outcomes. Least well studied are the interactions with capital market shocks, and room for improvement remains in integrating both human and financial capital market shocks.

## Benchmarks for Pension Performance

Before concluding this discussion of pension plan performance, it is important to briefly mention the wide range of benchmarks or concepts offered by which system outcomes have been judged (Mitchell 2008). Some

**Table 5.5    Sensitivity of Optimal DB Pension Replacement Rate to Human Capital Risk**

| Sensitivity to human capital risk | Optimal DB replacement ratio (%) |
| --- | --- |
| Earnings growth (% per year) | |
| 0 | 28 |
| 1 | 26 |
| 2 | 24 |
| Wage variability factor | |
| 0.5 | 56 |
| 1.0 | 28 |
| 1.5 | 3 |

*Source:* Derived from McCarthy 2003.
*Note:* Wage variability refers to a factor by which the temporary and permanent components of wage variability are multiplied to illustrate the effect of variation in wages. Base value is 1.0.

authors project annual retirement benefits paid from a national social security or company-based DB plan and compare these to a measure of national average wages (OECD 2007). Others convert annual retirement benefit flows into pension wealth, or the lifetime expected present value of promised pension benefits, as a way to determine a pension plan's generosity over the entire lifetime. In doing so, of course, the latter measure incorporates longevity into the pension performance value. For funded DC systems, analysts compute projected account balances at retirement (for example, Poterba, Venti, and Wise 2007). It is also conventional to use a "replacement rate" concept, or the ratio of pension payments compared to an income standard; the latter could refer to a worker's own final or career pay, or to some national average pay level (for example, Whitehouse 2007). The success of a pension system can alternatively be measured by the rate of return provided on invested assets. The following discussion briefly outlines the performance targets most employed in the policy and academic literature on benefit payouts.

### Performance Target: Adequacy

One benchmark in wide use in the West compares benefits paid by a pension system (or projected to be paid) to some minimum criterion, where the latter is usually a country's income-based poverty line, the minimum wage level, or a national average earnings measure. Adequacy metrics of this type have been used, for instance, by Citro and Michael (1995), who compare pension system income payments over time or across countries, usually for a hypothetical "average" or representative individual selected by the authors. This measure is useful in that it allows computation of how many people fall short of the minimum income line and how large their shortfalls may be. On the other hand, very interesting recent research by Meyer and Sullivan (2009) shows that income and consumption measures of deep poverty and poverty gaps in the United States have actually moved in opposite directions over the last 20 years: income poverty rates have risen but consumption poverty has fallen. For this reason, it is necessary to carefully define what is meant by "adequacy" in attempting to judge whether a pension system is performing adequately.

### Performance Target: Income Replacement Rate

A different and widely used concept for measuring pension system performance is the so-called income replacement rate. In the literature a replacement rate refers to the amount of income a retiree receives from his or her pension compared to some active worker income level (OECD 2007, 2009). Target replacement rates of, say, 75 percent are often recommended by financial planners for clients who cannot otherwise estimate what income they will need in retirement (Palmer 2004; VanDerhei 2006).[21] A lower target replacement rate might be sensible if workers anticipate lower expenditures (and perhaps lower taxes) after leaving the labor market.

Implementing the replacement rate concept accordingly requires comparing two (more-or-less) readily observable economic flows, namely, workers' market income and retirees' retirement benefits; pension systems would then be judged more successful when the replacement rate is higher. Despite the simplicity of this concept, however, in practice people come up with very different measures. For instance, analysts disagree about *what period* to cover with regard to the earnings in the numerator. Some compare pension benefits with a worker's own labor earnings immediately before retirement; others make the comparison with a worker's own pre-retirement pay in a few peak years; and still others compare retirement benefits to the worker's entire career average pay.[22] (As an example, the U.S. Social Security system computes retirement benefits as a fraction of a worker's own pre-retirement earnings indexed for labor income growth; see Bosworth, Burtless, and Steuerle 2000). Also, analysts disagree on whether the replacement rate should compare benefits to gross (that is, pretax) or net (after-tax) incomes (Munnell, Webb, and Delorme 2006). A third issue is that benefits may be worth much more early in retirement than they are later, for instance, if benefit payments are not inflation indexed. In such a case, what might appear to be an initially generous replacement rate will be eroded over time. A fourth consideration is that focusing on retirement benefits overlooks how long benefits will be paid (for example, for a term, or until death of the individual and his or her partner). A fifth issue is that replacement rates should, by rights, be adjusted for household composition; it is widely agreed that one person requires fewer resources than a couple, and that children residing in their families have distinct consumption needs (Hurd and Rohwedder 2008).[23] Additional complexities in measuring relative benefit generosity include that not all benefits are life annuities. Hence what might appear to be a generous benefit at one point in time might become less generous if, for instance, the retiree exhausts his or her resources because of overspending, poor planning, or other shocks (Brown and others 2008). The point is that it is therefore critical not only to assess replacement rate outcomes in a static sense, but also to track the trajectory of replacement rates over the retirement period to assess the risk of failure relative to some minimum target (VanDerhei 2006).

Other considerations regarding the use of benefit replacement rates as a criterion for pension plan performance include the possibility that retirees' expenses might differ from those of younger persons. Thus non-workers will not need to incur commuting costs and outlays for tools or clothing used on the job or child-care expenses; in this case, daily expenses might be lower, and so benefit income may stretch farther. On the other hand, some expenditures, such as medical costs, are substantially higher for retirees, and these costs tend to rise with age. Also, in the context of pension reform assessments, it is important to note that observed replacement rates will inevitably be endogenous: that is, the value of pension benefits paid is usually a function of when the worker retires, with the formula paying less to those who leave the job market early. In such a situation, an observed low replacement rate could indicate either a poorly performing system or the outcome of a program that permits workers to consume more leisure by leaving their jobs early.[24] For this reason, it is useful to measure replacement rates for some simulated or hypothetical worker at given ages (for example, the earliest age at which benefits can be received, the normal retirement age).

***Dynamic considerations.*** Where possible, policy makers seeking to assess pension outcomes must focus not simply on static benefit outcome projections, but also on dynamic models that can include stochastic elements. To date, many authors have found ways to allow investment performance to be treated as stochastic, but as is explained in more detail below, one of the key factors determining pension outcomes is human capital risk.

Few existing models do a very good job including this important stochastic factor driving pension outcomes.

***Replacement rates in practice.*** In many policy settings, pension replacement rate computations are conducted using static projection models for representative or hypothetical individuals. Such an approach is most invaluable for actuarial models of benefit formulas and taxes, nicely exemplified in the Pension Reform Toolkit developed by the World Bank (World Bank 2008). This model has been used in over 80 countries to evaluate long-term flows of pension system revenues and expenditures, as well as to generate projected benefit amounts that can be used to compute replacement rate and adequacy measures. Similarly the OECD (2009) has produced several illustrative benefit computations for countries across the OECD, Africa, the Middle East, Eastern Europe, and Latin America. These replacement rates are measured as individual pension entitlements compared to individual earnings while working. The earnings measures used are the average of a hypothetical individual's lifetime earnings, where planners revalue those earnings in line with the growth of average earnings in the economy. Whitehouse (2008) calculates both gross and net replacement rates, with net replacement rates subtracting out taxes on earnings and taxes on benefits.

An alternative approach computes replacement rates for actual rather than hypothetical workers. This is a data-intensive effort because it can be implemented only if a country has good longitudinal earnings histories for actual workers. Mitchell and Philips (2006) compare replacement rate measures estimated for hypothetical workers with those computed using actual earnings data; they conclude that actual workers had many more gaps in their earnings than hypothetical workers. Because the U.S. pension system uses a progressive benefit formula, the results for actual workers generated higher replacement rates than would otherwise be concluded using hypothetical workers.[25]

***A caveat on consumption smoothing.*** A final point regarding pension outcomes measures is that replacement rates have been criticized by some analysts as a poor measure of retirement well-being. The main reason is that the economic life-cycle model of consumption and saving proposes that rational optimizing employees will seek to smooth the marginal utility of consumption over time, which is not equivalent to targeting a particular income replacement rate (Scholz, Seshadri, and Khitatrakun 2006). The point is that consumption patterns for many people rationally change post-retirement because their time is worth less in retirement than while working. As a result, retirees will naturally tend to substitute time for expenditure after leaving the job market, meaning that it is cheaper to live in retirement (Aguiar and Hurst 2005). As Skinner (2007: 21) notes, "planning for consumption smoothing doesn't mean one has to maintain consumption spending through retirement."

Another consideration is that in-kind benefits are often not included in the metric of resources available to retirees, to some extent because it may be difficult to measure the value of food or transport subsidies, provided medical care, or the like.[26] Such shortcomings in the computation of income replacement rates have led some planners to move away from the simple measure of income replacement rates toward measures that involve adjustments, such as for the imputed rent on housing. Each of these points serves to weaken the theoretical underpinning for focusing on a simple retirement replacement rate goal.

### Performance Target: Efficiency

An alternative indicator of pension performance could be the system's efficiency, again a concept that can be measured in many different ways. One approach focuses on the level of fees and charges levied by the pension system (Mitchell 1998; Turner and Witte 2008). From this perspective, scale economies may arise because of fixed costs and as a result of how the pension system is organized. For instance, when a DC plan has a single pool of assets managed centrally, it may have lower administrative costs than the same plan with numerous individual accounts in which each account holder is permitted to decide how his or her own assets are allocated. Economies also occur with experience, so that older plans may be more efficient than younger plans because of learning by doing. An alternative measure of efficiency is tied to the rates of return received on pension funds. For example, a DC plan could charge low fees but be inefficient because of the lack of diversification provided by the offered investment menu (Tang and Mitchell 2008).

In sum, a commonly used measure of pension system outcomes, namely, benefit replacement rates, has been challenged for a number of theoretical and conceptual reasons. Nevertheless some analysts will still use an average target replacement rate of around 75 percent, but a more sophisticated approach is to instead emphasize adequacy targets, perhaps adjusted for household size and composition, benefits in kind, and taxes and transfers. Naturally, whatever metric is proposed, the challenge for policy makers interested in measuring outcomes is the reality that longitudinal microeconomic data are needed to simulate, project, and assess lifetime labor income patterns and benefit outcomes.

## Conclusions and Policy Implications

This chapter emphasizes the key importance of integrating human capital and financial market risks into any assessment of pension system performance. The most relevant human capital risks discussed include volatility of labor earnings, uncertainty in hours of work and the length of the work life, and longevity in retirement. The chapter has shown how fluctuations in wage rates, unemployment, and hours of work can produce very different pension outcomes and, at the extensive margin, how the length of the work and retirement periods also shapes retirement payouts. In fact, the recent literature suggests that labor income uncertainty may be quantitatively more important than financial capital risk in determining retirement well-being for most people, insofar as their labor market earnings represent their primary form of wealth. We also show that the next generation of pension models will need to be more thoughtful in specifying what the sensible pension performance standards should be, moving beyond a simple income replacement rate notion to take into account consumption, leisure, and life spans.

Analysis of pension outcomes and the impact of pension policy changes would be greatly facilitated by access to new microeconomic longitudinal data sources. Of most value would be information tracking individual workers over time, particularly panel data linked to administrative records. For example, the United Kingdom, United States, and several European nations are now gathering such data on lifetime earnings as well as employment and pension contribution patterns that are linked to sociodemographic detail about respondents. Similar efforts are now under way in Chile with the Social Protection Survey, the Republic of Korea with the Korean Health and Retirement study, Japan with the Japanese Survey of Health and Retirement, and China with the CHARLS study. These data sets will be invaluable in providing a more realistic picture of the variability in labor earnings and employment patterns over the life cycle, patterns of contributions to pensions, and correlations between the capital market and labor income patterns.

It is also necessary to link these to "metafiles" containing information on pension parameters as well as those of other related programs. For instance, if the goal is to model the range of benefit outcomes under a specific DB plan, the analyst must know the rules pertinent to job changing or layoffs, vesting and backloading of benefit formulas, and the risk of DB plan closure due to either plan termination or sponsor bankruptcy.[27] Similar parameters would be required for CDC plans, along with some forecast of benefit and contribution adjustments when times require them. Without the richness of microlevel data, it will be difficult to test and model distributional outcomes from pension plan performance. When such detail is lacking, retirement analysts can use so-called hypothetical workers, designed to describe the life cycle of "representative" people of different types. Even here, it is important not to assume hypothetical profiles with full-time steady employment over a long career; otherwise one may overstate pension contributions, accumulations, and eventual retirement benefits (Pfau 2008). This is particularly important for modeling DC pension systems that could be anticipated to result in higher account balances than would actually apply to real-world workers.

In conclusion, recent research strongly indicates that both financial and human capital volatility must be taken into account when assessing pension performance metrics. In particular, retirement investment strategies and the associated benchmarks against which asset management performance is assessed should make explicit the desired benefit or income replacement targets, and the modeling must take due account of variable wage and labor earnings patterns, variable patterns of labor force attachment, and unevenness in pension contribution rates. Furthermore, these human capital aspects, including work hours and retirement ages, are plausibly highly correlated with financial market shocks, as the financial market crisis has made abundantly clear. To fully address the particular needs of the retirement income provision to which they are directed, the formulation of optimal portfolio strategies and performance evaluation benchmarks should therefore take into consideration the full scope of these human capital risks in addition to the financial parameters on which they have traditionally been based.

## Notes

1. See, for example, relevant papers in this volume, including Antolín and Tapia (chapter 2) and Walker and Iglesias (chapter 3).

2. Pension accumulations in OECD countries dropped by an estimated $5 trillion in 2008 because of the financial crisis (OECD 2008).

3. Jeanette Neumann, "Argentina Nationalizes Pension Funds; Analysts Say a Mixed Bag," www.startribune.com/business/34837309.html.

4. Also note that many workers have both DB and DC plans. In some countries firms that offer separate DB and DC plans with no interaction between the two are deemed to be hybrid plans as, for example, in Canada (Wesbroom and Reay 2005). About 14 percent of the U.S. private sector workforce participated in both DB and DC plans provided by their employer (Buessing and Soto 2006).

5. Some large plans have established pension "ladders," with formulas that explicitly determine the indexation rate applied to average wages and to benefits in payment at different plan funding levels. The adjustments tend to be made primarily through changes in indexation rates rather than through changes in contribution rates. These plans appeal to employers because the employer bears less risk than in a traditional DB plan. They can appeal to employees because the employee bears less risk than in a traditional DC plan.

6. Other scholars working with actual earnings trajectories include Mitchell, Moore, and Phillips (2000), Mitchell, Phillips, and Au (2007), and Nichols and Favreault (2008).

7. Another problem arising from volatile employment patterns is that workers may lose their pension entitlement because of poor documentation, or because the plan sponsor may have changed location, changed names, been bought out or merged with another firm, or gone out of business. This occurs in both DB and DC plans but is more prevalent in DB plans because they are less likely to provide portability (Bruce, Turner, and Lee 2005). Because of these changes, workers may encounter difficulties finding their pension plans to claim benefits.

8. Efforts to link life-cycle employment volatility and pension outcomes are few, mainly because of the difficulty of obtaining microeconomic longitudinal data on the patterns of real workers' contributions to their pension plans. In the United States, the evidence suggests that DC plan participants are persistent in making contributions, but the contribution rates vary over time. Thus Smith, Johnson, and Muller (2004) followed employees in 401(k) plans for a dozen years and reported that only 27 percent of those studied made persistent contributions at a stable contribution rate for the entire period. Of the remainder, 24 percent increased their contribution rates over time, 8 percent decreased their payments, 19 percent had breaks in their contribution patterns, and 23 percent had fluctuating contributions. Using tax data for 1987–96, Smith (2001) found substantial drop-off rates in workers' contributions to individual retirement accounts (IRAs); only 45 percent were still contributing in 1992, and 40 percent contributing through 1996, of those who contributed in 1987. In the U.K. context, Smith found a link between pension contributions and changes in income needs measured by changes in financial circumstances, such as health shocks, having a baby, or moving to a new house (www.bris.ac.uk/Depts/CMPO/workingpapers/wp139.pdf).

In Canada about half of participants in registered retirement savings plans (or individual account plans) contributed in only one or two of the three years between 1991 and 1993 (Maser 1995).

9. O'Connor-Grant, "Putnam Finds Diminishing 401(k) Contributions," http://www.onwallstreet.com/news/putnam-finds-diminishing-401k-contributions-613601-1.html.

10. In other countries, pre-retirement access to pension funds by workers is not permitted.

11. Burtless (2000), for example, evaluates the impact of fluctuations in financial markets using U.S. historical data for a hypothetical worker in a DC plan; the author concludes that variations in capital returns and the discount rate for an annuity conversion can change the value of retirement income relative to pre-retirement earnings by 20-110 percent of pre-retirement earnings. For workers with a DB plan, the employer bears the risk of fluctuation in the underlying assets, whereas in hybrid CDC plans, this risk is shared between employers and employees.

12. In a few instances, aggregate models have been expanded to incorporate some stochastic features; for instance, Burdick and Manchester (2003) use MINT to examine Social Security system finances in the United States, and Van Rooij, Siegmann, and Vlaar (2005) use the PALMNET model to evaluate the future status of pension plans in the Netherlands.

13. For instance, Poterba, Venti, and Wise (2007) do not model capital market risk in making their projections. Rather, they assume that 401(k) portfolios are allocated 60/40 to large capitalization equities and corporate bonds and that the average returns on corporate equities are equivalent to about 9.2 percent real and 3.2 percent on bonds. Further, they omit any impact of investment fees on net rates of return. They report average (mean) account balances. Given the skewness in account balances, with a small number of people having large balances, median account balances would be more indicative of the account balances of the typical participant. Account balances at the bottom and top deciles would provide information about the extremes. They do not report replacement rates but calculate the ratio of total 401(k) assets to gross domestic product.

14. Surveys of this literature include Dupont, Hagneré, and Touzé (2003) and Baroni and Richiardi (2007); examples of software include Destinie (Crenner 2008) in France, Cosi and Midas (Dekkers and others, http://www.statcan.gc.ca/conferences/ima-aim2009/session2e-fra.htm) in Belgium, and PENSIM (Curry 1996) in the United Kingdom.

15. Both the MINT model and the ICI model are mainly used for pension policy outcomes analysis. The MINT model matches Social Security earnings records to data from the Census Bureau's Survey of Income and Program

Participation (SIPP). Both the ICI model and DYNASIM can be used to study distributional issues and aggregate policy costs and effects. The new ICI model is similar to PENSIM in its focus on how job changes affect pension outcomes (Sabelhaus and Brady 2008). Holden and VanDerhei (2002a, b) use the EBRI-ICI 401(k) Accumulation Projection model to project the proportion of pre-retirement income that will be replaced by 401(k) assets. They incorporate uncertainty by each year determining whether a person contributes based on the percentage of workers at his or her age, tenure, and salary level that participate. Similarly, a probability is assigned to determine whether a participant would take a loan or a pre-retirement withdrawal from his or her 401(k) plan. Loans and pre-retirement withdrawals are not allowed in most countries. Each year in the projections, rates of return are randomly assigned from the historic range of rates of return for different asset classes. In addition, the authors investigate the effects of capital market risk by running different scenarios in which they limit the range of rates of return to simulate a worst case scenario, or the effects of timing of a brief bear or bull market at different points of a worker's career or retirement. The Congressional Budget Office (2004a, b) projects asset flows into and out of DB, DC, and IRA plans. The studies assume that future participation and contribution rates will equal the age-specific rates in 1997. These studies do not consider the future spread of 401(k) plans or the effects of demographic trends on the accumulation in personal retirement plans. Poterba, Venti, and Wise (2007) project future levels of U.S. 401(k) account balances as of age 65 for cohorts for the years between 2000 and 2040. Those authors note that projected account balances depend critically on assumed rates of return: if one assumes the historical average, average account balances are projected to amount to about $452,000 (in 2000 dollars); however, if the historical average less 300 basis points is assumed, averages will be only $269,000. To derive these estimates requires a large number of assumptions. Worker earnings are projected using the Health and Retirement Study. The intermediate earnings growth rate is used from the 2005 Annual Report of the Trustees of the Social Security Administration. Pension participation rates, job separation rates, and taking lump-sum distributions at job separation are aspects of human capital risk or of behavior that they consider. Job separation rates are based on the 1998 SIPP based on five-year age intervals. Separation rates vary by age but not by time on the job. SIPP data from various years are used to track the spread of 401(k) plans and to project future participation rates. Based on these data, the authors assume that the future annual rate of increase in 401(k) participation rates declines by 0.12 percent per year. The probability that the worker takes a lump-sum distribution given job separation is taken from the Health and Retirement Survey. Based on data from the 2003 SIPP, a combined employer-employee contribution rate of 10 percent is assumed, which does not vary across workers or over time.

16. Horneff and others (2007) review this rapidly expanding literature.

17. When annuities are fairly priced, that study shows that a 40-year-old investor lacking any bequest motive would trade half of his or her liquid wealth to gain access to the annuity; with a moderate bequest motive, the person would still exchange one-third of his or her wealth to gain access to annuities. When reasonable loads and asymmetric mortality distributions are included, the utility gains are still worth over one-third of financial wealth.

18. See the studies reviewed in Chai and others (2009).

19. This discussion is related to, but distinct from, the debate over whether a Value at Risk (VaR) approach often used by money managers is helpful in the DC context. In the DB context, a conditional Value at Risk (CVaR) model has been found to be quite useful in guiding investment decision making; see Maurer, Mitchell, and Rogalla (2009b).

20. This discussion is related to, but distinct from, the debate over whether a VaR approach often used by money managers is useful in the DC context. For instance, Blake, Cairns, and Dowd (2000) note that VaR results depend on the fund's asset allocation strategy; that model assumes fixed retirement ages and no annuities, as distinct from the models discussed above.

21. Rates in the range of 70 to 80 percent are often proposed as sensible target replacement rates for retirement benefits in the United States, with the caveat that low-income workers may require higher replacement rates because they consume a higher percentage of their pre-retirement income when working (Scholz and Seshadri 2008). The U.S. Department of Labor (2008) has recommended target replacement rates of at least 80 to 90 percent.

22. For instance, Biggs and Springstead (2008) use four different measures of pre-retirement earnings to compute alternative replacement rate measures: what they call "final" earnings (average real earnings in the five years preceding retirement), average lifetime wage-indexed earnings, average price-indexed earnings, and average real income computed based on the present value of real lifetime earnings. Of course, the average lifetime earnings measures ignore when the earnings are received.

23. It has been argued that the preferred way to compute replacement rate targets would not seek to maintain constant *household* consumption levels, but rather constant per capita consumption trajectories for those people *remaining* in the household. For instance, Kotlikoff (2008) argues in favor of lower replacement rates than commonly used, noting that while raising children, adults with a typical family budget cannot consume very much. He calculates a target replacement rate of 42 percent for a couple with two children; the couple with no children has a target rate of 52 percent. Kotlikoff argues that conventional saving rate measures call for much higher saving than would be economically justified if the target were to smooth consumption per person over time.

24. Also, those desiring to retire earlier will need to have a higher saving rate to finance their longer years of retirement. This higher savings rate depresses their pre-retirement net income and hence consumption, which, in turn, reduces the level of consumption relative to income that they need to replace in retirement (Schieber 1998). Accordingly, target replacement rates will be lower, the earlier is the target retirement age.

25. Using data from the U.S. Bureau of Labor Statistics' Consumer Expenditure Survey, the Aon/Georgia State RETIRE Project shows that low-earner couples have benefit replacement rates of 85 percent, middle-earner couples 75 percent, and high-income couples 78 percent (Palmer 2004).

26. For instance, when a retiree owns his or her home, the flow of housing services received by the retiree should be computed as valuable consumption; some researchers therefore add into pre- and post-retirement income streams an imputed value for such housing services (Munnell, Webb, and Delorme 2006).

27. The U.S. Pension Benefit Guaranty Corporation has devised a stochastic model known as the Pension Insurance Modeling System to assess how benefit claims evolve over time, taking into account demographic change, pension funding, and the chance of corporate bankruptcy. A short overview of this appears in the PBGC annual report (http://www.pbgc.org/docs/2008_annual _report.pdf).

## References

Agnew, Julie. 2004. "An Analysis of How Individuals React to Market Returns in One 401(k) Plan." Unpublished manuscript, College of William and Mary, Williamsburg, VA.

Aguiar, Mark, and Eric Hurst. 2005. "Consumption versus Expenditure." *Journal of Political Economy* 113 (5): 919–48.

Arenas de Mesa, Alberto, David Bravo, Jere R. Behrman, Olivia S. Mitchell, and Petra E. Todd. 2008. "The Chilean Pension Reform Turns 25: Lessons from the Social Protection Survey." In *Lessons from Pension Reform in the Americas*, ed. S. Kay and T. Sinha, 23–58. Oxford: Oxford University Press.

Bailey, Clive, and John Turner. 2001. "Strategies to Reduce Contribution Evasion in Social Security Financing." *World Development* 29: 385–93.

Baroni, Elisa, and Matteo Richiardi. 2007. "Orcutt's Vision, 50 Years On." Yale Economics Working Papers, Yale University, New Haven, CT. http://www .elisabaroni.com/download/orcutt.pdf.

Bernal, N., A. Munoz, H. Perea, J. Tejada, and D. Tuesta. 2008. *Una Mirada al Sistema Peruano de Pensiones.* Lima: BBVA.

Berstein, Solange, Guillermo Larraín, and Felipe Pino. 2005. "Cobertura, densidad y pensiones en Chile: proyecciones a 20 años plazo." SAFP Documento de Trabajo no. 12, Santiago.

Biggs, Andrew G., and Glenn R. Springstead. 2008. "Alternate Measures of Replacement Rates for Social Security Benefits and Retirement Income." *Social Security Bulletin* 68 (2): 1–19.

Blake, David, Andrew Cairns, and Kevin Dowd. 2001. "PensionMetrics: Stochastic Pension Plan Design and Value at Risk during the Accumulation Phase." *Insurance: Mathematics & Economics* 29: 187–215.

———. 2007. "The Impact of Occupation and Gender on the Pensions from Defined Contribution Plans." *Geneva Papers on Risk & Insurance* 32: 458–82.

Bosch, Mariano, and William F. Maloney. 2006. "Gross Worker Flows in the Presence of Informal Labor Markets: The Mexican Experience 1987–2002." CEP Discussion Paper, Center for Economic Performance, London.

Bosworth, Barry, Gary Burtless, and C. Eugene Steuerle. 2000. "Lifetime Earnings Patterns, the Distribution of Future Social Security Benefits, and the Impact of Pension Reform." *Social Security Bulletin* 63 (4): 74–98.

Bovenberg, Lans. n.d. "The Dutch Collective Pension System: Best of Both Worlds?" Netspar Working Papers, Tilburg University, Tilburg, the Netherlands.

Brown, Jeffrey R. 2008. "Guaranteed Trouble: The Economic Effects of the Pension Benefit Guaranty Corporation." *Journal of Economic Perspectives* 22 (1): 177–98.

Brown, Jeffrey R., Jeffrey King, Sendhil Mulainathan, and Marian V. Wrobel. 2008. "Why Don't the People Insure Late Life Consumption? A Framing Explanation of the Under-annuitization Puzzle." TIAA-CREF Research Dialogue, April, TIAA-CREF, New York.

Bruce, Ellen, John A. Turner, and Donsoo Lee. 2005. "Lost Pensions: An Empirical Investigation." *Benefits Quarterly* 21 (1): 42–48.

Bucheli, Marisa, Alvaro Forteza, and Ianina Rossi. 2007. "Work History and the Access to Contributory Pensions: The Case of Uruguay." Document no. 16/07, October, Departmento de Economía, Universidad de la República, Montevideo, Uruguay.

Buessing, Marric, and Mauricio Soto. 2006. "The State of Private Pensions: Current 5500 Data." Center for Retirement Research, Issue Brief no. 42, February, Boston College, Boston.

Burdick, Clark, and Joyce Manchester. 2003. "Stochastic Models of the Social Security Trust Funds." Research and Statistics Note 2003-01, Social Security Administration, Washington, DC.

Burtless, Gary. 2000. "How Would Financial Risk Affect Retirement Income under Individual Accounts?" Center for Retirement Research, no. 5, October, Boston College, Boston.

Butrica, Barbara A., Eric Toder, and Desmond J. Toohey. 2008. "Boomers at the Bottom: How Will Low Income Boomers Cope with Retirement?" AARP Public Policy Institute Research Report 2008-07, AARP, Washington, DC.

Campbell, John Y., Joao F. Cocco, Francisco J. Gomes, and Pascal J. Maenhout. 1999. "Investing Retirement Wealth: A Life-Cycle Model." Harvard Institute of Economic Research Discussion Paper no. 1896, Harvard University, Cambridge, MA.

Chai, Jingjing, Wolfram Horneff, Raimond Maurer, and Olivia S. Mitchell. 2009. "Extending Life Cycle Models of Optimal Portfolio Choice: Integrating Flexible Work, Endogenous Retirement, and Investment Decisions with Lifetime Payouts." NBER Working Paper 15079.

Citro, Connie F., and Robert T. Michael, eds. 1995. *Measuring Poverty: A New Approach.* Washington, DC: National Academy Press.

Cocco, Joao, Francisco Gomes, and Pascal Maenhout. 2005. "Consumption and Portfolio Choice over the Life Cycle." *Review of Financial Studies* 18: 491–533.

Cohen, Bruce, and Brian Fitzgerald. 2007. *The Pension Puzzle.* 3rd ed. Mississauga, Ontario: John Wiley & Sons Canada.

Congressional Budget Office (CBO). 2004a. "A Model to Project Flows into and Out of Tax-Deferred Retirement Saving Accounts." CBO Technical Paper 2004 15, CBO, Washington, DC. http://www.cbo.gov/ftpdocs/63xx/doc6335/BP-2004-15.pdf.

———. 2004b. "Tax-Deferred Retirement Saving." CBO Paper, May, CBO, Washington, DC.

Crenner, Emmanuelle. 2008. "Effects of the French Pension Reforms on Living Standards of Retirees: Intergenerational Comparisons." Paper presented at the Conference of the International Association of Research on Income and Wealth, Portoroz, Slovenia, August 24–28.

Curry, Chris. 1996. "PENSIM: A Dynamic Simulation Model of Pensioners' Income." Government Economic Service Working Paper no. 129. Analytical Services Division, Department of Social Security, London.

Dupont, G., C. Hagneré, and V. Touzé. 2003. "Les modèles de microsimulation dynamique dans l'analyse des réformes des systèmes de retraites une tentative de bilan." (Dynamic Microsimulation Models Used to Analyze Retirement System Reforms: An Essay of Synthesis). *Economie et Prevision* 160–61: 167–91.

Favre, Michel, Angel Melguizo, Angel Muñoz, and Joaquin Vial. 2006. *A 25 Años del la reforma del sistema previsional chileno: evaluación y propuestas de ajuste.* Santiago, Chile: BBVA.

Ferris, Shauna. 2005. "Ansett's Superannuation Fund: A Case Study in Insolvency." In *Retirement Provision in Scary Markets,* ed. Hazel Bateman, 161–86. Cheltenham, U.K.: Edward Elgar.

Gomes, Francisco, Lawrence Kotlikoff, and Luis M. Viceira. 2008. "Optimal Life-Cycle Investing with Flexible Labor Supply: A Welfare Analysis of Life-Cycle Funds." *American Economic Review: Papers & Proceedings* 98: 297–303.

Gruber, Jonathan, and David A. Wise, eds. 2007. *Social Security Programs and Retirement around the World: Micro-Estimation.* Chicago: University of Chicago Press.

Gustman, Alan, and Thomas Steinmeier. 2002. "Retirement and the Stock Market Bubble." NBER Working Paper 9404.

Hermes, Sharon. 2009. "Private Pension Reform and Personal Accounts in the UK: Implications for Women." *Advances in Industrial and Labor Relations* 16: 161–80.

Hinz, Richard P., Martin R. Holmer, and Joseph S. Piacentini. 2001. "The Accidental Pension: Miracle Cure or Retirement Roulette." Paper presented at the IZA Conference on Pension Reform and Labor Markets, Berlin, Germany, May 19.

Holden, Sarah, and Jack VanDerhei. 2002a. "EBRI/ICI 401(k) Accumulation Projection Model and Appendix." *Perspective.* Investment Company Institute. Vol. 8, no. 3a, November.

———. 2002b. "Can 401(k) Accumulations Generate Significant Income for Future Retirees?" *Perspective* (Investment Company Institute) vol. 8, no. 3, November.

Holmer, Martin R. 2006. "PENSIM Analysis of Impact of Regulation on Defined-Contribution Default Investments." Working Paper, U.S. Department of Labor, Washington, DC.

Horneff, Wolfram, Raimond Maurer, Olivia S. Mitchell, and Ivicia Dus. 2007. "Following the Rules: Integrating Asset Allocation and Annuitization in Retirement Portfolios." *Insurance: Mathematics and Economics* 42: 396–408.

Horneff, Wolfram, Raimond Maurer, Olivia S. Mitchell, and Michael Z. Stamos. 2009. "Asset Allocation and Location over the Life Cycle with Investment-Linked Survival-Contingent Payouts." *Journal of Banking and Finance* 33 (9): 1688–99.

Hurd, Michael D., and Susann Rohwedder. 2008. "Adequacy of Economic Resources in Retirement and Returns-to-Scale in Retirement." Working Paper 2008-174, May, Michigan Retirement Research Center, Ann Arbor, MI.

Kotlikoff, Lawrence J. 2008. "The Economics Approach to Financial Planning." *Journal of Financial Planning* (March): 40–48.

Laise, Eleanor. 2009. "Odds-on Imperfection: Monte Carlo Simulation. Financial-Planning Tool Fails to Gauge Extreme Events." *Wall Street Journal*, May 2. http://online.wsj.com/article/SB124121875397178921.html.

LeBlanc, Pierre. 2002. "Essays on Tax-Deferred Savings in Canada." PhD dissertation, Harvard University.

Maser, Karen. 1995. "Who's Saving for Retirement?" *Perspectives* (Statistics Canada) (winter): 14–19.

Maurer, Raimond, Olivia S. Mitchell, and Ralph Rogalla. 2009a. "The Effect of Uncertain Labor Income and Social Security on Lifecycle Portfolios." Working Paper, Pension Research Council, Wharton School, Philadelphia.

———. 2009b. "Managing Contribution and Capital Market Risk in a Funded Public Defined Benefit Plan: Impact of CVaR Cost Constraints." *Insurance: Mathematics & Economics* 45: 25–34.

Maurer, Raimond, and Christian Schlag. 2003. "Money-Back Guarantees in Individual Pension Accounts: Evidence from the German Pension Reform." In *The Pension Challenge: Risk Transfers and Retirement Income Security,* ed. O. S. Mitchell and K. Smetters, 187–213. Oxford: Oxford University Press.

Mazumder, Bhashkar. 2001. "The Mismeasurement of Permanent Earnings: New Evidence from Social Security Earnings Data." Working Paper 2001-24, Federal Reserve Bank of Chicago, Chicago.

McCarthy, David. 2003. "A Life-Cycle Analysis of Defined Benefit Pension Plans." *Journal of Pensions Economics and Finance* 2 (2): 99–126.

McGill, Dan, K. Brown, John Haley, Sylvester Schieber, and Mark Warshawsky. 2009. *Fundamentals of Private Pensions.* 9th ed. Oxford: Oxford University Press.

Meyer, Bruce D., and James X. Sullivan. 2009. "Five Decades of Consumption and Income Poverty." NBER Working Paper 14827. March.

Mitchell, Olivia S. 1998. "Administrative Costs of Public and Private Pension Plans." In *Privatizing Social Security,* ed. M. Feldstein, 403–56. Chicago: University of Chicago Press.

———. 2008. "New Directions for Pension System Performance Measurement." Paper presented at the International Seminar "Pensions for the Future: Developing Individually Funded Programs" held by the International Federation of Pension Fund Administrators (FIAP) and the Peruvian Association of Private Pension Fund Administrators. Lima, Peru.

Mitchell, Olivia S., James Moore, and John Phillips. 2000. "Explaining Retirement Saving Shortfalls." In *Forecasting Retirement Needs and Retirement Wealth,* ed. O. S. Mitchell, B. Hammond, and A. Rappaport, 139–66. Philadelphia: University of Pennsylvania Press.

Mitchell, Olivia S., and John Phillips. 2006. "Social Security Replacement Rates for Alternative Earnings Benchmarks." *Benefits Quarterly* (fourth quarter): 37–47.

Mitchell, Olivia S., John Phillips, and Andrew Au. 2007. "Lifetime Earnings Variability and Retirement Shortfalls." In *Retirement Provision in Scary Markets*, ed. H. Bateman, 78–99. Cheltenham, U.K.: Edward Elgar.

Munnell, Alicia, Anthony Webb, and Luke Delorme. 2006. "Retirements at Risk: A New National Retirement Risk Index." June, Center for Retirement Research, Boston College, Boston.

Nichols, Austin, and Melissa M. Favreault. 2008. "The Impact of Changing Earnings Volatility on Retirement Wealth." Paper presented at the 10th Annual Joint Conference of the Retirement Research Consortium, Washington, DC, August 7–8.

Organisation for Economic Co-operation and Development (OECD). 2007. *Pensions at a Glance: Public Policies across OECD Countries*. Paris: OECD.

———. 2008. *Pension Markets in Focus*. OECD, Paris.

———. 2009. *Pensions at a Glance: Retirement Income Systems in OECD Countries*. Paris: OECD.

Orcutt, Guy H. 1957. "A New Type of Socio Economic System." *Review of Economics and Statistics* 58: 773–97.

Palmer, Bruce A. 2004. "2004 GSU/Aon RETIRE Project Report." Center for Risk Management and Insurance Research, Georgia State University, Atlanta.

Pfau, Wade D. 2008. "Assessing the Applicability of Hypothetical Workers for Defined-Contribution Pensions." GRIPS Policy Information Center Discussion Paper no. 07-11, National Graduate Institute for Policy Studies, Tokyo.

Poterba, James, Steve Venti, and David A. Wise. 2007. "New Estimates of the Future Path of 401(k) Assets." NBER Working Paper no. 13083, May.

Sabelhaus, John. 2008. "CBOLT Documentation." Background Paper, Congressional Budget Office, Washington, DC.

Sabelhaus, John, and Peter Brady. 2008. "The Role of Defined Contribution Accounts in Future Retirement Income Security: A Dynamic Microsimulation Approach." May, Investment Company Institute, Washington, DC.

Sarney, Mark. 2008. "Distributional Effects of Increasing the Benefit Computation Period." Policy Brief no. 2008 02. Social Security Administration, Office of Policy, Washington, DC.

Schieber, Sylvester J. 1998. Deriving Pretreatment Income Replacement Rates and the Savings Rates Needed to Meet Them. *Benefits Quarterly* 14 (2): 53–69.

Scholz, John Karl, and Ananth Seshadri. 2008. "Are All Americans Saving 'Optimally' for Retirement?" Paper presented at the 10th Annual Joint Conference of the Retirement Research Consortium, Washington, DC, August 7–8. http://crr.bc.edu/images/stories/Conference papers/4_1.pdf.

Scholz, John Karl, and Ananth Seshadri, and Surachai Khitatrakun. 2006. "Are Americans Saving 'Optimally' for Retirement?" *Journal of Political Economy* 116: 607–43.

Seligman, Jason S., and Jeffrey B. Wenger. 2005. "Asynchronous Risk, Unemployment, Equity Markets, and Retirement Savings." Working Paper no. 05–114, Upjohn Institute, Kalamazoo, MI. http://www.upjohninst.org/publications/wp/05–114.pdf.

Skinner, Jonathan. 2007. "Are You Sure You Are Saving Enough for Retirement?" NBER Working Paper 12981.

Smith, Karen, Richard Johnson, and Leslie Muller. 2004. "Deferring Income in Employer-Sponsored Retirement Plans: The Dynamics of Participant Contributions." *National Tax Journal* 57 (3): 639–70.

Smith, Paul. 2001. "A Longer Term Perspective on IRA Participation: Evidence from a Panel of Tax Returns." U.S. Office of Tax Analysis, Department of the Treasury, Washington, DC.

Soares, Chris, and Mark Warshawsky. 2002. "Annuity Risk: Volatility and Inflation Exposure in Payments from Immediate Life Annuities." Paper presented at the Center for Research in Pension and Welfare Policies, Conference "Developing an Annuity Market in Europe," Turin, Italy.

Tang, Ning, and Olivia S. Mitchell. 2008. "The Efficiency of Pension Plan Investment Menus: Investment Choices in Defined Contribution Pension Plans." Working Paper no. WP2008-02, June, Pension Research Council, Wharton School, Philadelphia.

Turner, John A., and David M. Rajnes. 2003. "Rate of Return Guarantees for Voluntary Defined Contribution Plans." In *Risk Transfers and Retirement Income Security*, ed. Olivia S. Mitchell and Kent Smetters, 251–67. Oxford: Oxford University Press.

Turner, John A., and Hazel A. Witte. 2008. "Fee Disclosure to Pension Participants: Establishing Minimum Requirements." Report to the International Centre for Pension Management, University of Toronto, Toronto, Canada.

U.S. Department of Labor, Employee Benefits Security Administration. 2008. "Taking the Mystery Out of Retirement Planning." U.S. Department of Labor, Washington, DC.

VanDerhei, Jack. 2006. "Measuring Retirement Income Adequacy: Calculating Realistic Income Replacement Rates." *EBRI Issue Brief* no. 297 (September): 1–35.

van Rooij, Maarten, Arjen Siegmann, and Peter Vlaar. 2005. "PALMNET: A Pension Asset and Liability Model for the Netherlands." DNB Research Memorandum no. 760, February, DNB, Amsterdam.

Wesbroom, Kevin, and Tim Reay. 2005. "Hybrid Pension Plans: UK and International Experience." Research Report 271, U.K. Department for Work and Pensions, London.

Whitehouse, Edward. 2007. *Pensions Panorama: Retirement Income Systems in 53 Countries.* Washington, DC: World Bank.

World Bank. 2008. "Modeling Pension Reform: The World Bank's Pension Reform Options Simulation Toolkit." World Bank, Washington, DC. http://siteresources .worldbank.org/INTPENSIONS/Resources/395443-1121194657824/ PRPNoteModeling.pdf.

# CHAPTER 6

# Pension Funds, Life-Cycle Asset Allocation, and Performance Evaluation

## Fabio C. Bagliano, Carolina Fugazza, and Giovanna Nicodano

Current efforts to measure the performance of defined contribution (DC) pension funds are nearly exclusively derived from those developed to evaluate mutual funds. These methods simply equate a higher return per unit of risk with better performance. As discussed in chapter 3, this assumption might be appropriate if the members of the fund all have preferences that are defined exclusively in terms of the mean and the variance of portfolio returns.[1] However, as introduced in chapter 5, a range of other factors, including the presence of a mandatory social insurance system, potentially differing income replacement objectives, variations in lifetime earnings patterns, and differences in risk appetite, as well as a variety of other potential factors that will vary in relation to the setting and characteristics of the covered population, may help to define a performance measurement metric for pension funds.

In nearly all cases, workers contribute to a pension fund to enhance the ability to smooth consumption after retirement because the pension provided by a first-pillar program is insufficient to achieve the desired level of income replacement. In a few countries the funded program is designed to be the primary source of retirement income. In either case, the optimal asset allocation should take into account, together with the asset return distributions and the risk aversion parameter that enter a standard portfolio choice problem, the expected value of other sources of pension income as well as the worker's life expectancy. Because the pension transfer is usually a fraction of labor income during the last working year (which is, in turn, the outcome of the worker's employment history and the risk associated with this), the optimal asset allocation should explicitly consider the trade-off between gains from investing in high-risk premium assets with the needs to hedge labor income shocks.

Adopting a life-cycle perspective, this chapter explores a number of the key methodological issues that must be resolved to include other determinants of optimal portfolios for retirement, such as other sources of retirement income, volatility of labor earnings, and potential correlations between financial and labor markets. The methods proposed are then used to develop a simple model that is calibrated to deliver quantitative estimates of an optimal portfolio allocation for DC pension funds of various characteristics and evaluate the sensitivity of the asset allocation within this portfolio to variations of the parameters from which it is derived. The discussion then addresses practical issues in the application of a theoretically optimal portfolio by considering whether the cost of implementation is likely to be associated with commensurate welfare gains, and it concludes by proposing a welfare-based performance metric.

The model that is presented in this chapter is derived from the literature on strategic asset allocation for long-term investors. The recent increase in the prevalence of DC pension programs, and the associated decline in defined benefit (DB) plans in settings in which they had been common, has reinforced the focus on determining optimal investment policies for this form of retirement savings plan. Substantial progress over the traditional (mean-variance, one-period) approach that still forms the basis for much practical financial advice has been made in recent years, exemplified by Campbell and Viceira (2002), which is often cited as seminal work in this area of financial theory. Long investment horizons, the presence of risky labor income, and consideration of illiquid assets, such as real estate, have been gradually incorporated into the analysis of optimal portfolio choice. Moreover, the conditions under which conventional financial advice (such as the suggestion that investors should switch from stock to bonds as they age, and that more risk-averse investors should hold a larger fraction of their risky portfolio in bonds) is broadly consistent with optimal asset allocation policies have been developed through this work. The key intuition is that optimal portfolios for long-term investors may not be the same as for short-term investors because of a different judgment of assets' riskiness, and because of the crucial role played by (nontradable) human wealth in investors' overall asset portfolio.

The life-cycle model presented features two risky assets and one riskless asset. These are parameterized by the first two moments of their return distribution and correspond to domestic stocks, bonds, and bills. As shown in Bodie, Merton, and Samuelson (1992) and Cocco, Gomes, and Maenhout (2005), early in a worker's life the average asset allocation is tilted toward the high-risk premium asset because labor income provides an effective hedge against financial risks. In contrast, in the two decades before retirement, the allocation gradually shifts to less risky bonds because income profiles peak at about age 45.

Although these patterns are associated with the given values of the parameters that describe both workers' human capital and investment opportunities, as well as with the institutional framework, this chapter performs sensitivity analysis along several important dimensions. The first examines the relationship of optimal asset allocation to the labor income profile. For instance, a construction worker may face a higher variance of uninsurable labor income shocks than a teacher (Campbell and others 2001); alternatively, the correlation between stock returns and labor income may be higher for a self-employed individual or a manager than for a public sector employee. If such differences have negligible effects on optimal asset allocation, the pension plan could offer the same option to all participants without any differences in its utility. Instead, in the simulations in this chapter, optimal portfolio shares are found to be highly heterogeneous across coeval agents (despite their common life expectancy, retirement age, and replacement ratios) because of individual-specific labor income shocks. Dispersion decreases as workers approach retirement, the greater the labor income–stock return correlation. As this increases, the histories of labor incomes tend to converge over time, leading to a convergence in the associated optimal portfolio choices. These results suggest that the optimal allocation should be implemented through diversified investment options for most occupations and age brackets.

The assumed underlying pension transfer in the present model is a fixed annuity (provided by an unmodeled first pillar or DB program)[2] that is proportional to labor income in the last working year. The replacement ratios for such programs vary widely across countries, as documented by the OECD (2007), ranging from 34.4 percent in United Kingdom to 95.7 percent in Greece. Such differences also depend on the inflation indexation of pension annuities, which is often less than the measured increase in prices; this implies a reduced average replacement ratio. By measuring the sensitivity of optimal portfolio composition with respect to the replacement ratio, this chapter considers whether optimal pension fund portfolio policies should vary across countries for given members' types. When the replacement ratio falls, the simulations reveal that agents save more during their working life in anticipation of lower pension incomes, thus accumulating a higher level of financial wealth. This activity results in a lower optimal share of stocks at all ages and for all values of the labor income–stock return correlation when risk aversion remains unchanged. Stated differently, with higher financial wealth, a given labor income becomes less apt to offset bad financial outcomes. The model therefore indicates that asset allocation in low replacement ratio countries should be more conservative because workers' contributions to pension funds would be higher.

Computing the optimal life-cycle asset allocation allows this to be used as a performance evaluation benchmark that explicitly considers the role of funded pension savings in smoothing participants' lifetime consumption risk. Based on the model, the analysis is extended to suggest an integrated approach to evaluating pension funds' performance. This approach considers the ratio of the worker's ex ante maximum welfare under optimal asset allocation to his or her welfare under the pension fund actual asset allocation: the higher the ratio, the worse the pension fund performance. This combines potentially lower performance resulting from a lower return per unit of financial risk, the focus of standard metrics, with poor matching between the pension fund portfolio and its members' labor income and pension risks.

An important practical question, however, is whether the costs of developing portfolios tailored to age, labor income risk, and other worker-specific characteristics are commensurate with gains in welfare that might result. To provide some initial insight into this question, this chapter assesses the welfare costs of implementing two simpler strategies, namely, an age rule and a strategy with portfolio shares fixed at one-third for each of the three financial assets under consideration, echoing the $1/N$ rule of DeMiguel, Garlappi, and Uppal (2008), which has been found to outperform several portfolio strategies in ex post portfolio experiments. The simulation results suggest that this portfolio strategy is likely to be cost efficient for both high-wealth and highly risk-averse, average-wealth workers in medium-to-high replacement ratio countries. In these cases the welfare costs of the suboptimal one-third rule are often lower than

50 basis points each year in terms of welfare-equivalent consumption, which is likely to be lower than the management cost differential.

The remainder of the chapter is organized into four sections. The main theoretical principles relevant for pension fund strategic asset allocation are outlined in the next section 2. The following presents the simple life-cycle model, showing how it can be calibrated to deliver quantitative predictions on optimal portfolio allocation. Potential welfare metrics for pension funds' performance evaluation then are introduced and discussed to address whether such optimal portfolios are practical to implement and to suggest application in measuring portfolio performance. A final section summarizes the main conclusions.

## Methodological Issues in Developing Optimal Portfolios That Include Pension-Specific Parameters

Financial theory provides simple asset allocation rules for an investor maximizing utility when (1) this is defined as expected (financial) wealth at the end of a single-period horizon $(E_tW_{t+1})$, (2) there is no labor income, and (3) specific assumptions are made regarding the form of the utility function and the distribution of asset returns. Within this standard framework the main assumptions include the following: (1) a *constant* degree of *relative risk aversion* is assumed (a simplifying assumption broadly consistent with long-run features of the economy, such as the stationary behavior of interest rates and risk premia in the face of long-run growth in consumption and wealth), (2) investors have power utility, and (3) returns are lognormally distributed. The underlying theory posits that investors trade off mean expected returns of the portfolio against variance, obtaining in the case of one risky and one riskless asset the following optimal portfolio distribution:

$$\alpha_t = \frac{E_t r_{t+1} - r_{t+1}^f + \frac{\sigma_t^2}{2}}{\gamma \sigma_t^2},$$

where $r_{t+1} = \log(1+R_{t+1})$ and $r_{t+1}^f = \log(1+R_{t+1}^f)$ are the continuously compounded returns on the risky and riskless asset, respectively, $\sigma_t^2$ is the conditional variance of the risky return, and $\gamma$ is the constant relative risk aversion parameter.[3] This result is equivalent to the prediction of the simple mean-variance analysis, and the equivalence extends also to the case of many risky assets, with affecting only the scale of the risky asset portfolio but not its composition among different asset classes.

The optimal investment strategy may substantially differ from the above one-period (that is, myopic) rule if the investment horizon extends over multiple periods and when a human wealth component is added to financial wealth. Extending the analysis to these two conditions is outlined below.

### Multiperiod Investment Horizons

When the investor has a long-term investment horizon, maximizes the expected utility of wealth $K$ periods in the future ($E_t W_{t+K}$), lognormally distributes returns, and is allowed to rebalance his or her portfolio in each period, the optimal portfolio choice coincides with the (myopic) choice of a one-period investor under the following two sets of conditions:[4]

- The investor has power utility, and returns are independent and identically distributed (i.i.d.).
- The investor has log utility ($\gamma=1$), and returns need not be i.i.d. In fact, this investor will maximize expected log return, and the $K$-period log return is the sum of one-period returns: therefore, with rebalancing, the sum is maximized by making each period the optimal one-period choice.

These relationships have been well understood in the financial literature since the contributions of Samuelson (1969) and Merton (1969, 1971).

The myopic strategy can also be found to be optimal when the investor is concerned with the level of *consumption* in each period (and not only with a terminal value for financial wealth). In this framework, the joint consumption-saving and asset allocation problem is often formulated in an infinite-horizon setting, yielding portfolio rules that depend on preference parameters and state variables, but not on time. The length of the effective investment horizon is governed by the choice of a rate of time preference to discount future utility. With power utility, under the assumption that the investor's consumption to wealth ratio is constant, the consumption capital asset pricing model (CCAPM; Hansen and Singleton 1983) implies that (with denoting log consumption and log wealth):

$$E_t r_{t+1} - r_{t+1}^f + \frac{\sigma_t^2}{2} = \gamma \operatorname{cov}_t(r_{t+1}, \Delta c_{t+1}) = \gamma \operatorname{cov}_t(r_{t+1}, \Delta w_{t+1}) = \gamma \alpha_t \sigma_t^2,$$

where the second equality is derived from the assumption of a constant consumption-wealth ratio. The optimal share of the risky asset is therefore the same as in the myopic case:

$$\alpha_t = \frac{E_t r_{t+1} - r_{t+1}^f + \frac{\sigma_t^2}{2}}{\gamma \sigma_t^2}.$$

This equivalence result is valid also in the case of multiple risky assets. The constant consumption-wealth ratio is justified under i.i.d. returns (implying that there are no changes in investment opportunities over time) or in the special case of log utility ($\gamma=1$, implying that the income and substitution effects of varying investment opportunities cancel out exactly, leaving the ratio unaffected).

All the above results have been obtained under the assumption of constant relative risk aversion and power utility. This formulation is highly restrictive under (at least) one important respect: it links risk aversion ($\gamma$) and the elasticity of intertemporal substitution ($1/\gamma$) very tightly, the latter concept capturing the agent's willingness to substitute consumption over time. Epstein and Zin (1989, 1991) adopt a more flexible framework in which scale independence is preserved but risk aversion and intertemporal substitution are governed by two independent parameters ($\gamma$ and $\psi$, respectively). The main result is that risk aversion remains the main determinant of portfolio choice, whereas the elasticity of intertemporal substitution has a major effect on consumption decisions but only marginally affects portfolio decisions. With Epstein-Zin preferences, in the case of one risky asset, the premium over the safe asset is given by

$$E_t r_{t+1} - r_{t+1}^f + \frac{\sigma_t^2}{2} = \theta \frac{\mathrm{cov}_t(r_{t+1}, \Delta c_{t+1})}{\psi} + (1-\theta)\mathrm{cov}_t(r_{t+1}, r_{t+1}^p),$$

where $\theta = (1 - \gamma)/(1 - 1/\psi)$ and $r^p$ is the continuously compounded portfolio return. The risk premium is a weighted average of the asset return's covariance with consumption divided by $\psi$ (a CCAPM term) and the covariance with the portfolio return (as in the traditional capital asset pricing model). Under power utility, $\theta = 1$, and only the CCAPM term is present. The two conditions for optimal myopic portfolio choice apply in this case as well:

- If asset returns are i.i.d., then the consumption-wealth ratio is constant, and covariance with consumption growth equals covariance with portfolio return. In this case

$$E_t r_{t+1} - r_{t+1}^f + \frac{\sigma_t^2}{2} = \gamma \, \mathrm{cov}_t(r_{t+1}, r_{t+1}^p).$$

This implies the myopic portfolio rule.

- Alternatively, if $\gamma = 1$, then $\theta = 0$ and the risk premium is simply $\text{cov}_t(r_{t+1}, r_{t+1}^p)$, again implying optimality of the myopic portfolio rule.

Therefore, what is required for optimality of the myopic portfolio choice is a unit relative risk aversion, not a unit elasticity of intertemporal substitution.

## Portfolio Choice with Variations in Investment Opportunities

The portfolio choice for a long-term investor can differ in important ways from the myopic rule when investment opportunities are time varying. Investment opportunities can vary over time because of variable real interest rates and variable risk premia. Campbell and Viceira (1999, 2001), among others, study the two cases separately, deriving the optimal portfolio policies for an infinite-horizon investor with Epstein-Zin preferences and no labor income.

Preliminarily, following Campbell (1993, 1996), a linear approximation of the budget constraint is derived, and the expected risk premium on the risky asset is expressed in terms only of parameters and covariances between the risky return and current and expected future portfolio returns

$$E_t r_{t+1} - r_{t+1}^f + \frac{\sigma_t^2}{2} = \gamma \, \text{cov}_t(r_{t+1}, r_{t+1}^p)$$

$$+ (\gamma - 1) \text{cov}_t \left( r_{t+1}, (E_{t+1} - E_t) \sum_{j=1}^{\infty} \rho^j r_{t+1+j}^p \right), \qquad (1)$$

where $\rho$ is a constant of linearization and the last term captures the covariance between the current risky return, and the revision in expected future portfolio returns due to the accrual of new information between $t$ and $t+1$. Then equation (1) can be applied to portfolio choice under specific assumptions on the behavior of returns over time.

If only *variations in the riskless interest rate* are considered, as in Campbell and Viceira (2001), with constant variances and risk premia, then $(E_{t+1} - E_t)\sum_{j=1}^{\infty}\rho^j r_{t+1+j}^p = (E_{t+1} - E_t)\sum_{j=1}^{\infty}\rho^j r_{t+1+j}^f$, and with a single risky asset we have $\text{cov}_t(r_{t+1}, r_{t+1}^p) = \alpha_t^2 \sigma_t^2$. From equation (1) the optimal portfolio weight on the risky asset is then given by

$$\alpha_t = \underbrace{\frac{1}{\gamma}\frac{E_t r_{t+1} - r_{t+1}^f + \frac{\sigma_t^2}{2}}{\sigma_t^2}}_{\text{myopic demand}} + \underbrace{(1-\frac{1}{\gamma})\frac{\text{cov}_t\left(r_{t+1}, -(E_{t+1}-E_t)\Sigma_{j=1}^{\infty}\rho^j r_{t+1+j}^f\right)}{\sigma_t^2}}_{\text{intertemporal hedging demand}} . \quad (2)$$

In addition to the asset's risk premium relative to its variance, which determines the myopic demand for the asset, a second demand component is relevant (for $\gamma \neq 1$). This component (related to the asset return's covariance with reductions in expected future riskless interest rates, relative to its variance) captures the intertemporal hedging demand of Merton (1973), whose weight tends toward one as $\gamma$ increases. The risky asset is held not only for its expected premium, but also because it hedges future expected changes in the portfolio return (due to changes in the riskless rate), compensating the investor for the loss in interest income. This role remains when risk aversion is increased, and the myopic component of demand moves toward zero. In practical terms, inflation-indexed long-term bonds or, less effectively, nominal long-term bonds can provide this kind of intertemporal hedging because their returns covary with declines in the level of interest rates.

A second empirically relevant case of time-varying investment opportunities involves *variable premia on the risky assets.* Campbell and Viceira (1999) explore the implications of variable risk premia for optimal asset allocation in the case of only one risky asset and a constant riskless rate. Here time-varying investment opportunities are captured by a variable, mean-reverting excess return on the risky asset. Formally,

$$r_{t+1} = E_t r_{t+1} + u_{t+1},$$

$$E_t r_{t+1} - r^f + \frac{\sigma_u^2}{2} = x_t,$$

$$x_{t+1} = \mu + \varphi (x_t - \mu) + \eta_{t+1},$$

where the state variable $x_t$ summarizes investment opportunities at time $t$. Innovations $u_{t+1}$ and $\eta_{t+1}$ may be correlated, with covariance $\sigma_{\eta u}$. This covariance generates intertemporal hedging demand for the risky asset by long-term investors because it measures the ability of the risky asset to effectively hedge changes in investment opportunities. In fact,

$$\text{cov}_t(r_{t+1}, x_{t+1}) = \text{cov}_t(r_{t+1}, r_{t+2}) = \sigma_{\eta u},$$

so that, in the empirically relevant case $\sigma_{\eta u} < 0$, there is mean reversion in the risky asset return: an unexpectedly high return today reduces expected returns in the future. Under this set of assumptions, the optimal portfolio share of the risky asset contains the two components, as in equation (2):

$$
\alpha_t = \underbrace{\frac{1}{\gamma} \frac{E_t r_{t+1} - r_{t+1}^f + \frac{\sigma_u^2}{2}}{\sigma_u^2}}_{\text{myopic demand}}
$$

$$
\underbrace{+ (1 - \frac{1}{\gamma}) \left( \frac{-\sigma_{\eta u}}{\sigma_u^2} \right) \left[ b_1(\mu\varphi) + b_2(\varphi) \frac{E_t r_{t+1} - r_{t+1}^f + \frac{\sigma_u^2}{2}}{\sigma_u^2} \right]}_{\text{intertemporal hedging demand}}, \quad (3)
$$

where $b_1(\mu, \phi)$ is positive and increasing in $\mu$ and decreasing in $\phi$, and $b_2(\phi)$ is positive and increasing in $\phi$. The intertemporal hedging demand is captured by the term involving $\sigma_{\eta u}$: in the empirically relevant case $\sigma_{\eta u} < 0$ (and $\mu > 0$) a sufficiently risk-averse investor ($\gamma > 1$) will hold a larger portfolio share in the risky asset than a myopic one, exploiting the possibility of hedging expected future changes in investment opportunities. Overall, a conservative long-run investor should respond to mean-reverting risky returns by increasing his or her average portfolio share invested in the risky asset.

## Asset Allocation with Human Wealth

The results for optimal asset allocation mentioned so far apply in the case of fully tradable financial wealth. Adding a nontradable human wealth component (that is, the expected present discounted value of future labor earnings) is an important step toward the construction of models useful to establish practical asset allocation strategies of long-term investors, such as pension funds. In this case the analysis above must be suitably adapted, as first done by Bodie, Merton, and Samuelson (1992). Here the discussion briefly considers several cases of increasing complexity.

### Baseline Case: Riskless Labor Income
The simplest case to analyze is the asset allocation choice of an investor endowed with power utility and a nonstochastic labor income faced with one riskless and one risky asset. In this case (nontradable) human wealth

$H_t$ is the present discounted value of all future earnings discounted at the riskless rate and is equivalent to the holding of the riskless asset. Therefore, the investor will choose the portfolio share of the risky asset $\sigma_t$ so as to make the nominal holdings of the asset equal to the optimal holdings in the unconstrained case of fully tradable (financial and human) wealth $\hat{\alpha}_t$:

$$\alpha_t = \frac{\hat{\alpha}_t(W_t + H_t)}{W_t} = \frac{E_t r_{t+1} - r^f + \frac{\sigma^2}{2}}{\gamma \sigma^2}\left(1 + \frac{H_t}{W_t}\right) \geq \hat{\alpha}_t. \tag{4}$$

Thus, in the presence of riskless nontradable human wealth, the investor's financial portfolio will be tilted toward the risky asset. The share $\sigma_t$ is increasing in the ratio $H_t/W_t$ and therefore changes over the investor's life cycle for (at least) two reasons: (1) along the life cycle, $H$ changes relative to $W$, being higher at the beginning of the working life and lower at retirement; and (2) it changes with financial asset returns: when the risky asset performs well, $W$ increases relative to $H$ and the optimal share of the risky asset decreases, with the investor rebalancing his or her portfolio away from the risky asset.

More complicated cases are now analyzed, under the simplifying assumptions of power utility, i.i.d. financial asset returns (ruling out time-varying investment opportunities), and no life-cycle perspective (that is, either a single period or an infinite investment horizon with fixed probability of retirement is considered). An explicit life-cycle perspective will be adopted in the operative model of the next section.

### Adding Labor Income Uncertainty

The investor has a one-period horizon (so that no saving decision is involved) and earns a lognormally distributed labor income $l_t$, potentially correlated with the return on the risky asset: $\mathrm{cov}_t(l_{t+1}, r_{t+1}) \equiv \sigma_{lu}$. In this setting the optimal portfolio rule is given by

$$\alpha_t = \frac{1}{\rho}\left(\frac{E_t r_{t+1} - r^f + \frac{\sigma_u^2}{2}}{\gamma \sigma_u^2}\right) + \overbrace{\left(1 - \frac{1}{\rho}\right)\left(\frac{\sigma_{lu}}{\sigma_u^2}\right)}^{(-)}, \tag{5}$$

$$\underbrace{\phantom{\left(1 - \frac{1}{\rho}\right)\left(\frac{\sigma_{lu}}{\sigma_u^2}\right)}}_{\text{labor income hedging demand}}$$

where $\rho = (1 + \overline{H/W})^{-1} < 1$ (with $\overline{H/W}$ being the average human to financial wealth ratio) captures the elasticity of consumption to financial wealth and plays a crucial role in linking consumption to the optimal portfolio choice. The first component of the risky asset share in equation (5) is the optimal share when labor income risk is idiosyncratic (that is, $\sigma_{lu} = 0$), confirming the result (because $1/\rho > 1$) that the optimal share of the risky asset is higher than in the absence of labor income, when all wealth is tradable. The second is an income-hedging component. The risky asset is desirable if it allows an investor to hedge consumption against low realizations of labor income: if $\sigma_{lu} < 0$, the risky asset is a good hedge, and this increases its portfolio share.

### Adding Flexible Labor Supply

If labor supply can be flexibly adjusted by the investor, he or she can compensate for losses in the financial portfolio by increasing work effort: this additional margin of adjustment makes the investor more willing to take on financial risk, as shown by Bodie, Merton, and Samuelson (1992). In this extended setting, the optimal share of the risky asset is

$$\alpha_t = \frac{1}{\beta_w}\left(\frac{E_t r_{t+1} - r^f + \frac{\sigma_u^2}{2}}{\gamma \sigma_u^2}\right) + \overbrace{\left(1 - \frac{1}{\rho}\right)(1+v)\left(\frac{\sigma_{zu}}{\sigma_u^2}\right)}^{(-)}, \qquad (6)$$

where

$$\beta_w = \frac{\rho}{1+(1-\rho)\,\gamma v},$$

with $v$ capturing the elasticity of labor supply to the real wage and $\sigma_{zu}$ measuring the covariance between risky returns and the real wage (as $v \to 0$, labor supply becomes infinitely inelastic and $\beta_w \to \rho$ as in the case of fixed labor supply: in all cases $0 \le \beta_w \le \rho$). The ability to adjust labor supply increases the risky asset share ($\beta_w \le \rho$) if wages are uncorrelated with risky returns, and as the elasticity of labor supply increases, the portfolio share increases. The sensitivity of the portfolio allocation to a nonzero $\sigma_{zu}$ is measured by $(1 - 1/\rho)(1 + v)$ and becomes increasingly negative as $v$ increases: investors with a flexible labor supply are particularly willing to hedge wage risk because they respond to fluctuations in the real wage by changing their work effort, and thus the effects of wage shocks on their labor income are magnified.

### Extension to a Long-Horizon Setting

Following Viceira (2001), the investor has an infinite horizon (which makes decision rules time invariant), with a positive probability of retirement $\pi^r$ (that is, a zero-labor income state) in each period. The expected time until retirement, $1/\pi^r$, is the effective investor's retirement horizon. After retirement the investor may die with probability $\pi^d$ in each period, so that $1/\pi^d$ is his or her expected lifetime after retirement. Labor income is subject only to permanent shocks (a log-random walk process with drift), so that income growth is

$$\Delta l_{t+1} = g + \xi_{t+1}$$

with

$$cov_t(r_{t+1}, \Delta l_{t+1}) = cov_t(u_{t+1}, \xi_{t+1}) = \sigma_{u\xi}.$$

In each period the investor can be in either of two states (retired or employed), and the solution to the intertemporal optimization problem depends on the state. For a *retired* investor the optimal portfolio share of the risky asset $\alpha^r$ is simply given by the myopic solution

$$\alpha_t^r = \frac{E_t r_{t+1} - r^f + \frac{\sigma_u^2}{2}}{\gamma \sigma_u^2}.$$

For an *employed investor* the (approximate) portfolio share of the risky asset, $\alpha^e$, is

$$\alpha_t^e = \frac{1}{\bar{b}_1}\left(\frac{E_t r_{t+1} - r^f + \frac{\sigma_u^2}{2}}{\gamma \sigma_u^2}\right) - \left(\frac{\pi^e(1-b_1^e)}{\bar{b}_1}\right)\left(\frac{\sigma_{u\xi}}{\sigma_u^2}\right), \tag{7}$$

where $0 < b_1^e < 1$ is the elasticity of consumption to financial wealth for an employed investor, and $\bar{b}_1 = \pi^e b_1^e + (1-\pi^e)$ is the average consumption elasticity over the two states (the elasticity in the retirement case being one). Given $b_1^e < 1$, negative shocks to financial wealth do not cause a proportional reduction in consumption because the employed investor can use labor income to shield consumption from unexpected declines in financial wealth.

The general form of the rule is the same as in the single-period case, with two components, the latter depending on the correlation between labor income and return shocks, thus having the nature of a hedging demand. In fact, when labor income is idiosyncratic ($\sigma_{u\xi} = 0$), only the first component is present, with the average wealth elasticity of consumption to wealth $\bar{b}_1 < 1$. Therefore, the optimal allocation to the risky asset is larger for employed investors than for retired investors. The second term represents the income hedging component of optimal allocation, with a sign opposite to the sign of $\sigma_{u\xi}$ (negative correlation implying that the risky asset is a good hedge against bad labor income realizations).

## A Basic Life-Cycle Model

A fundamental insight from the methodological innovations surveyed in the preceding section (introducing uninsurable labor income risk and extending the analysis to a multiperiod or an infinite investment horizon) is that the optimal asset allocation depends crucially on the ratio of discounted expected future labor income (that is, human capital) to accumulated financial wealth. This ratio typically changes over the investor's life cycle in a way that simple assumptions of a stochastic process generating labor income are not able to capture. Instead, a model with a more realistic age profile of labor income (making human wealth increase relative to financial wealth in the early part of the working life and then decline in the years before retirement) is needed to address the issue of how investors should optimally adjust their financial portfolio over their life cycle.

Adopting an explicit life-cycle perspective, this section presents a model, built mainly on Campbell and others (2001); Cocco, Gomes, and Maenhout (2005); and Gomes and Michaelides (2004, 2005), that can be used to generate optimal portfolio choice over the life cycle.

This discussion does not allow for excess return predictability and other forms of changing investment opportunities over time, as in Michaelides (2002) and Koijen, Nijman, and Werker (2009). Although both papers document market-timing effects on asset allocations when parameters of the return distributions are known with certainty, considerable debate still exists as to the ex post value of market timing (De Miguel et al. 2008) and return predictability in general (Fugazza, Guidolin, and Nicodano 2008; Goyal and Welch 2008) when such parameters are estimated by an asset manager.

### The Model

This discussion creates a model for an investor that maximizes the expected discounted utility of consumption over his or her entire life. Although the maximum length of the life span is $T$ periods, its effective length is governed by age-dependent life expectancy. At each date $t$, the survival probability of being alive at date $t + 1$ is $p_t$, the conditional survival probability at $t$. The investor starts working at age $t_0$ and retires with certainty at age $t_0 + K$. The investor's $i$ preferences at date $t$ are described by a time-separable power utility function:

$$\frac{C_{it_0}^{1-\gamma}}{1-\gamma} + E_{t_0}\left[\sum_{j=1}^{T}\beta^j\left(\prod_{k=0}^{j-1}p_{t_0+k}\right)\frac{C_{it_0+j}^{1-\gamma}}{1-\gamma}\right],$$

where $C_{it}$ is the level of consumption at time $t$, $\beta < 1$ is an utility discount factor, and $\gamma$ is the constant relative risk aversion parameter.[5] Utility derived from leaving a bequest, introduced by Cocco, Gomes, and Maenhout (2005), is ruled out. Moreover, the discussion does not model labor supply decisions, whereby ignoring the insurance property of flexible work effort (allowing investors to compensate for bad financial returns with higher labor income), as in Gomes, Kotlikoff, and Viceira (2008).

*Labor and retirement income.* Available resources to finance consumption over the life cycle are derived from accumulated financial wealth and from the stream of labor income. At each date $t$ during the working life, the exogenous labor income $Y_{it}$ is assumed to be governed by a deterministic age-dependent growth process $f(t, Z_{it})$ and is subject to both a permanent $u_{it}$ and a transitory $n_{it}$ shock, the latter being uncorrelated across investors. Formally, the logarithm of $Y_{it}$ is represented by

$$\log Y_{it} = f(t, Z_{it}) + u_{it} + n_{it}, \quad t_0 \leq t \leq t_0 + K. \tag{8}$$

More specifically, $f(t, Z_{it})$ denotes the deterministic trend component of permanent income, which depends on age $t$ and on a vector of individual characteristics $Z_{it}$, such as gender, marital status, household composition, and education. Uncertainty of labor income is captured by the two stochastic processes, $u_{it}$ and $n_{it}$, driving the permanent and the transitory components, respectively. Consistent with the available empirical evidence, the permanent disturbance is assumed to follow a random walk process:

$$u_{it} = u_{it-1} + \varepsilon_{it}, \tag{9}$$

where $\varepsilon_{it}$ is distributed as $N(0, \sigma_\varepsilon^2)$ and is uncorrelated with the idiosyncratic temporary shock $n_{it}$, distributed as $N(0, \sigma_n^2)$. Finally, the permanent disturbance $\varepsilon_{it}$ is made up of an aggregate component, common to all investors, $\xi_t \sim N(0, \sigma_\xi^2)$, and an idiosyncratic component, $\omega_{it} \sim N(0, \sigma_\omega^2)$, uncorrelated across investors:

$$\varepsilon_{it} = \xi_t + \omega_{it}. \tag{10}$$

As specified below, correlation is allowed for between the aggregate permanent shock to labor income $\xi_t$ and variations in the risky asset returns.

During retirement, income is certain and equal to a fixed proportion $\lambda$ of the permanent component of the last working year income:

$$\log Y_{it} = \log \lambda + f(t_{0+K}, Z_{it_{0+K}}) + u_{it_{0+K}}, \quad t_0 + K < t \le T \tag{11}$$

where the level of the replacement rate $\lambda$ is meant to capture at least some of the features of common pubic social insurance systems. Other, less restrictive, modeling strategies are possible. For example, Campbell and others (2001) model a system of mandatory saving for retirement as a given fraction of the (stochastic) labor income that the investor must save for retirement and invest in the riskless asset, with no possibility of consuming it or borrowing against it. At retirement the value of the wealth so accumulated is transformed into a riskless annuity until death.

***Investment opportunities.*** Here savings are allowed to be invested in a short-term riskless asset, yielding each period a constant gross real return $R^f$, and in two risky assets, called *stocks* and *bonds*. The risky assets yield stochastic gross real returns $R_t^s$ and $R_t^b$, respectively. This discussion maintains that the investment opportunities in the risky assets do not vary over time and model excess returns of stocks and bonds over the riskless asset as

$$R_t^s - R^f = \mu^s + \varepsilon_t^s, \tag{12}$$

$$R_t^h - R^f = \mu^b + \varepsilon_t^b, \tag{13}$$

where $\mu^s$ and $\mu^b$ are the expected stock and bond premia, and $\varepsilon_t^s$ and $\varepsilon_t^b$ are normally distributed variations, with mean zero and variances $\sigma_s^2$ and $\sigma_b^2$, respectively. The two disturbances are allowed to be correlated, with correlation $\rho_{sb}$. Moreover, the innovation on the stock return is allowed to be correlated with the aggregate permanent disturbance to the labor income, denoting this correlation by $\rho_{sY}$.

At the beginning of each period, financial resources available for consumption and saving are given by the sum of accumulated financial wealth $W_{it}$ plus current labor income $Y_{it}$, which here is called *cash on hand* $X_{it} = W_{it} + Y_{it}$. Given the chosen level of current consumption $C_{it}$, next-period cash on hand is given by

$$X_{it+1} = (X_{it} - C_{it})R_{it}^P + Y_{it+1},\qquad (14)$$

where $R_{it}^P$ is the portfolio return

$$R_{it}^P = \alpha_{it}^s R_t^s + \alpha_{it}^b R_t^b + (1 - \alpha_{it}^s - \alpha_{it}^b)R^f,\qquad (15)$$

with $\alpha_{it}^s$, $\alpha_{it}^b$, and $(1 - \alpha_{it}^s - \alpha_{it}^b)$ denoting the shares of the investor's portfolio invested in stocks, bonds, and the riskless asset, respectively. Short sales are not allowed, and it is assumed that the investor is liquidity constrained, so that the nominal amount invested in each of the three financial assets is $F_{it} \geq 0$, $S_{it} \geq 0$, and $B_{it} \geq 0$, respectively, for the riskless asset, stocks, and bonds, and the portfolio shares are non-negative in each period.

Optimal asset allocation and savings for the purpose of providing retirement income also depend on investment opportunities during retirement. The simulations presented below concern the case when the pension fund continues to optimally invest the retiree's savings into the same three assets. However, the results concerning asset allocation appear to be qualitatively similar in unreported simulations based on the assumption that retirees invest in the riskless asset only.

***Solving the life-cycle problem.*** In this standard intertemporal optimization framework, the investor maximizes the expected discounted utility over the lifetime, by choosing the consumption and the portfolio rules derived from the assumptions about labor income and asset returns. Formally, the optimization problem is written as

$$\max_{\{C_{it}\}_{t_0}^{T-1},\{\alpha_{it}^s,\alpha_{it}^b\}_{t_0}^{T-1}} \left( \frac{C_{it_0}^{1-\gamma}}{1-\gamma} + E_{t_0}\left[ \sum_{j=1}^{T}\beta^j\left(\prod_{k=0}^{j-1}p_{t_0+k}\right)\frac{C_{it_0+j}^{1-\gamma}}{1-\gamma} \right] \right)$$

$$s.t.\quad X_{it+1} = (X_{it} - C_{it})\left(\alpha_{it}^s R_t^s + \alpha_{it}^b R_t^b + (1 - \alpha_{it}^s - \alpha_{it}^b)R^f\right) + Y_{it+1},\qquad (16)$$

with the labor income and retirement processes specified above and the presence of short sales and borrowing constraints.

Given the intertemporal nature of the problem, it can be restated in a recursive form, rewriting the value of the optimization problem at the beginning of period as a function of the maximized current utility and of the value of the problem at $t + 1$ (Bellman equation):

$$V_{it}(X_{it}, u_{it}) = \max_{\{C_{it}\}_{t_0}^{T-1}, \{\alpha_{it}^s, \alpha_{it}^b\}_{t_0}^{T-1}} \left( \frac{C_{it}^{1-\gamma}}{1-\gamma} + \beta p_t E_t \left[ V_{it+1}(X_{it_{+1}}, u_{it+1}) \right] \right). \qquad (17)$$

At each time $t$ the value function $V_{it}$ describes the maximized value of the problem as a function of the two state variables, the level of cash on hand at the beginning of time $t$, $X_{it}$, and $u_{it}$, the level of the stochastic permanent component of income at beginning of $t$.

To reduce the dimensionality of the original problem to one with a state variable, the homogeneity of degree $(1 - \gamma)$ of the utility function is exploited, and the entire problem is normalized by the permanent component of income $u_{it}$. Thus, rewrite equation (17) can be rewritten as as

$$V_{it}(X_{it}) = \max_{\{C_{it}\}_{t_0}^{T-1}, \{\alpha_{it}^s, \alpha_{it}^b\}_{t_0}^{T-1}} \left( \frac{C_{it}^{1-\gamma}}{1-\gamma} + \beta p_t E_t \left[ V_{it+1}(X_{it+1}) \right] \right). \qquad (18)$$

The problem has no closed-form solution, hence the optimal values for consumption and portfolio allocation at each point in time have to be derived numerically. To accomplish this, a backward induction procedure is applied to obtain optimal consumption and portfolio rules in terms of the state variable starting from the last (possible) period of life $T$.

In particular, the solution for period $T$ is trivial, considering that, because there is no allowance for positive bequest, it is optimal to consume all the available resources (that is, $C_{iT} = X_{iT}$), implying that

$$V_{iT}(X_T) = \frac{X_{iT}^{1-\gamma}}{1-\gamma}. \qquad (19)$$

The value function at coincides with the direct utility function over the cash on hand available at the beginning of the period. Proceeding backward, for every period, $t = T - 1, T - 2, \ldots, t_0$, and for each possible value of the state variable (the initial level of cash on hand at $t$) the optimal rules for consumption and the assets' portfolio shares are obtained from the Bellman equation (17) using the grid search method.[6] From the Bellman equation, for each level of the state variable $X_{it}$, the value function at the beginning of time $t$, $V_{it}(X_{it})$, is obtained by picking the level of consumption and of portfolio shares that maximizes the sum of the utility from current consumption $U(C_{it})$ plus the discounted expected value from continuation, $\beta p_t E_t V_{it+1}(X_{it+1})$. The latter value is computed using $V_{it+1}(X_{it+1})$, obtained from the previous iteration. In particular, given $V_{it+1}(X_{it+1})$, the expectation term is evaluated in two steps. Numerical integration is used, performed by means of the standard Gaussian-Hermite quadrature method to approximate the distribution of shocks to labor income and asset returns. Then cubic spline interpolation is employed to evaluate the value function at points that do not lie on the state space grid.

## Simulation Results

The numerical solution method briefly outlined above yields, for each set of parameters chosen, the optimal policy functions for the level of consumption and the shares of the financial portfolio invested in the riskless asset, stocks, and bonds as functions of the level of cash on hand. Using those optimal rules, it is then possible to simulate the life-cycle consumption and asset allocation choices of a large number of individuals with differing characteristics. This section describes results obtained from this procedure, focusing first on a benchmark case and then presenting extensions along various dimensions.

*Calibration.* Parameter calibration concerns the investor's preferences, the features of the labor income process during working life and retirement, and the moments of the risky asset returns. To obtain results for a benchmark case, plausible sets of parameters have been chosen, mainly derived from the United States and based on Cocco, Gomes, and Maenhout (2005) and Gomes and Michaelides (2004, 2005).

The investor begins his or her working life at the age of 20 and works for (a maximum of) 45 periods ($K$) before retiring at the age of 65. After retirement, he or she can live for a maximum of 35 periods until the age of 100. In each period the conditional probability of being alive in the next period $p_t$ is taken from the life expectancy tables of the U.S. National Center for Health Statistics. In regard to preferences, the utility discount factor is set at $\beta = 0.96$, and the coefficient of relative risk aversion $\gamma = 5$ (capturing an intermediate degree of risk aversion).

The labor income process is calibrated using the estimated parameters for U.S. households with a high school education (but not a college degree) in Cocco, Gomes, and Maenhout (2005). The age-dependent trend is captured by a third-order polynomial in age, delivering the typical hump-shaped profile until retirement, depicted as the dash-dotted line in figure 6.1. After retirement, income is a constant proportion $\lambda$ of the final (permanent) labor income, with $\lambda = 0.68$. The solid line in the figure portrays the whole deterministic trend $f(t, Z_{it})$, used in the simulations below, which also allows for other personal characteristics. In the benchmark case, the variances of the permanent and transitory shocks ($\varepsilon_{it}$ and $n_{it}$, respectively) are $\sigma_\varepsilon^2 = 0.0106$ and $\sigma_n^2 = 0.0738$; in some of the extensions below those parameters are allowed to vary (to explore the effects of increasing labor income uncertainty), but the permanent-transitory ratio is kept roughly constant at the 0.14 level. The riskless (constant) interest rate is set at 0.02, with expected stock and bond premia $\mu^s$ and $\mu^b$ fixed at 0.04 and 0.02, respectively. The standard deviations of the returns innovations are set at $\sigma_s = 0.157$ and $\sigma_b = 0.08$; in the benchmark case, their correlation is fixed at a positive but relatively small value: $\rho_{sb} = 0.2$, a value calibrated on the historical annual correlation in the United States and close to the choice of Gomes and Michaelides (2004). Finally, $\rho_{sY} = 0$ is set in the benchmark case, imposing a zero correlation between stock return innovations and aggregate permanent labor income disturbances.

**Figure 6.1    Labor Income Process**

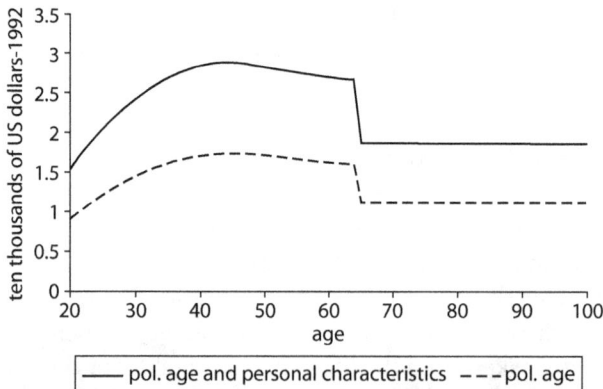

Source: Authors' elaborations on calibrations by Cocco et al. 2005.
Note: Fitted polynomial in age and personal characteristics derived according to calibrations by Cocco et al. (2005) for households with high school education.

**Benchmark results.** In the simulations, cross-sectional averages were taken of 10,000 individuals over their life cycle. Figure 6.2 displays the simulation results for the patterns of consumption, labor income, and accumulated financial wealth for the working life and the retirement period in the benchmark case. The typical life-cycle profile for consumption is generated. Binding liquidity constraints cause consumption to closely track labor income until the 35–40 age range, when the consumption path becomes less steep and financial wealth is accumulated at a faster rate. After retirement at 65, wealth is gradually decumulated, and consumption decreases to converge to retirement income in the last possible period of life.

Before this discussion presents the age profile of optimal portfolio shares, figures 6.3 and 6.4 display the optimal policy rules for the risky asset shares $\alpha_{it}^s$ and $\alpha_{it}^b$ as functions of the level of (normalized) cash on hand (the problem's state variable). In each figure the optimal fraction of the portfolio invested in stocks and bonds is plotted against cash on hand for investors of four different ages (20, 30, 55, and 75). The basic intuition that should guide the interpretation of these optimal policies, on which the following simulation results are based, is that labor income is

**Figure 6.2    Life-Cycle Profiles of Consumption, Income, and Wealth**

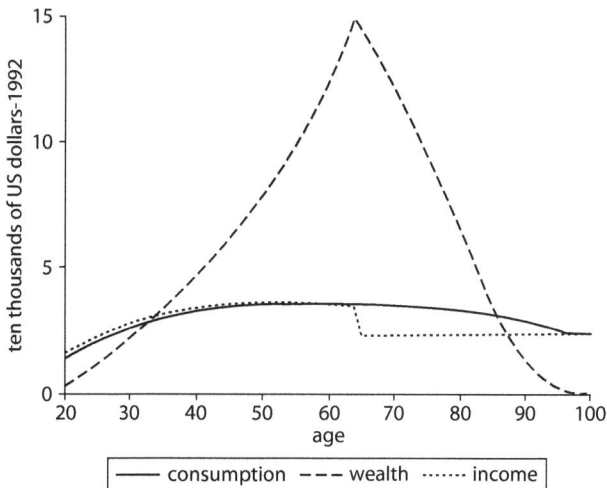

*Source:* Authors' simulations.
*Note:* Age profiles for consumption, income, and wealth averaged over all simulations. Parameters are set as in the benchmark case: risk aversion 5, replacement ratio 0.68, correlation between stock and bond returns 0.2, zero correlation between stock returns and labor income.

**Figure 6.3    Policy Functions: Sensitivity to Stocks**

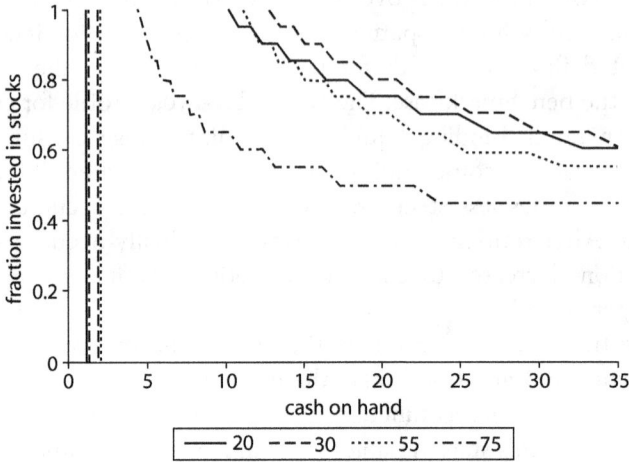

*Source:* Authors' simulations.
*Note:* Policy functions for the portfolio shares invested in stocks at different ages. Parameters are set as in the benchmark case: risk aversion 5, replacement ratio 0.68, correlation between stocks and bonds 0.2, zero correlation between stock returns and labor income.

**Figure 6.4    Policy Functions: Sensitivity to Bonds**

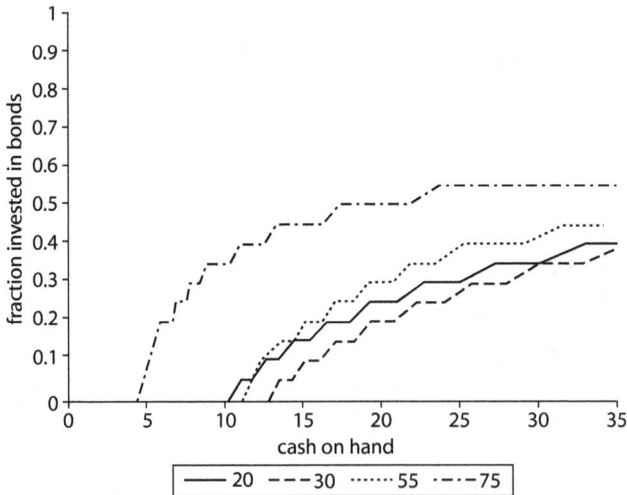

*Source:* Authors' simulations.
*Note:* Policy functions for the portfolio shares invested in bonds at different ages.

viewed by the investor as an implicit holding of an asset. Although in the present setting labor income is uncertain (it is subject to both permanent and transitory shocks), as long as the correlation of asset return variations and labor income disturbances is not too large, labor income is more similar to the risk-free than to the risky assets.[7] Therefore, when the present discounted value of the expected future labor income stream (that is, human capital) constitutes a sizeable portion of overall wealth, the investor is induced to tilt his or her portfolio toward the risky assets. The proportion of human capital in relation to total wealth is widely different across investors of different ages and is consequently one of the main determinants of the portfolio composition derived from the model.

As can be seen in figures 6.3 and 6.4, in the case of an investor age 75, the certain retirement income derived from the universal pension system based on final years earnings acts like a riskless asset. This causes the relatively poor investors (with a small amount of accumulated wealth and current income) to hold a financial portfolio entirely invested in stocks.[8] Wealthier investors, on the other hand, will hold a lower portfolio share in stocks (and increase their holdings of bonds) because for them the proportion of the overall wealth implicitly invested in the riskless asset is lower. At age 55 the investor has a decade remaining of relatively high expected labor income before retirement, and he or she will tend to balance this implicit holding of a low-risk asset with a financial portfolio more heavily invested in risky stocks than older investors. The optimal asset allocation shown in figures 6.3 and 6.4 is shifted outward in relation to the 75-year-old investor for all levels of cash on hand.[9] The same intuition applies to earlier ages, for which the optimal stock and bond policies shift gradually outward as younger investors are considered. The only exception to this pattern occurs for the very young investors (approximately in the 20–25 age range), for whom the labor income profile is increasing very steeply, making it optimal to hold portfolios more invested in stocks (in the figures, the policy functions shift outward in the 20–25 age range).

On the basis of the optimal investment policies, the mean portfolio shares of stocks and bonds for the simulations of the 10,000 individuals are plotted in figure 6.5(a) in relation to their age. The age-related profiles for stocks and bonds are mainly determined by the fact that over the life cycle the proportion of overall wealth implicitly invested in the riskless asset through expected labor incomes varies. It is large for young investors and declines as retirement approaches. In fact, younger individuals are

**Figure 6.5    Age Profiles of Optimal Stock and Bond Holdings (Averages)**

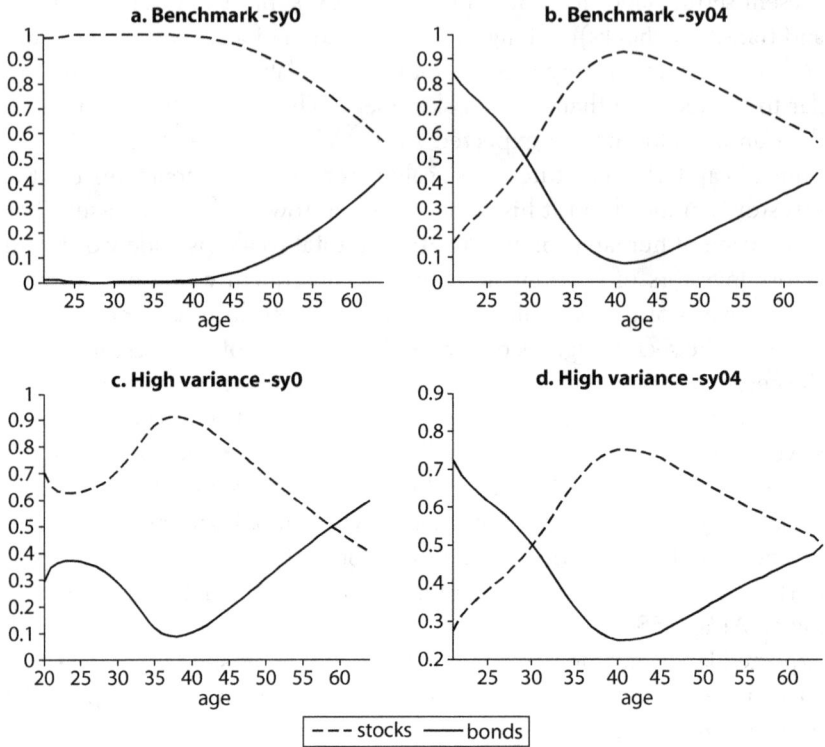

*Source:* Authors' simulations.
*Note:* Mean share profiles, as a function of age, for stocks (dashed-dotted) and bonds (solid). The replacement ratio is equal to 0.68, the correlation between stock and bond returns is set to 0.2, and the one between stocks and labor income (sy) is 0 in the upper and 0.4 in the lower panel. The variance of permanent and transitory shocks is 0.0106 and 0.0738 (benchmark) and 0.0408 and 0.269, respectively (high variance).

expected to invest their entire portfolio in stocks until approximately age 40. Middle-age investors (between 40 and the retirement age of 65) gradually shift the composition of their portfolio away from stocks and into bonds, to reach shares of 60 percent and 40 percent, respectively, at the retirement date. Throughout, the holdings of the riskless asset are kept at a minimum, which is very often zero. Only very young investors keep a small fraction of their portfolio in the riskless asset.

Overall, the rule of thumb that recommends holding a retirement savings portfolio's share of risky stocks that is equal to minus the investor's age (so that $\alpha_{age}^s = (100 - age)/100$), implying a gradual shift toward bonds as the individual ages, is similar to the optimal investment policies derived from the simulations. However, in the benchmark case described above, the decumulation of stocks is not the linear pattern suggested by the simple age-dependent rule under which the stock share is being reduced from 80 percent at the age of 20 to reach 35 percent at retirement. A more rigorous comparison of the optimal investment policy with the simple age rule is provided below.

*Sensitivity of asset allocation to labor income risk.* To evaluate the robustness of the results and to explore the sensitivity of optimal asset allocation to changes in the main parameters of the model, the benchmark case can be modified along a number of dimensions. These include varying the degree of risk aversion, different assumptions about the relationship between age and labor earnings, and different assumptions about the moments of the asset return distributions. This section focuses on two important dimensions and their interactions to capture changes in labor income uncertainty: the correlation between stock return variations and the aggregate permanent shock to labor income ($\rho_{sY}$), which is set to zero in the benchmark case, and then the variances of the permanent and transitory disturbances driving the stochastic part of labor income ($\sigma_\varepsilon^2 = 0.0106$ and $\sigma_n^2 = 0.0738$ in the benchmark case). Figure 6.5 displays the mean shares of the portfolios for stocks and bonds in relation to age over the accumulation period beginning from age of 20 to the retirement age of 65.

First, the stock return variability is allowed to be positively correlated with the variations in labor income. Empirical estimates of this correlation from the United States include values not significantly different from zero in Cocco, Gomes, and Michaelides (2005) for households with any level of educational attainment to the relatively high values reported by Campbell and others (2001) and Campbell and Viceira (2002), ranging from 0.33 for households with no high school education to 0.52 for college graduates. Because the present calibration of labor income reflects the features of households with a high school education, an intermediate value of $\rho_{sY} = 0.4$ is chosen, close to the value of 0.37 used by Campbell and Viceira (2002). Figure 6.5(b) displays the optimal portfolio shares of stocks and bonds when $\rho_{sY} = 0.4$.

The general pattern of asset allocation obtained in the benchmark case (figure 5[a]) is confirmed for middle-aged workers, whereas for younger workers (in the 20–40 age range) optimal portfolio shares differ sharply. The positive correlation between labor income shocks and stock returns makes labor income closer to an implicit holding of stocks rather than holding of a riskless asset. Younger investors, for whom human capital is a substantial fraction of overall wealth, are therefore heavily exposed to stock market risk and will find it optimal to offset such risk by holding a relatively lower fraction of their financial portfolio in stocks. This effect decreases as workers get older, resulting in a gradual increase in the portfolio share of stocks until about the age of 40. Finally, as the retirement age approaches, the size of human capital decreases and the investor shifts his or her portfolio composition again toward safer bonds; this yields a hump-shaped profile for the optimal share of stocks during working life.

The effects of increasing labor income risk on optimal asset allocation over the working life are portrayed in figures 6.5(c) and 6.5(d). Both sets of simulations increase the variance of both the permanent and the transitory stochastic components of labor income, setting these to $\sigma_\varepsilon^2 = 0.0408$ and $\sigma_n^2 = 0.269$, and keeping their ratio approximately equal to that used in the benchmark case. Panel c plots the results for $\rho_{sY} = 0$ as in the benchmark case, whereas panel d shows optimal portfolio shares when $\rho_{sY} = 0.4$. When there is no correlation between labor income and stock returns, the effect of increasing labor income risk is stronger, with higher labor income risk reducing the optimal share of stocks in the portfolio at any age. As panel c shows, the (average) investor holds a diversified portfolio of risky assets even at a very young age and starts decumulating stocks and increasing the bond share from the age of about 40. At retirement, the share of stocks is much lower than in the benchmark case, reaching about 0.4, with a correspondingly higher fraction invested in bonds.

A similar effect is detected also in the case of positive correlation between stock returns and labor income shocks ($\rho_{sY} = 0.4$). Comparing the portfolio shares in panel d (with high labor income risk) with those in panel b (with low income risk), the investor is expected to choose a lower proportion of stocks at any age. At retirement the share of stocks is significantly lower than in the case of reduced labor income risk.

*Optimal portfolio shares heterogeneity.* So far simulation results have been presented in terms of the average optimal portfolio shares across the investor population. However, in the present framework the presence of idiosyncratic labor income shocks may generate substantial heterogeneity in the pattern of financial wealth accumulation over time. This potentially can lead to a wide dispersion of the optimal portfolio shares across individuals of the same age who have widely different levels of accumulated wealth. The degree of heterogeneity in the optimal asset allocation may be an important element in evaluating the performance of pension funds managing individual accounts, whereby each member's asset allocation is adjusted over time on the basis of age and of the history of individual labor income. For this reason, in exploring the sensitivity of the benchmark results to variations in risk aversion $(\gamma)$, the replacement ratio $(\lambda)$,[10] and the correlation between labor income shocks and stock return variations $(\rho_{sY})$, this discussion focuses on the main features of the whole distribution of optimal portfolio shares across the investors' population. Figures 6.6–6.10 display for each age the median and the 5th and 95th percentiles of the distribution of optimal stock and bond portfolio shares.

In figure 6.6 panels a and b present the distribution of portfolio shares for the benchmark values of risk aversion $(\gamma = 5)$, the replacement ratio $(\lambda = 0.68)$, and the two values of the labor income–stock return correlation $(\rho_{sY} = 0$ and $0.4)$ already used in figures 6.5(a)–(b). Panel c highlights the role of the correlation between labor income shocks and stock returns by assuming that $\rho_{sY} = 1$. Note that even this extreme value for $\rho_{sY}$ does not imply a (counterfactually) high correlation between the stock return innovation and the growth rate of individual labor income because the latter includes a sizeable idiosyncratic component that is uncorrelated with stock returns.[11]

**Figure 6.6    Age Profiles of Optimal Stock and Bond Holdings, Benchmark Case**
*(percentiles)*

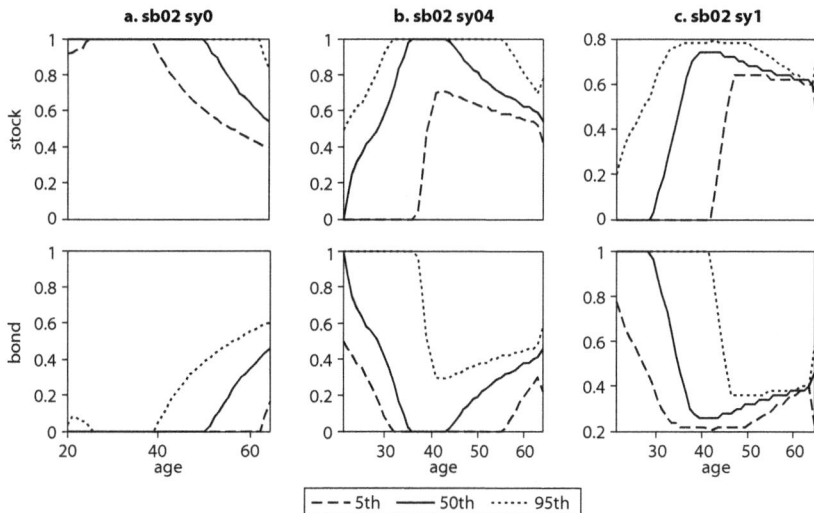

Source: Authors' simulations.
Note: Share profiles, as a function of age, for stocks and bonds. The solid line represents the shape of the median portfolio share, and the (dotted) dashed lines refer to the (5th) 95th percentiles. The replacement ratio is equal to 0.68, the correlation between stock and bond returns (sb) is set to 0.2, and the correlation between stocks and labor income (sy) varies between 0 and 1.

**Figure 6.7    Age Profiles of Optimal Stock and Bond Holdings, High Risk Aversion**
*(percentiles)*

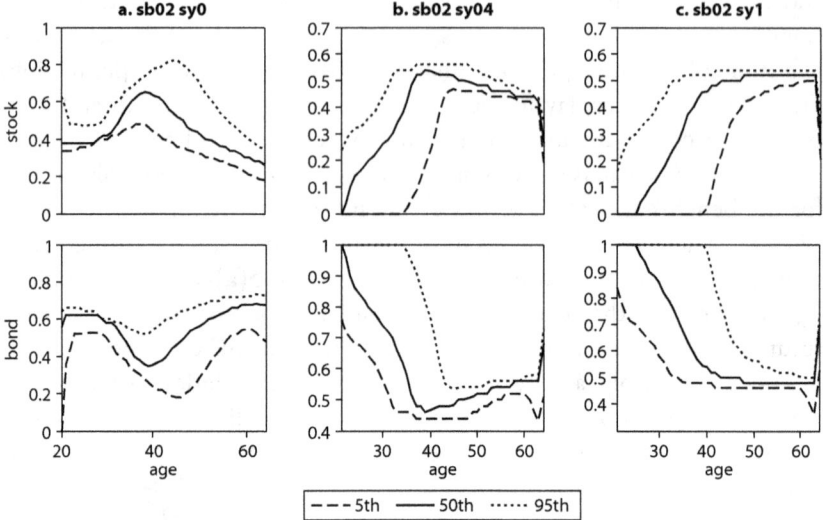

*Note:* Share profiles, as a function of age, for stocks and bonds. The solid line represents the shape of the median portfolio share, and the (dotted) dashed lines refer to the (5th) 95th percentiles. The replacement ratio is equal to 0.68, the correlation between stock and bond returns (sb) is set to 0.2, and the correlation between stocks and labor income (sy) varies between 0 and 1.

The results confirm that as $\rho_{sY}$ increases, young workers would optimally invest less in stocks, gradually raising the share of the riskier asset until the age of 40 (Benzoni, Collin-Dufresne, and Goldstein 2007). In the case of $\rho_{sY} = 1$ the highest stock share in the financial portfolio never exceeds 80 percent. In all panels the distribution of portfolio shares is highly heterogeneous because of the presence of idiosyncratic labor income shocks (with the exception of young workers in the case of $\rho_{sY} = 0$, who invest the entire portfolio in stocks to compensate for the relatively riskless nature of their human capital). However, interesting patterns can be detected. The dispersion among workers decreases as they approach retirement, and this decrease is greater the higher the labor income–stock return correlation. As $\rho_{sY}$ increases, the histories of labor incomes and the optimal associated portfolio choices tend to converge over time.

The effects of high risk aversion ($\gamma = 15$) are explored in figure 6.7. As expected, the share of stocks is significantly reduced at all ages and for all values of the labor income–stock return correlation. The hump-shaped

**Figure 6.8    Age Profiles of Optimal Stock and Bond Holdings, Low Replacement Ratio**
*(percentiles)*

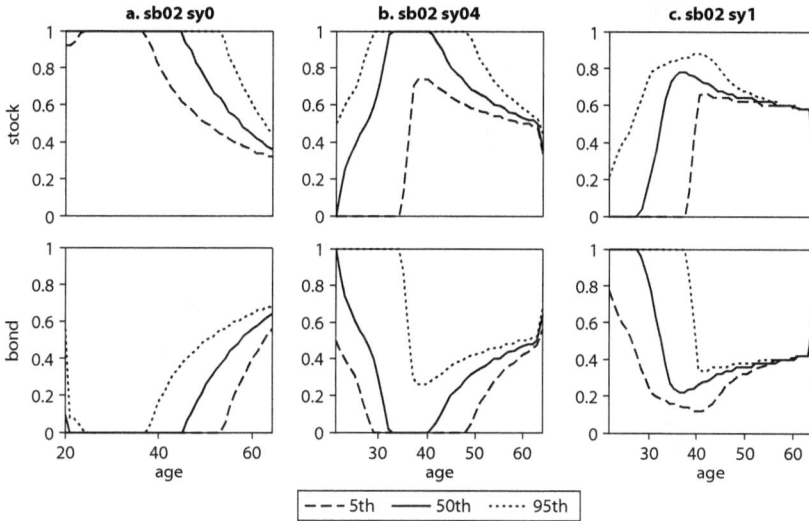

*Source:* Authors' simulations.
*Note:* Share profiles, as a function of age, for stocks and bonds. The solid line represents the shape of the median portfolio share, and the (dotted) dashed lines refer to the (5th) 95th percentiles. The replacement ratio is equal to 0.40, the correlation between stock and bond returns (sb) is set to 0.2, and the correlation between stocks and labor income (sy) varies between 0 and 1.

pattern of the optimal stock share during working life now also appears in the case of $\rho_{sY} = 0$. To assess the effects on optimal asset allocation of the generosity of the first-pillar pension system (whose features are summarized by the level of the replacement ratio $\lambda$, set at 0.68 in the benchmark case), figures 6.8 and 6.9 display portfolio shares for two different values of the replacement ratio, 0.40 and 0.80, respectively, that are estimated using the benchmark risk aversion of $\gamma = 5$. When the replacement ratio is 0.40, anticipating relatively low pension incomes, individuals are expected to save more during their working life, accumulating a higher level of financial wealth. This leads to a lower optimal share of stocks at all ages and for all values of the labor income–stock return correlation. Finally, figure 6.10 displays asset allocation choices in the case of only partial price indexation of pension income. In the present framework all income flows are expressed in real terms, which amounts to an implicit assumption of full indexation of pension income. Partial indexation is simply modeled as a 2 percent decrease in the replacement ratio $\lambda$ from the benchmark value of 0.68 at age 65, to reach 0.34 at year 100.

**Figure 6.9    Age Profiles of Optimal Stock and Bond Holdings, High Replacement Rate** *(percentiles)*

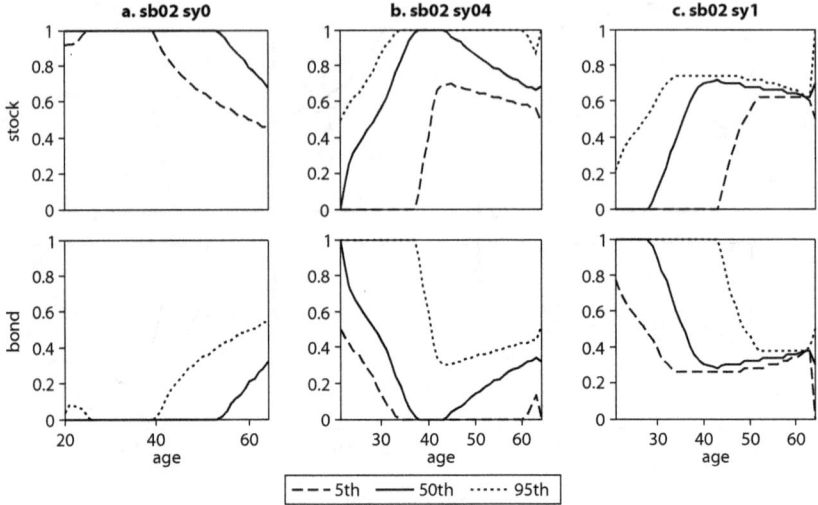

*Source:* Authors' simulations.
*Note:* Share profiles, as a function of age, for stocks and bonds. The solid line represents the shape of the median portfolio share, and the (dotted) dashed lines refer to the (5th) 95th percentiles. The replacement ratio is equal to 0.80, the correlation between stock and bond returns (sb) is set to 0.2, and the correlation between stocks and labor income (sy) varies between 0 and 1.

From figures 6.6–6.7 and 6.8–6.9 a general pattern emerges as to the dispersion in the portfolio shares, which decreases as the retirement age approaches, and the more so the higher the risk aversion parameter and the lower the replacement ratio. Indeed, the higher the risk aversion and the lower the replacement ratio, the higher the saving and the larger the accumulation of financial wealth over the working life. This, according to the policy functions shown in figure 6.3, implies a reduced sensitivity of portfolio composition to the level of human capital. This insensitivity is stronger the closer the worker is to the retirement age, when financial wealth reaches the maximum level.

## *Welfare Costs of Suboptimal Asset Allocations*
Tailoring asset allocations to the specificities of workers' income patterns may involve considerable management fees that are not included in the present model. This inevitably raises the question of whether the gains associated with these additional costs are warranted. To practically assess the welfare gains from optimal asset allocation relative to simpler alternative

**Figure 6.10    Age Profiles of Optimal Stock and Bond Holdings, Decreasing Replacement Ratio**
*(percentiles)*

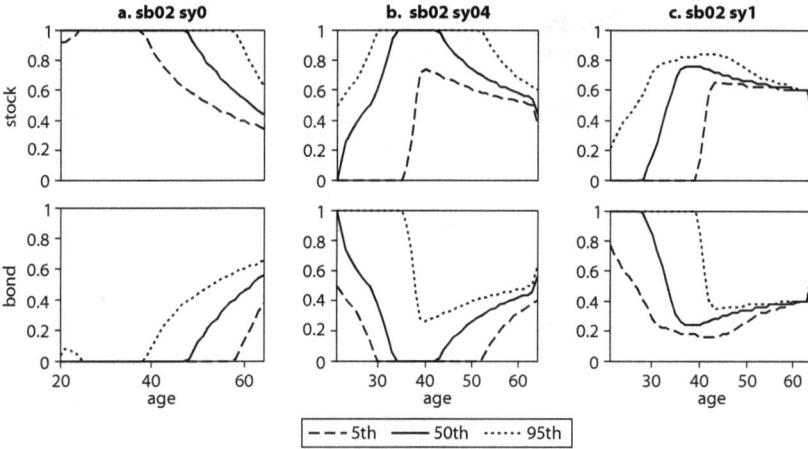

Source: Authors' simulations.
Note: Share profiles, as a function of age, for stocks and bonds. The solid line represents the shape of the median portfolio share, and the (dotted) dashed lines refer to the (5th) 95th percentiles. Pension treatments at the beginning of retirement correspond to a replacement ratio of 0.68 and then decrease by 0.02 per year due to inflation (which implies an average replacement ratio of about 0.45 over all retirement ages). The correlation between stock and bond returns (sb) is set to 0.2, and the correlation between stocks and labor income (sy) varies between 0 and 1.

investment strategies, table 6.1 shows the welfare gains of the optimal strategy computed as the yearly percentage increase in consumption that would be provided by the optimal asset allocation relative to two alternative strategies that would be simpler and less expensive to implement.

The first alternative strategy is a common age-related rule-of-thumb approach in which the portfolio share of the risky assets is set at (100 – age) percent and equally allocated between stocks and bonds. This mirrors the relationship between the average proportion invested in stocks and the fund's horizon for many so-called "target date funds," which is approximately linear with a slope of –1.[12] The second alternative strategy fixes portfolio shares at one-third for each financial asset in the present model. This mirrors the 1/N rule of DeMiguel, Garlappi, and Uppal (2008), which systematically outperforms several optimal asset allocation strategies in ex post portfolio experiments.

Table 6.1 shows the welfare cost of each suboptimal strategy for the two values of risk aversion ($\gamma= 5$ and $15$) and the three values of $\rho_{sY}$ considered in the simulations above. For each parameter combination, the

**Table 6.1    Welfare Gains**

| | Risk aversion 5 | | Risk aversion 15 | |
|---|---|---|---|---|
| | $\rho_{sy} = 0$ | | | |
| | (100–age)/2 | 1/3 | (100–age)/2 | 1/3 |
| Mean | 0.021 | 0.018 | 0.015 | 0.013 |
| 5th percentile | 0.032 | 0.027 | 0.043 | 0.037 |
| 50th percentile | 0.024 | 0.021 | 0.012 | 0.011 |
| 95th percentile | 0.004 | 0.003 | 0.004 | 0.004 |
| | $\rho_{sy} = 0.4$ | | | |
| | (100–age)/2 | 1/3 | (100–age)/2 | 1/3 |
| Mean | 0.012 | 0.012 | 0.012 | 0.011 |
| 5th percentile | 0.027 | 0.022 | 0.036 | 0.034 |
| 50th percentile | 0.013 | 0.011 | 0.006 | 0.005 |
| 95th percentile | 0.001 | 0.001 | 0.002 | 0.001 |
| | $\rho_{sy} = 1$ | | | |
| | (100–age)/2 | 1/3 | (100–age)/2 | 1/3 |
| Mean | 0.012 | 0.011 | 0.011 | 0.010 |
| 5th percentile | 0.025 | 0.023 | 0.032 | 0.031 |
| 50th percentile | 0.012 | 0.011 | 0.005 | 0.005 |
| 95th percentile | 0.002 | 0.001 | 0.002 | 0.002 |

*Source:* Authors' simulations.
*Note:* Welfare gains of the optimal strategy are reported relative to two suboptimal strategies, for example, the age rule in the first column and the 1/N rule in the second column. Welfare gains are the yearly percentage increase in consumption granted by the optimal asset allocation. The correlation between labor income risk and stock returns (the risk aversion parameter) increases from the top (left) to the bottom (right) panel. Each panel reports mean welfare gains for the overall population, as well as gains corresponding to percentiles of financial wealth accumulated at age 65.

table reports the mean welfare cost for the overall population and the welfare costs corresponding to the 5th, 50th, and 95th percentiles of the distribution of accumulated financial wealth at age 65.

Several results stand out. First, the magnitude of the mean welfare costs is broadly in the range of 1–3 percent, consistent with that found by Cocco, Gomes, and Maenhout (2005). Second, welfare costs of the alternative suboptimal approaches fall as risk aversion increases because high risk aversion implies reduced exposure to the stock market—and risky assets in general. Looking at the cost distribution conditional on wealth, welfare costs increase as financial wealth falls because a high human-to-financial-wealth ratio implies a relatively high optimal exposure to the stock market. Third, higher welfare costs are associated with lower values of the labor income–stock return correlation because of the more important role of the stock market in hedging background risk.

Last but not least, the $1/N$ strategy performs consistently better than the "age rule," showing lower mean welfare costs for all parameter combinations. Tabulated results suggest that an unconditional $1/N$ asset allocation is likely to be cost efficient for a high-wealth worker in medium to high replacement ratio countries. It is noteworthy that the $1/N$ rule implies a reduction of 49 basis points every year in terms of equivalent consumption for a highly risk-averse worker with median wealth and intermediate labor income correlation with stock returns. According to Blake (2008), the annual fee for active portfolio management charged by pension funds ranges from 20 to 75 basis points per year depending on the assets under management. Thus, the reduction in welfare (as measured by equivalent consumption flow) due to these simple asset allocation methods is lower than the maximum management fee. Moreover, such a reduction refers to the benchmark of an optimal asset allocation chosen by an investor who knows precisely the distribution of both labor income and asset returns. This represents a very high standard for comparison because asset managers typically make mistakes when estimating the parameters of such distributions, a fact that explains why a $1/N$ allocation usually outperforms optimal strategies in ex post experiments.

## Welfare Ratios for Performance Evaluation

The methods used to evaluate DC pension funds are typically similar to those used to evaluate mutual fund performance. These studies often examine the performance of delegated fund managers, which justifies the practice of using these methods. These performance evaluations are based either on the return of the managed portfolio relative to that of an appropriate benchmark or directly in relation to the distribution of portfolio holdings (see Ferson and Khang 2002). The investor horizon is usually assumed to be short, and when it is relatively long, as in Blake, Lehmann, and Timmermann (1999), the question being asked concerns whether performance is due to strategic asset allocation, as opposed to short-term market timing and security selection. Rarely do these studies assess performance at the pension plan level. However, recently Bauer and Frehen (2008)[13] evaluated U.S. pension funds plans against their internal benchmark portfolios.[14]

In principle, return-based performance evaluation is appropriate if the worker's preferences are defined over consumption and there are nontraded assets, as in the present life-cycle model. The benchmark portfolio must, however, be the optimal portfolio for hedging fluctuations in the intertemporal marginal rates of substitution of any marginal investor. However, the benchmarks used typically reflect the state of empirical asset pricing and constraints on available data (Lehmann and Timmermann 2008). Thus, standard performance evaluation practice relies on the idea that a higher return-to-risk differential equates to better performance. This overlooks the important parameters discussed above, including the pension fund's ability to hedge labor income risk and the role of other pension income of plan participants.

Computing the optimal life-cycle asset allocation permits evaluation of a pension fund's performance with reference to a benchmark that explicitly accounts for the pension plan's role in smoothing consumption risk. An integrated approach to the application of this method could be to take the ratio of the worker's ex ante maximum welfare under optimal asset allocation, $V_0(R_{it}^{P*})$, by his or her welfare level under the actual pension fund asset allocation, $V_0(R_{it}^{PF})$:

$$WR1 \equiv \frac{V_0(R_{it}^{P*})}{V_0(R_{it}^{PF})},$$

where $R_{it}^{P*}$ and $R_{it}^{PF}$ are the optimal and actual portfolio return—net of management costs—for member at time $t$.[15] More precisely, $R_{it}^{PF}$ are simulated returns that are extracted from the estimated empirical distribution of pension fund returns. Similarly, $V_0(R_{it}^{PF})$ results from the simulation of optimal consumption and savings decisions for pension members, without optimizing for the asset allocation. In this formulation the higher the value of the welfare ratio $WR1$, the worse the pension fund performance. It is important to note that a lower ratio may be due not only to a higher return per unit of financial risk earned by the pension fund, but also to a better matching between the pension fund portfolio and its members' labor income and pension risks.

Table 6.2 displays welfare ratios $WR1$ computed for various combinations of risk aversion, the replacement ratio, and the correlation between shocks and labor income and stock returns. In the table it is assumed that the fund follows a suboptimal strategy (the age rule) that is insensitive to members' incomes and replacement ratios, yielding a Sharpe ratio equal to 0.34. The average Sharpe ratio of the optimal rule is consistently lower, from a minimum of 0.24 for $\lambda = 0.8$ and $\rho_{sY} = 0$ to a maximum of 0.31 for $\lambda = 0.4$ and $\rho_{sY} = 1$. Thus, performance evaluated according to a standard return-to-risk metric is worse for the optimal than for the age rule. The picture changes when we look at the proposed welfare metric, which

**Table 6.2    Welfare Ratios**

| | Risk aversion 5 | | |
|---|---|---|---|
| Replacement ratio | 0.68 | 0.4 | 0.8 |
| | | $\rho_{sy} = 0$ | |
| Sharpe ratio | | | |
| Optimal | 0.260 | 0.286 | 0.244 |
| Age rule | 0.337 | 0.337 | 0.337 |
| Welfare ratio | | | |
| Mean | 1.051 | 1.096 | 1.044 |
| 5th percentile | 1.101 | 1.096 | 1.048 |
| 50th percentile | 1.056 | 1.074 | 1.057 |
| 95th percentile | 1.014 | 1.011 | 1.007 |
| | | $\rho_{sy} = 0.4$ | |
| Sharpe ratio | | | |
| Optimal | 0.273 | 0.310 | 0.257 |
| Age rule | 0.337 | 0.337 | 0.337 |
| Welfare ratio | | | |
| Mean | 1.033 | 1.049 | 1.028 |
| 5th percentile | 1.049 | 1.076 | 1.028 |
| 50th percentile | 1.040 | 1.054 | 1.032 |
| 95th percentile | 1.009 | 1.012 | 1.007 |
| | | $\rho_{sy} = 1$ | |
| Sharpe ratio | | | |
| Optimal | 0.296 | 0.314 | 0.264 |
| Age rule | 0.337 | 0.337 | 0.337 |
| Welfare ratio | | | |
| Mean | 1.025 | 1.037 | 1.020 |
| 5th percentile | 1.042 | 1.029 | 1.032 |
| 50th percentile | 1.031 | 1.043 | 1.021 |
| 95th percentile | 1.002 | 1.009 | 1.002 |

*Source:* Authors' simulations.
*Note:* The upper part of each panel displays the Sharpe ratio of the portfolios under both the optimal asset allocation and the asset allocation followed by the worker's pension plan, for example, the age rule. The lower part of
each panel reports the worker's ex ante welfare under the optimal asset allocation divided by his or her ex ante
welfare level under the age rule. Both mean welfare ratio for the overall population as well as welfare ratios corresponding to percentiles of financial wealth accumulated at age 65 appear in each panel. Results are ordered
according to both labor income–stock return correlation (0, 0.4, and 1) and replacement ratio (0.4, 0.68, and 0.8);
other parameters are set as in the benchmark case.

always exceeds one; this indicates a higher welfare associated with the
optimal asset allocation. Also note that the value of pension funds in
smoothing consumption risk is higher the lower are both the member's
income and the country's replacement ratio. In fact, the higher values for
the welfare ratio (1.1) obtain for the fifth income percentile and $\lambda = 0.40$

or 0.68. Such figures are associated with $\rho_{sY} = 0$, that is, a case in which the low correlation between income and stock returns allow for a better hedging of labor income shocks.

Another property of this metric is that it allows for cross-country performance comparisons, even if countries differ in labor income profiles, replacement ratios, inflation protection for pension annuities, and life expectancy. These parameters enter both the numerator and the denominator of $WR1$. The cross-country distribution of this ratio is affected only by how well pension funds perform their consumption smoothing role in addressing the main criticisms of standard performance measures discussed in chapter 3.

It is well known that the investable asset menu in certain countries is restricted by regulation, as outlined in chapter 2. If this is the case, the numerator of the welfare ratio should be computed conditional on the country's investable asset menu so as to evaluate the pension fund manager's ability. If the regulator wants to assess the costs from restricting the asset menu for retirees, then an appropriate ratio could be calculated as

$$WR2 \equiv \frac{V_0(R_{it}^{P*})}{V_0(R_{it}^{P*restricted})}.$$

In this ratio the optimal asset allocation enters both the numerator and the denominator, but the asset menu in the numerator is an internationally available one.

The previous section argues that the strategy dominates the optimal asset allocation when the costs of tailoring the asset allocation to workers' profiles exceed their benefits, that is, when the differential in management fees is sufficiently high. In such a case, it could be appropriate to substitute the numerator with the ex ante welfare achieved when portfolio returns are associated with the strategy,[16] obtaining

$$WR3 \equiv \frac{V_0(R_t^P(1/N))}{V_0(R_{it}^{PF})}.$$

## Conclusions

Modern finance theory suggests that levels of financial wealth in relation to other sources of wealth (most prominently social insurance benefits and future labor income) and the features of the labor income stream over the investor's life cycle are crucial determinants of an optimal investment policy. Models that incorporate these characteristics and generate realistic patterns of life-cycle consumption and wealth accumulation can advance the design and evaluation of investment policies for DC pension funds. This is most readily accomplished through the estimation of optimal portfolios for retirement savings investors of varying characteristics that are derived from a model that considers the multiple time period relevant to pension savings, life-cycle patterns of consumption and savings, risks associated with future earnings, dynamic responses in labor supply to variations in earnings, characteristics of other retirement income sources, and correlations between these aspects of human capital and the return on the assets of the portfolio. In addition to informing the design of investment options, an optimal portfolio developed in this way can provide a benchmark for the performance measurement of pension funds, advancing the value of performance measurement beyond what is achieved through standard methods that consider only returns and variance over short time horizons.

To illustrate how these concepts can be implemented and to obtain a benchmark asset allocation, such a model is proposed and results are estimated for 10,000 individuals. In this simulation exercise, the available financial assets include a riskless short-term asset, a high-risk premium asset, and a low-risk premium asset, with potentially correlated returns. The calibrated version of the model uses U.S. stock index and bond index returns. However, any pair of assets (or baskets of assets, such as the Fama-French portfolios) can be accommodated, to the extent that their mean returns, variances, and covariances can be estimated precisely. Although the simulations are based on U.S. data, the model can be used for assessing pension fund performance in other countries conditional on the availability of labor income profiles suggested in chapter 5.

The benchmark results indicate significant variations in the optimal portfolios across the main categories of parameters, including age, income level, and generosity of an earnings-based pubic retirement system. Evaluation of potential individual-level variations in risk aversion and the correlation of earnings and asset returns indicate that these factors introduce meaningful differences in optimal portfolios as well. These results suggest that the capacity for pension funds to effectively deliver retirement income can be enhanced through the development of a range of benchmark portfolios beyond the more conventional mean-variance–based approaches common to the industry that incorporate standard life-cycle principles and are developed in consideration of a set of differences in these factors. A key practical question regarding implementation of such an approach to guide investment management is whether the additional value is commensurate with the costs. Preliminary evaluation of the gains in return from this type of optimization indicates that the gains in return from active management may be similar to the costs of implementation relative to simpler passive or naive strategies. It is, however, possible to evaluate the performance and the associated participants' welfare when the funds implement simpler rules that partially account for the heterogeneity of optimal portfolio shares, for example, by grouping members into age classes and applying the optimal "median" share to all members in a specified class. This suggests that optimal portfolios may be more useful as comparative benchmarks against which the outcomes of the actual portfolio composition are measured rather than as guidelines for investment management. In addition to providing a pension-specific performance measure, estimating optimal portfolios can support the selection from a relatively narrow group of portfolio options by individuals and the selection of default options in pension system design.

Adopting this approach will require the use of overall performance measurement metrics that consider measures of welfare gains. One approach that is proposed would be to compare the welfare outcomes of the optimal portfolio that considers consumption smoothing and income risk-hedging properties against the outcome of an actual portfolio. This, however, will require an evolution of thinking beyond conventional mean variance methods because it is found that the Sharpe ratios for a standard portfolio exceed those of a theoretically optimal portfolio, whereas the welfare-based metric ranks the benchmark higher because it optimally smoothes consumption risk. This simulation exemplifies how performance evaluation is affected by both institutional design and investor heterogeneity. For instance, the role of pension funds in optimally smoothing consumption risk tends to be higher for lower-income members and replacement ratios. This indicates that further work is required to incorporate specific utility functions and alternative characterization of preferences before such an approach could be fully implemented.

Returns on foreign assets should be expressed in foreign currency, with currency risk fully hedged, because explicit dynamics of the exchange rate does not exist in this simple version of the model. Furthermore, the model can be used in its current version in economies in which inflation is not highly volatile because the model assumes constant inflation.

## Notes

1. The investor may also have more elaborate preferences that, combined with investment opportunities, reduce to mean variance preferences.

2. Koijen, Nijman, and Werker (2006) argue that it is suboptimal relative to alternative annuity designs, despite its diffusion across pension systems.

3. When $\gamma = 1$, the investor has log utility and chooses the portfolio with the highest log return; when $\gamma > 1$, the investor prefers a safer portfolio by penalizing the return variance; when $\gamma < 1$, the investor prefers a riskier portfolio.

4. If rebalancing is not allowed (as under a buy-and-hold strategy), with i.i.d. returns over time, all mean returns and variances for individual assets are scaled up by the same factor $K$, and the one-period portfolio solution is still optimal for a $K$-period investor. This result holds exactly in continuous time and only approximately in discrete time. However, Barberis (2000) shows that if uncertainty on the mean and variance of asset returns is introduced, the portfolio share of the risky asset $\alpha_t$ decreases as the investment horizon lengthens.

5. As already mentioned, assuming power utility with relative risk aversion coefficient constrains the intertemporal elasticity of substitution to be equal to $1/\gamma$. Moreover, $\gamma$ also governs the degree of relative prudence of the consumer $RP$, related to the curvature of the marginal utility and measured by

$$RP = -\frac{CU'''(C)}{U''(C)} = 1 + \gamma.$$

Relative prudence is a key determinant of the consumer's optimal reaction to changes in the degree of income uncertainty.

6. According to this method, the problem is solved over a grid of values covering the space of the state variables and the controls to ensure that the solution found is a global optimum.

7. Recall that in the benchmark case there is a zero correlation between stock return and labor income innovations: $\rho_{sY} = 0$.

8. The portfolio shares of the risky assets are not defined for extremely low values of cash on hand because the investor (of any age) has no savings in this case.

9. The stepwise appearance of the policy rules is due to the choice of the grid in the numerical solution procedure. The use of a finer grid would deliver smoother policies, at the cost of additional computing time.

10. Changes in retirement age are not analyzed; see Bodie and others (2004), who investigate this in a general life-cycle setting with stochastic wage, labor supply flexibility, and habit formation.

11. In fact, using equations (8), (9), and (10) it is possible to express the correlation between the growth rate of individual labor income ($\Delta \log Y_{it}$) and the stock return innovation ($\varepsilon_t^s$) in terms of $\rho_{sY}$ and the variances of the aggregate and idiosyncratic labor income shocks as

$$corr(\Delta \log Y_{it}, \varepsilon_t^s) = \frac{1}{\sqrt{\dfrac{\sigma_\varepsilon^2}{\sigma_n^2} + \sigma_n^2}} \cdot \rho_{sY} \leq \rho_{sY}.$$

Using the present benchmark value for $\sigma_n^2 = 0.0738$, an upper bound is derived for $corr(\Delta \log Y_{it}, \varepsilon_t^s)$:

$$corr(\Delta \log Y_{it}, \varepsilon_t^s) \leq 0.28 \cdot \rho_{sY}.$$

Therefore, the values for $\rho_{sY}$ used in the present simulations (0.4 and 1) correspond to (relatively low) values for $corr(\Delta \log Y_{it}, \varepsilon_t^s)$ of (at most) 0.11 and 0.26, respectively.

12. Bodie and Treussard (2008) adopt another variant of this formula: starting the process of saving for retirement 40 years before the target retirement date, they set the initial proportion invested in equity to 80 percent, letting it fall to 40 percent at the target date. Thus the formula for the equity percentage $T$ years from the target date is $40 + T$.

13. Rob Bauer and Rick G. P. Frehen, "The Performance of US Pension Funds," available at www.ssrn.com.

14. Elton, Gruber, and Blake (2006) investigate whether 401(k) plans offer their participants appropriate investment opportunities such that they can span the frontier generated by an adequate set of alternative investment choices.

15. Estimated management fees should be subtracted from portfolio returns when computing workers' wealth accumulation.

16. In general, the numerator should be associated with the best suboptimal strategy, taking into account management costs.

## References

Antolín, Pablo. 2008. "Pension Fund Performance." OECD Working Paper on Insurance and Private Pensions no. 20. OECD, Paris.

Barberis, Nicholas. 2000. "Investing for the Long-Run When Returns Are Predictable." *Journal of Finance* 56: 1247–92.

Benzoni, Luca, and Olena Chyruk. 2009. "Investing over the Life Cycle with Long-Run Labor Income Risk." Draft, Federal Reserve Bank of Chicago.

Benzoni, Luca, Pierre Collin-Dufresne, and Robert S. Goldstein. 2007. "Portfolio Choice over the Life-Cycle: When the Stock and Labor Markets Are Cointegrated." *Journal of Finance* 62 (5): 2123–67.

Blake, David. 2008. "It Is All Back to Front: Critical Issues in the Design of Defined Contribution Pension Plans." In *Frontiers in Pension Finance*, ed. D. Broeders, S. Eijffinger, and A. Houben, 99–165. Cheltenham, UK: Edward Elgar.

Blake, David, Bruce N. Lehmann, and Allan G. Timmermann. 1999. "Asset Allocation Dynamics and Pension Fund Performance." *Journal of Business* 72: 429–61.

Bodie, Zvi, Jérôme Detemple, S. Otruba, and S. Walter. 2004. "Optimal Consumption-Portfolio Choices and Retirement Planning." *Journal of Economic Dynamics and Control* 28 (6): 1115–48.

Bodie Zvi, Robert C. Merton, and William Samuelson. 1992. "Labor Supply Flexibility and Portfolio Choice in a Life Cycle Model." *Journal of Economic Dynamics and Control* 16: 427–49.

Bodie, Zvi, and Jonathan Treussard. 2008. "Making Investment Choices as Simple as Possible: An Analysis of Target Date Retirement Funds." Draft, Boston University.

Cairns, Andrew J. G., David Blake, and Kevin Dowd. 2006. "Stochastic Lifestyling: Optimal Dynamic Asset Allocation for Defined Contribution Pension Plans." *Journal of Economic Dynamics and Control* 30: 843–77.

Campbell, John Y. 1993. "Intertemporal Asset Pricing without Consumption Data." *American Economic Review* 83: 487–512.

———. 1996. "Understanding Risk and Return." *Journal of Political Economy* 104: 298–345.

Campbell, John Y., Joao Cocco, Francisco Gomes, and Paul Maenhout, 2001. "Investing Retirement Wealth: A Life-Cycle Model." In *Risk Aspects of Investment-Based Social Security Reform*, ed. J. Y. Campbell and M. Feldstein, 439–82. Chicago: University of Chicago Press.

Campbell, John Y., and Luis Viceira. 1999. "Consumption and Portfolio Decisions When Expected Returns Are Time Varying." *Quarterly Journal of Economics* 114: 433–95.

———. 2001. "Who Should Buy Long-Term Bonds?" *American Economic Review* 91: 99–127.

———. 2002. *Strategic Asset Allocation: Portfolio Choice for Long-Term Investors*. Oxford: Oxford University Press.

Cocco, Joao. 2004. "Portfolio Choice in the Presence of Housing." *Review of Financial Studies* 18: 535–67.

Cocco, Joao, Francisco Gomes, and Paul Maenhout. 2005. "Consumption and Portfolio Choice over the Life Cycle." *Review of Financial Studies* 18: 491–533.

DeMiguel, Victor, Lorenzo Garlappi, and Raman Uppal. 2008. "Optimal versus Naive Diversification: How Inefficient Is the 1/N Portfolio Strategy?" *Review of Financial Studies* 22: 1915–53.

Elton, Edwin, Martin J. Gruber, and Christopher R. Blake. 2006. "Participant Reaction and the Performance of Funds Offered by 401(k) Plans." EFA Zurich Meetings.

Epstein, Larry, and Stanley Zin. 1989. "Substitution, Risk Aversion, and the Temporal Behavior of Consumption and Asset Returns: A Theoretical Framework." *Econometrica* 57: 937–69.

———. 1991. "Substitution, Risk Aversion, and the Temporal Behavior of Consumption and Asset Returns: An Empirical Investigation." *Journal of Political Economy* 99: 263–86.

Ferson, Wayne, and Kenneth Khang. 2002. "Conditional Performance Measurement Using Portfolio Weights: Evidence for Pension Funds." *Journal of Financial Economics* 65: 249–81.

Fugazza, Carolina, Massimo Guidolin, and Giovanna Nicodano. 2008. "Time and Risk Diversification in Real Estate Investments: Assessing the Ex Post Economic Value." *Real Estate Economics* 37 (3): 341–81.

Gomes, Francisco J., Laurence J. Kotlikoff, and Luis M. Viceira. 2008. "Optimal Life-Cycle Investing with Flexible Labor Supply: A Welfare Analysis of Life-Cycle Funds." *American Economic Review* 98 (2): 297–303.

Gomes, Francisco J., and A. Michaelides. 2004. "A Human Capital Explanation for an Asset Allocation Puzzle." Draft, London School of Economics.

———. 2005. "Optimal Life-Cycle Asset Allocation: Understanding the Empirical Evidence." *Journal of Finance* 60: 869–904.

Goyal, Amit, and Ivo Welch. 2008. "A Comprehensive Look at the Empirical Performance of Equity Premium Prediction." *Review of Financial Studies* 21 (4): 1453–54.

Hansen, Lars P., and Kenneth J. Singleton. 1983. "Stochastic Consumption, Risk Aversion, and the Temporal Behavior of Asset Returns." *Journal of Political Economy* 91: 249–68.

Jagannathan, Ravi, and Narayana R. Kocherlakota. 1996. "Why Should Older People Invest Less in Stocks than Younger People?" *Federal Reserve Bank of Minneapolis Quarterly Review* 20: 11–23.

Koijen, Ralph S. J., Theo Nijman, and Bas J. M. Werker. 2009. "Optimal Annuity Risk Management." Netspar Discussion Paper, Netspar.

———. 2009. "When Can Life-Cycle Investors Benefit from Time-Varying Bond Risk Premia?" *Review of Financial Studies*, forthcoming.

Lehmann, Bruce, and Allan Timmermann. 2008. "Performance Measurement and Evaluation." In *Handbook of Financial Intermediation and Banking*, ed. A. Boot and A. Thakor, 191–259. Amsterdam: North-Holland.

Merton, Robert C. 1969. "Lifetime Portfolio Selection under Uncertainty: The Continuous Time Case." *Review of Economics and Statistics* 51: 247–57.

———. 1971. "Optimum Consumption and Portfolio Rules in a Continuous-Time Model." *Journal of Economic Theory* 3: 373–413.

———. 1973. "An Intertemporal Capital Asset Pricing Model." *Econometrica* 41: 867–87.

Michaelides, Alexander. 2002. "Portfolio Choice, Liquidity Constraints and Stock Market Mean Reversion." Draft, London School of Economics.

Organisation for Economic Co-operation and Development (OECD). 2007. "Pensions at a Glance: Public Policies across OECD Countries." OECD, Paris.

Samuelson, Paul A. 1969. "Lifetime Portfolio Selection by Dynamic Stochastic Programming." *Review of Economics and Statistics* 51: 239–46.

Viceira, Luis. 2001. "Optimal Portfolio Choice for Long-Horizon Investors with Nontradable Labor Income." *Journal of Finance* 56: 433–70.

# CHAPTER 7

# Application of Advances in Financial Theory and Evidence to Pension Fund Design in Developing Economies

**Luis M. Viceira**

The two previous chapters provided a conceptual introduction to the many potential issues related to the unique investment objectives of pension funds as well as the challenges of incorporating individual pattern of earnings and other aspects of human capital risks into the formulation of an investment performance benchmark. Chapter 6 addresses some of the key methodological issues in undertaking this challenging task and provides an initial exercise in developing optimal portfolios for groups of individuals with varying characteristics. It also provides insights into the relative importance of several basic parameters that enter into the development of such a metric. This chapter extends the discussion by addressing issues related to the key issues of asset management for such a portfolio and provides an example of how these conceptual issues could be applied to develop an optimal portfolio in a developing country by applying the principles that have been articulated in the case of Chile.

The chapter begins by adding to the conceptual discussion with an overview of trends in retirement income provision and how these accentuate the importance of a benchmark that is specific to the emerging forms of pension systems. The next section discusses some of the limitations of defined contribution (DC)–based pension systems, and the following section discusses the current policy proposals to confront these limitations. Then we will examine the economic arguments for the adoption of some of these proposals, as well as the design of investment options in DC pension systems in developing economies from the perspective of the theory and practice of long-term investing. A simulation study of the performance of different plan designs in a realistically calibrated setting is presented using data from an example of the developing country that has been at the forefront of the transition to a predominantly DC pension system, Chile. The chapter concludes with general observations on how this study can be applied to the design of pension systems in developing economies.

## Global Trends of DC Pension Systems

The provision of income at retirement is experiencing structural changes in many developed economies. Traditionally social insurance systems and voluntary or mandatory defined benefit (DB) pension plans provided employees with a stable and usually generous income stream at retirement. In recent years this system has been replaced by another that relies much more heavily on individuals to finance their own retirement though their participation in DC pension arrangements. In those plans, income at retirement is typically not guaranteed; instead, individuals finance their retirement from the assets that they have accumulated in their pension account through their working lives. The size of those assets depends on the individual's own lifetime contribution and investment decisions.

The United States is perhaps the developed economy in which this transition from DB to DC plans has been more pronounced. Using data from the Survey of Consumer Finances, Munnell and Sundén (2006) show that about 62 percent of employees with pension coverage in the United States in 1983 were covered exclusively by a traditional DB pension plan; an additional 25 percent were covered by both a traditional DB pension plan and a DC plan. By 2004, however, the proportion of employees covered exclusively by a traditional DB plan had declined to only 20 percent, and the proportion of those covered by both a DC plan and a DB plan had declined to 17 percent. The remaining 63 percent of employees depended exclusively on a DC plan to finance their retirement, in addition to their Social Security benefits.

A number of factors explain the decline in coverage by traditional DB plans in developed economies. The "perfect storm" of the early part of the first decade of this century, with declining stock market valuations and interest rates, produced a dramatic worsening of funding ratios in most corporate and public DB pension plans, as assets declined while liabilities increased. Numerous corporate DB pension plans disappeared, and many of the remaining plans were frozen for existing participants and closed to new participants. Increased global competition in product markets has also made it expensive for private sector employers to sponsor traditional DB plans, especially for those with a more mature employee population. Most if not all new employers do not offer DB plans and opt instead for offering DC plans. The significant increase in dependency ratios in developed economies is also affecting the funding cost of publicly sponsored DB plans. Increased flexibility and mobility in labor markets also favor the adoption of DC plans for their portability.

Many of the factors driving the transition toward a DC system in developed economies also affect developing economies. Developing economies are generally open and subject to global competition in product and capital markets. They typically have highly flexible labor markets as well. Although demographic profiles are more favorable in many developing economies, in others, such as those in Eastern and Central Europe, population aging is a concern. Thus, it is perhaps not surprising that as they create pension systems in the wake of the sustained economic growth of the last one or two decades, most of these economies have chosen to offer DC-based systems with mandatory participation instead of traditional DB plans.

Although DC-based pension systems offer flexibility and portability, they also present important policy challenges.

## Policy Challenges of DC Pension Systems

In a typical DC-based system, plan participants to varying degrees must decide on their own how much they want to contribute to the plan, and how they want to invest their contributions. In some systems plan sponsors also have the option to make contributions on behalf of the participant, which commonly take the form of matching contributions, that is, contributions that are made only if the participant decides to contribute on his or her own. Contributions from the participant and the plan sponsor are usually tax exempt, up to a certain limit. Unlike DB plans, in which the overall investment strategy is developed in consideration of the capacity of assets to deliver a specified level of retirement income (to match the liability of the public or private sponsor), DC plans typically require their members to make basic decisions about the investment strategy, usually by selecting from a menu of choices of investment funds. These systems often provide limited educational materials about how to make prudent investment decisions. They also designate a specific investment option as the default option in which contributions are invested when the plan participant does not make an active choice. Beyond that, each individual participant is responsible for deciding how to best invest his or her contributions.

For a self-directed DC plan to work, one needs to believe that plan participants can make sound saving and investment decisions, or at least that they can learn how to make those decisions. Unfortunately, the existing evidence in the United States about the behavior of plan participants regarding contribution and investment decisions suggests that too many participants do not appear to make sound decisions (Viceira 2007a; Mottola and Utkus 2009). Three problems are of particular concern. First, participation in these plans appears to be relatively low when it is voluntary; those people who participate tend to choose relatively low contribution rates, even if the plan sponsor offers matching contributions. Second, plan participants appear to suffer from inertia in their investment decisions. They tend to rebalance their portfolios very infrequently, and many simply let their contributions go into the investment default option in the plan, regardless of whether this investment option is appropriate for them. Third, investment portfolios are often not adequately diversified, suffer from performance chasing, or contain excessive holdings of a single investment option, such as company stock. These problems tend to be more prevalent among participants with low income and low education levels (Campbell 2006; Calvet, Campbell, and Sodini 2007, 2009).

The existing empirical evidence about participant behavior in DC pension systems in developing economies is scant. However, the limited evidence suggests that participants in those plans suffer from the same saving and investment maladies as plan participants in developed economies. In particular, low savings and inertia appear to be widespread in these plans.

Although participation is typically mandatory in DC pension systems in developing economies, such as those in Latin America and Central and Eastern Europe, it affects only those with stable employment in the formal sector of the economy. Because the informal sector is relatively large in many of these economies, and employment tends to be less stable than in developed economies, these systems suffer from low contribution density and irregular contributions over the life cycle of a significant fraction of the working population.

The Chilean experience suggests that participants in these systems also suffer from investment inertia. The Chilean system offers a handful of investment funds, each one designed to be appropriate for participants in a particular age bracket. Participants are assigned a particular age-appropriate fund when they join, and they are expected to rebalance toward other age-appropriate funds over time. In practice, a large fraction of members adopt the default investment option offered by the pension fund at the time they join and stay with this fund forever.

This experience with DC plans suggests that many DC plan participants are making suboptimal saving and investment decisions. These participants might benefit from having their assets managed professionally in consideration of a specific retirement income objective, as would happen if they were in a traditional DB pension plan. Yet forces of global competition are likely to make it difficult to move back to the traditional DB-based pension system. Ideally, it would be desirable to have a pension system that preserves portability and flexibility, while minimizing the potential opportunity costs of self-directed investing and saving by individuals with a lack of financial sophistication. Recent developments in pension fund design as well as in the theory of long-term asset allocation suggest that it might be possible to move in this direction. If appropriately designed, a few investment options might suffice to achieve adequate diversification and rebalancing over the life cycle of a typical pension fund participant.

## Innovations in Pension Fund Design

In recent years, institutional investors, regulators, and academics have proposed changes to DC plans that address the problems of suboptimal contribution and diversification choices of DC plan participants. In essence, these proposals try to turn investors' inertia into a "force for good" by introducing default contribution and investment options that help participants overcome low contribution rates, lack of rebalancing and investment diversification, and other investment maladies.

Two proposals have been particularly successful in the United States following the enactment of the Pension Protection Act of 2006 (Viceira 2007a). One of them is the adoption of automatic enrollment clauses in

DC pension plans along the lines proposed by Thaler and Benartzi (2004) in their "Save More Tomorrow" program. The second one is the adoption, as a default investment, options of funds that provide automatic rebalancing and diversification across asset classes (Viceira 2007b). There are two main types of these funds used for this purpose in the United States: lifestyle funds, also known as balanced funds, and life-cycle funds. Lifestyle funds are funds that automatically rebalance their holdings toward a target asset mix that remains constant over time. For example, a fund might target a 60–40 percent mix of stocks and bonds; periodically the fund sells some of the holdings of the asset class that has outperformed over the period and uses the proceeds to invest in the asset class that has underperformed so as to keep the mix of stocks and bonds in the portfolio on target. Plan sponsors typically offer a collection of these funds, each one with a different target asset mix. Investors are expected to choose the fund that best fits their risk tolerance. These funds have been widely adopted by sponsors and regulators of DC pension plans in developing economies.

Life-cycle funds also rebalance automatically toward a target asset mix. However, this target asset mix does not stay constant over time; instead it becomes increasingly conservative over time until it reaches a certain target date, at which point the target asset mix remains constant. For example, a hypothetical life-cycle fund with a target date of 2045 and a five-year glide path might start with an initial target mix of 90 percent in stocks and 10 percent in bonds. The fund will automatically rebalance its holdings toward that target during the first five years of the life of the fund, at which point the target mix becomes 85 percent in stocks and 15 percent in bonds; every five years the stock allocation in the target mix decreases by five percentage points, and correspondingly the allocation to bonds increases by five percentage points, until in the year 2045 the target mix becomes 20 percent in stocks and 80 percent in bonds and stays there thereafter.

Plan sponsors typically offer a collection of life-cycle funds that differ on their target date, with funds with closer dates starting at more conservative allocations. Investors are expected to choose the fund whose target date is closest to their expected retirement date. These funds are becoming widely adopted by plan sponsors in DC pension plans in the United States, particularly after the U.S. Department of Labor granted a "safe harbor" provision for the adoption of these plans that protects the plan sponsor from liability for the investment results that may accrue to workers whose savings are invested in one of these funds as a default option.

## Life-Cycle Investing

Lifestyle funds are based on the idea of "risk-based investing," or the advice common among professional investment advisers that conservative (risk-averse) investors target a lower stock-bond asset ratio than aggressive investors. Life-cycle funds, on the other hand, are based on the idea of "age-based investing," or the idea also common among professional investment advisers that investors should target a lower stock-bond asset ratio as they age. Of course, conventional wisdom is not necessarily based on a solid scientific foundation. However, the modern theory of long-term asset allocation (Campbell and Viceira 2002) does provide a rationale for the asset allocation strategies pursued by both types of funds. This point is developed in Viceira (2009), who argues that life-cycle investing is a more appropriate asset allocation strategy from the perspective of working investors. To understand why, it is useful to consider the balance sheet of a typical working investor (figure 7.1). Working investors have two main assets in their balance sheets. One is their financial wealth, which they can easily trade and spend. The other asset is their human wealth (typically referred to as human capital), given by the present discounted value of their expected future labor earnings. Unlike financial wealth, human wealth is not tradable. Working investors can monetize only the dividends paid out by their human wealth over time, which are their labor earnings.

**Figure 7.1    Balance Sheet of Typical Plan Participant**

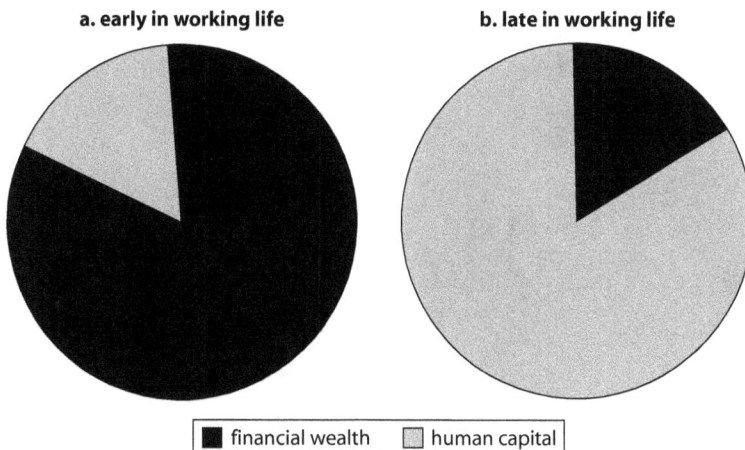

a. early in working life          b. late in working life

■ financial wealth    ▨ human capital

*Source:* Author.

For a typical working investor, human wealth represents that largest fraction of his or her total wealth at a young working age. The reason for this is that the investor has an expected lifetime of labor earnings ahead, but has not yet had an opportunity to accumulate substantial savings. As the investor ages, however, financial wealth increases through savings and the returns on invested savings, while human wealth shrinks because there are fewer years of expected labor earnings. Thus financial wealth represents the largest fraction of total wealth when the working investor approaches retirement.

These considerations raise the question of how working investors should take into account their human wealth when deciding how to invest their financial wealth. For working investors with safe jobs, human wealth represents a buffer against adverse outcomes in capital markets: they can finance consumption out of their stable labor earnings, and they can even replace lost financial wealth by increasing their labor supply. Therefore, from a financial perspective, the human wealth of working investors with safe jobs is equivalent to holding an implicit investment in bonds. These bond-equivalent holdings are large when the investor is young and decline as he or she ages (figure 7.2). This economic argument suggests that if the investor is willing to bear financial risk, it makes sense for him or her to tilt the composition of financial wealth toward risky assets, such as stocks, when he or she is young, and tilt it away from stocks

**Figure 7.2    Balance Sheet of Typical Plan Participant with a Safe Job**

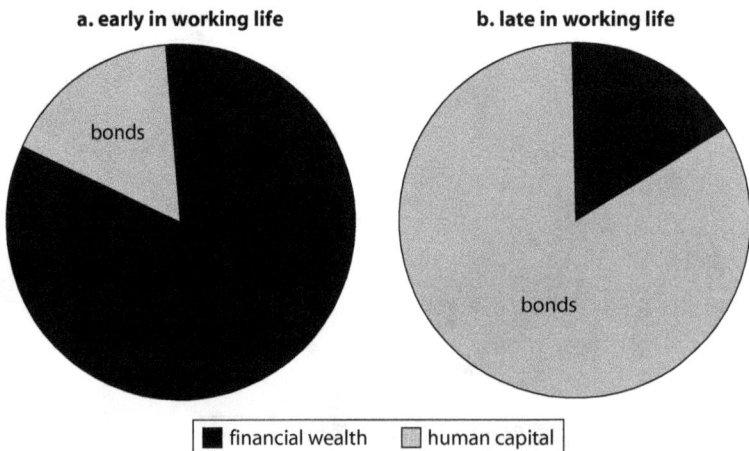

a. early in working life          b. late in working life

financial wealth    human capital

*Source:* Author.

as he or she grows older (Bodie, Merton, and Samuelson 1992). This is precisely the type of investment strategy built into life-cycle funds.

In practice, however, working investors face uncertain lifetime labor earnings. On the downside, they might experience periods of unemployment, adverse professional developments, declining real wages, or permanent disability. On the upside, they might experience unexpected positive developments, such as promotions or job offers. These adverse or favorable circumstances can be due to purely individual-specific reasons or to macroeconomic conditions.

Thus from the perspective of finance, one can think of human capital as a risky asset. As such, it is subject to both systematic or macroeconomic-related risk and idiosyncratic or individual-specific risk. Unlike tradable financial assets, individuals cannot ameliorate the idiosyncratic risk embedded in their human capital through diversification. Instead, the nonliquid nature of human wealth implies that they are forced to bear their human capital risk entirely.

Viceira (2001) studies the impact of both idiosyncratic and systematic labor income risk on portfolio choice. This study finds that working investors should optimally reduce their exposure to stocks if idiosyncratic labor income uncertainty increases. However, it is still optimal for them to follow a path in which they allocate more of their financial wealth to equities when young and less as they age. By contrast, this study finds that asset allocation over the life cycle is highly sensitive to the presence of systematic risk embedded in human capital, which the study measures as the correlation of labor income with stock returns. A positive correlation leads to a more conservative allocation path over the life cycle. For a high enough correlation, it might even be optimal for younger investors to tilt their allocations toward bonds, not stocks. Intuitively, this results from the fact that a positive correlation between labor income and stocks means that human capital is more "stock-like" than "bond-like." This relationship and its impact on asset allocation is also examined in the preceding chapter.

Figure 7.3 illustrates this relationship. It plots the life-cycle allocation to stocks and bonds of financial wealth for an investor whose risk tolerance is such that he or she is comfortable holding an overall exposure to equities equal to 60 percent of total wealth. When human capital is completely riskless (panel a), the investor allocates financial wealth to stocks for most of his or her working life and starts allocating part of financial wealth to bonds only as he or she approaches retirement. By contrast, when human capital is highly correlated with stocks, with an implicit exposure of 65 percent (panel b), the life-cycle allocation path reverses.

**Figure 7.3    Stylized Life-Cycle Asset Allocation**

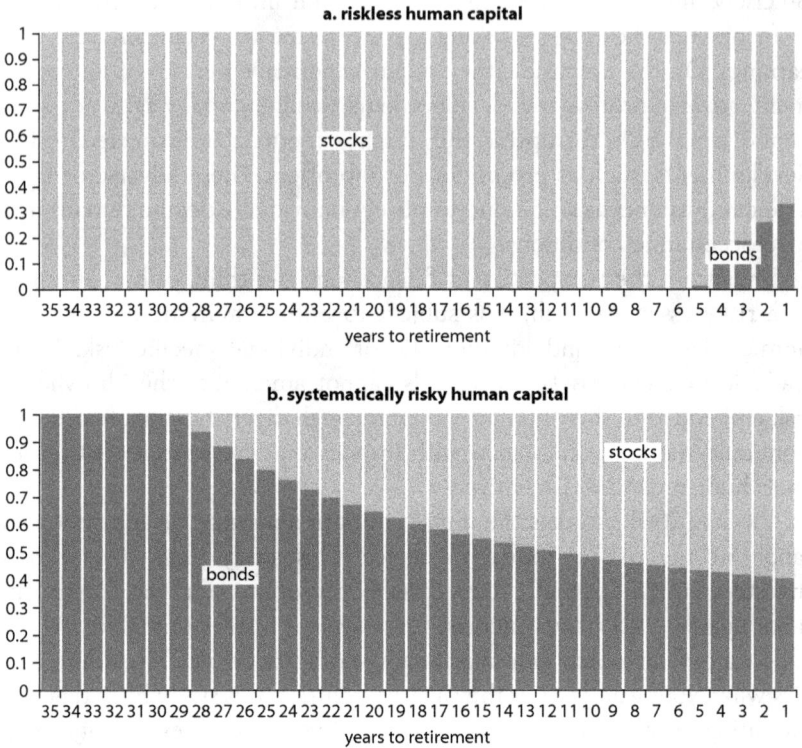

Source: Author.

The investor allocates financial wealth to bonds early in his or her working life and starts increasing allocation to stocks only as he or she approaches retirement. Therefore, investors whose human capital is highly correlated with the overall economy might want to follow a life-cycle path of investing that is the opposite of what standard life-cycle funds follow. Figure 7.3 illustrates two extreme characterizations of human capital. In recent work, Viceira (2001); Cocco, Gomes, and Maenhout (2005); Gomes, Kotlikoff, and Viceira (2008); and others have explored whether the basic conclusions about investing over the life cycle with safe human capital hold under a realistic characterization of labor income (or human capital) risk. These studies find that the basic conclusions of the stylized model of life-cycle portfolio allocation with riskless human capital still hold for plausible specifications of both systematic and idiosyncratic labor income uncertainty, albeit along more conservative life-cycle paths.

Figure 7.4 summarizes the results from these studies. It reproduces the optimal life-cycle allocation path to stocks and bonds found in Gomes, Kotlikoff, and Viceira (2008). This study presents a model of optimal life-cycle consumption, labor supply, asset accumulation, and portfolio decisions calibrated to match the typical life-cycle working hours and wage profile of a high school or college graduate in the United States, as well as his or her typical family size, housing expenditures, and Social Security benefits. The allocation path shown in figure 7.4 assumes a moderately risk-tolerant investor who on average would like to hold exposure to stocks in his or her portfolio given the positive risk premium on stocks. The allocation to stocks over the life cycle is large early in the life cycle and declines as the investor ages. This allocation path is considerably more conservative than the allocation path for the investor with perfectly riskless human capital shown in panel a of figure 7.3. The investor starts allocating to bonds at an early age, and the allocation to bonds increases rapidly in middle age.

It is important to note that the path shown in figure 7.4 also assumes that the investor will receive earnings-based defined benefits through a public social insurance system in retirement, in this case the Social Security system in the United States, which provides on average benefits

**Figure 7.4    Realistically Calibrated Life-Cycle Portfolio Allocation**

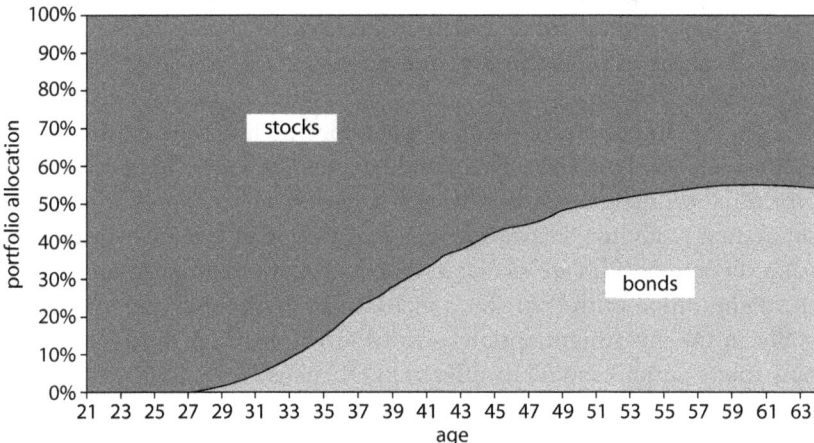

Source: Gomes, Kotlikoff, and Viceira 2008.

of about 40 percent of average lifetime earnings. In the absence of such benefits, the allocation path in figure 7.4 would be more conservative, although it would still have the same qualitative shape. To understand why Social Security benefits make working investors more willing to assume stock market risk in their financial portfolios, note that these benefits are functionally equivalent to receiving a riskless stream of labor income in retirement. Using the same logic to understand human capital as a financial asset, it is easily understandable why such benefits can be characterized as "bond-like" and as such will make the investor more willing to hold stocks in his or her financial portfolio. Thus the optimal life-cycle allocation path for employees who expect to receive traditional pensions in addition to the assets that they accumulate in their DC plan is more tilted toward equities than it would otherwise be in the absence of traditional pension benefits.

The asset allocation path shown in figure 7.4 is based on the estimated labor income uncertainty faced by a high school or college graduate in the United States. In developing economies, income uncertainty is likely to be exacerbated. One might also expect more dispersion in income profiles as well as in income uncertainty across the population. Accordingly, the optimal life-cycle asset allocation path for a typical working investor in these economies is likely to be more conservative than the one shown in figure 7.4, although it is unlikely that it will be similar to the reversed path shown in panel b of figure 7.3.

In summary, under plausible characterizations of labor income uncertainty, human capital arguments provide support for the age-based asset allocation strategies that life-cycle funds follow. It also provides a rationale for adopting these funds as default investment choices in pension systems. A number of important questions remain, however, that need careful consideration.

First, one important question is what specific life-cycle path to adopt in life-cycle fund offerings. This should depend on a careful assessment of typical labor income profiles in each country. This chapter will offer a simulation study for one developing economy, Chile, for which data on labor income profiles are available. A second important question is about the composition of the portfolios included in these funds and, more generally, in the investment options offered in DC plans. A third question is how many options should be offered in DC pension plans. Is it enough to offer a single life-cycle fund as the only investment option available to plan participants? A fourth question is the evaluation of performance of funds. The remainder of this chapter addresses these questions.

## Pension Fund Design in Developing Economies

The theory of long-term asset allocation provides insights for the design of investment options in DC pension plans. In the context of developing economies, pension fund design needs to address three particularly relevant issues: (1) the composition of fixed-income portfolios, (2) the composition of equity portfolios, and (3) currency hedging.

### Fixed-Income Portfolios

Most investment choices in DC pension plans in developing economies are "lifestyle"-type funds that, as a result of regulatory constraints, tend to be heavily weighted toward fixed-income instruments. Moreover, these large fixed-income allocations tend to be highly concentrated in domestic government bonds and cash instruments (short-term government bonds, money market instruments, and deposits). Table 7.1 shows the portfolio composition of a cross section of mandatory DC pension funds in developing economies as of December 2007. With the exception of Chile and Peru, all the funds have allocations to domestic government bonds and stable-value instruments well above 50 percent. In the case of the Slovak Republic and Uruguay the allocations are as high as 85 percent and 95 percent, respectively.

**Table 7.1    Portfolio Composition in Mandatory Pension Funds (December 2007)**

|  | Total fixed income (1) | Government instruments (2) | Total equity (3) | Foreign instruments (4) | Cash and CDs (5) | Government instruments + CDs (6) = (2) + (5) |
|---|---|---|---|---|---|---|
| Argentina | 52 | 51 | 33 | 8 | 4 | 55 |
| Chile | 27 | 8 | 54 | 36 | 18 | 26 |
| Colombia | 70 | 48 | 28 | 10 | 2 | 50 |
| Mexico | 80 | 69 | 4 | 0 | 6 | 76 |
| Peru | 44 | 22 | 54 | 13 | 2 | 24 |
| Uruguay | 87 | 87 | 0 | 0 | 8 | 95 |
| Croatia | 66 | 63 | 31 | 4 | 2 | 66 |
| Hungary | 64 | 61 | 30 | 0 | 1 | 62 |
| Poland | 62 | 60 | 35 | 1 | 3 | 63 |
| Slovak Republic | 38 | 38 | 10 | 10 | 48 | 85 |
| Average | 59 | 51 | 28 | 8 | 10 | 60 |
| Average (excluding Peru) | 61 | 54 | 25 | 8 | 10 | 64 |

*Source:* World Bank.

This heavy allocation to cash instruments, domestic government bonds, and closely related instruments is probably driven by two factors. First, it may be rooted in the conventional wisdom that cash instruments, money market funds, stable value funds, certificates of deposit, and similar investment vehicles are the safest assets because they minimize short-run return volatility. Second, fiscal deficit financing considerations are also likely to be at play, particularly in explaining the allocations to domestic government bonds, because governments of developing countries often attempt to utilize the predictable flows of pension contributions from mandatory systems to fulfill financing requirements. Unfortunately, the modern theory of long-term asset allocation suggests that the common practice of requiring pension funds to hold large holdings of domestic long-term nominal government bonds and deposits or cash-like instruments is not well aligned with the retirement income provision objectives of its members, even if the ultimate goal is to provide safe investment options.

Cash instruments, short-term government debt, and investment funds heavily weighted toward short-term debt instruments are not safe assets for long-term investors because they expose these investors to reinvestment risk. Because of their short maturity relative to the investment horizon of most plan participants, long-term investors need to follow a strategy of rolling over these instruments as they mature. This strategy is risky because the real rates at which investors can reinvest their cash holdings move considerably and persistently over time (Campbell and Viceira 2001, 2002; Campbell, Sunderam, and Viceira 2009). In particular, as the most recent experience suggests, low real interest rate regimes can persist for long periods. These instruments are also subject to short-term inflation risk. Although this is not a concern in developed economies with stable inflation, it can be an important concern in developing economies with volatile inflation. Long-term bonds protect investors from reinvestment risk because falls in interest rates are compensated with capital gains in the value of the bond. But long-term government bonds are typically instruments whose coupons and principal are fixed in nominal terms. This makes them risky investments for long-term investors because they are subject to long-term inflation risk: if realized and expected future inflation turn out to be larger than the rate of expected inflation built into the price of the bond at the time of its acquisition, the purchasing power of the coupons and principal of the bond will be eroded, and the bond will also experience capital losses.

Unfortunately, inflation risk can be important over a long horizon. Expected inflation in developed economies moves considerably over time and experiences both temporary and highly persistent changes (Campbell and Viceira 2001, 2002; Campbell, Sunderam, and Viceira 2009). In developing economies, long-term inflation risk is likely to be exacerbated, as the inflation experiences of many of these economies suggests.

In inflationary environments the only asset class that provides investors with protection from real interest rate uncertainty and from inflation uncertainty are inflation-linked bonds. Long-term inflation-indexed bonds (TIPS in the United States) protect investors from inflation risk by providing a predictable stream of real (inflation-adjusted) income. They protect investors from falls in interest rates because their prices adjust inversely to movements in real interest rates.

An investment in nominal bonds is a bet that inflation risk will be negligible in the future or, from a speculative perspective, that the economy will go through a period of deflation. In deflationary environments, inflation-indexed bonds still protect investors because their coupons and principal are constant in real terms. Although long-tem deflation is certainly a possibility, experience suggests that inflation is probably a bigger threat in developing economies.

Inflation-linked bonds have been labeled in the popular financial press as an "alternative" or "exotic" asset class. In fact, long-term inflation-indexed bonds are neither alternative nor exotic: they are the true riskless asset for long-term investors. As such, they should be at the core of the fixed-income investment options offered in any DC plan and at the core of the fixed-income allocation of life-cycle funds and lifestyle funds. Those plans that are oriented toward providing investors with a riskless default investment option should consider making an inflation-linked bond fund the default option for active participants in the plan.

Perhaps one reason why inflation-linked bonds are sometimes labeled "exotic assets" is because they are not readily available in many economies, particularly in developing economies. However, the experience has been that, when issued, there is ready demand for these bonds from long-term investors, such as traditional DB pension funds, endowments, and individual investors saving for retirement. Today governments and even private issuers in many developed economies issue inflation-indexed bonds on a regular basis, making these bonds readily available to investors. Governments in some developing economies have also started to issue such bonds; in some countries, such as Chile, inflation-indexed instruments have a long tradition, and they are the most liquid government bonds.

From the perspective of long-term investors, particularly working investors saving for retirement through DC pension plans, the issuance of inflation-indexed bonds by governments is welfare improving. Issuance of these bonds should also help governments reduce the cost of public deficit financing, because these bonds do not require compensation for inflation uncertainty. Of course, by eliminating the ability to inflate away government debt, these bonds are in some ways akin to foreign-currency–denominated debt, in the sense that straight default is the only possible way of reducing payments on these bonds.

In the absence of local inflation-linked bonds, Campbell, Viceira, and White (2003) show that investors in countries with volatile inflation at short and at long horizons can still gain inflation protection. They can do so by holding short-term bonds denominated in foreign currencies with stable inflation and real interest rates. This strategy is discussed in greater detail below.

### Equity Portfolios

In most developing economies, pension fund regulations limit the exposure to equities, and particularly the exposure to international equities, of DC pension plans. Although limiting overall equity holdings makes sense if the pension supervisor wants to set limits to the maximum risk exposure (although it should never be an excuse to implicitly make pension funds finance domestic fiscal deficits by forcing them to increase their holdings of government bonds), limiting international equity exposure might not be in the best interest of members. International diversification, with currency risk appropriately hedged, should have a first-order positive impact on improving the risk-return trade-off in equity allocations. In their classic study of the benefits of portfolio diversification, French and Poterba (1991) found substantial gains for U.S. investors from international equity diversification. These gains came from the historical imperfect correlation across international equity markets.

Although correlations of global stock markets that have increased recently might tend to diminish these advantages (figure 7.5), recent studies confirm the benefits of international diversification in equity portfolios and show that these benefits extend to investors in most developed economies (Dimson, Marsh, and Staunton 2002). Campbell, Serfaty-de Medeiros, and Viceira (2010) also find benefits to international diversification in bond portfolios. Goetzmann, Li, and Rouwenhorst (2004) take the long view and show that the correlations of international equity markets vary considerably over time. This variation appears to be related to differing degrees of global economic and financial integration, with greater average correlation at times of increased integration. To the extent that

**Figure 7.5     Correlations across International Equity Markets**

**a. 36-month rolling correlations of total returns on MSCI U.S. market index with total returns on MSCI World-Ex. U.S.**

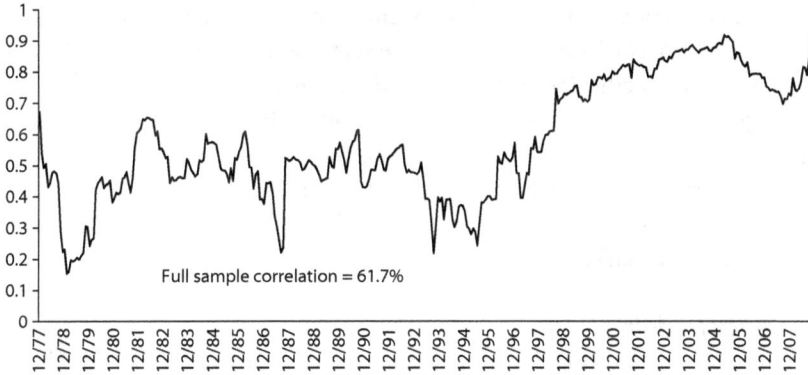

Full sample correlation = 61.7%

**b. 36-month rolling correlations of total returns on MSCI emerging market indexes with total returns on MSCI World**

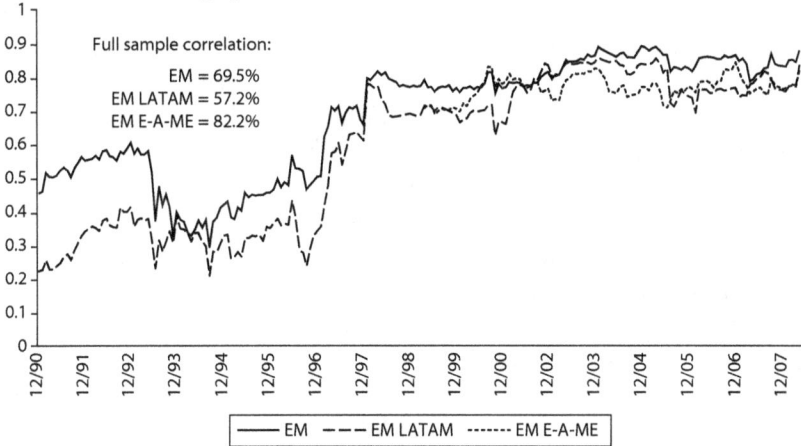

Full sample correlation:

EM = 69.5%
EM LATAM = 57.2%
EM E-A-ME = 82.2%

——— EM    – – – EM LATAM    ······· EM E-A-ME

*Source:* Author's calculations using monthly total returns (inclusive of dividends and price appreciation) on Morgan Stanley Capital International (MSCI) market capitalization weighted stock market indexes.
*Note:* EM = a comprehensive index of emerging stock markets; EM-E-A-ME = a comprehensive index of the emerging stock markets in Europe, Asia, and the Middle East; EM-LATAM = a comprehensive index of Latin American stock markets; MSCI US = U.S. stock market; World = a comprehensive index of global stock markets; World-Ex. U.S. = a global stock market index that excludes the U.S. stock market.

globalization might not be a permanent phenomenon (as evidenced by the recent decreases in trade and capital flows), the current lower (but still substantive) gains from international equity diversification might underestimate the long-run gains.

The benefits of international equity diversification are most likely to be even greater for investors in developing economies. Developing economies are typically characterized by small national stock markets subject to significant country-specific risk. For example, many of these economies do not have a widely diversified productive sector and instead are heavily concentrated in specific industries or services. This risk can be ameliorated through international diversification. Equity allocations in investment options in DC plans in developing economies should be held in the form of internationally diversified portfolios, with benchmarks oriented to reflect the performance of the world stock market portfolio rather than the local stock market.

### Currency Hedging

An important decision for internationally diversified equity and bond investors is to decide how much of the currency exposure implicit in their portfolios to hedge. A conventional practice among institutional investors in developed economies is to fully hedge the currency exposure of their international holdings of equities. This practice is optimal when equity excess returns are uncorrelated with currency excess returns (Solnik 1974). Indeed, Perold and Schulman (1988) find that U.S. investors can reduce volatility by fully hedging the currency exposure implicit in internationally diversified equity portfolios.

However, if equity (or bond) returns and currency returns are correlated, full currency hedging will not be the best approach to reduce portfolio risk. For example, if investors hold a portfolio of international equities, and excess returns on foreign equities are negatively correlated with foreign currency returns, holding currency exposure can help investors reduce the volatility of their speculative portfolio. Thus not hedging rather than hedging is what helps investors reduce portfolio risk.

Campbell, Serfaty-de Medeiros, and Viceira (2010) examine whether currency returns are in fact correlated with the returns on portfolios of international equities and bonds over the period 1975–2005. They derive the optimal risk-minimizing currency hedging policy for internationally diversified bond and equity investors implied by those correlations. They find that currencies traditionally considered as reserve currencies by international investors, such as the U.S. dollar, the euro, and the Swiss franc, tend to be negatively correlated with global stock markets. These currencies tend to appreciate when global stock markets fall and tend to depreciate when global stock markets rise. An immediate implication of this finding is that investors seeking to minimize the currency risk of their portfolios should not hedge their exposure to those currencies in global equity portfolios.

By contrast, they find that commodity-based currencies, such as the Australian dollar or the Canadian dollar, tend to be positively correlated with global stock markets, whereas other major currencies, such as the British pound or the Japanese yen, are largely uncorrelated with global stock markets. Thus investors should fully hedge the exposure to those currencies in equity portfolios to minimize portfolio risk. In the case of commodity-based currencies, it is even optimal to hold short positions that go beyond those required by full hedging.

In summary, Campbell, Serfaty-de Medeiros, and Viceira (2010) find that it is not optimal for internationally diversified equity investors to apply a single hedging policy across all major currencies to reduce risk. Rather, they should preserve their exposure to reserve currencies, while hedging their exposure to all other major currencies. Their study shows that investors based in developed economies can achieve highly economically and statistically significant gains relative to standard currency policies, such as full hedging, no hedging, or half-hedging.

The recent 2008 financial crisis has provided an informal corroboration of these findings because reserve currencies have tended to strengthen, whereas commodity currencies, such as the Australian dollar or the Chilean peso, have strongly depreciated. Investors in developing economies holding internationally diversified equity portfolios are likely to hold a very high proportion of their portfolios in the stock markets of developed economies. As such, the conclusions from the study by Campbell, Serfaty-de Medeiros, and Viceira (2010) apply to them. In fact, Walker (2008) finds that reserve currencies tend to appreciate with respect to emerging market currencies when global stock markets fall. Interestingly, Campbell and his colleagues find that global bond market returns are mostly uncorrelated with currency returns. They show that currency exposures in internationally diversified bond portfolios should be close to full hedging, with a modest long exposure to the U.S. dollar.

There is an additional argument for long-term investors in developing economies to hold exposure to reserve currencies. It is well known that holding foreign currency exposure may help reduce total portfolio volatility when there is no domestic asset that is riskless in real terms (Adler and Dumas 1983). At short horizons, this effect is unlikely to be important for investors in developed economies with stable inflation, but it can be important for investors in developing economies with volatile inflation.

At long horizons, Campbell, Viceira, and White (2003) show that investors interested in minimizing real interest rate risk can do so by holding portfolios of short-term government bonds denominated in euros and U.S. dollars because these two currencies have had relatively stable interest rates. In other words, in the absence of inflation-indexed bonds denominated in local currency, bills denominated in reserve currencies can help long-term investors mimic the properties of those bonds.

The ability of reserve currencies to hedge long-term real interest risk and inflation risk should be especially attractive to long-term investors in developing economies for at least two reasons. First, inflation-indexed bonds do not exist in many of these economies, and it has been argued that the inflation protection and interest rate risk protection that they provide is important for long-term investors. Second, bonds in those currencies are unlikely to default.

In summary, all these results suggest that reserve currencies—the U.S. dollar and the euro—can help long-term investors in developing economies to reduce short- and long-term portfolio volatility. These currencies can provide an attractive and stable store of value for these investors, particularly for DC plan participants.

## Performance Evaluation of Investment Options

The distribution of wealth at retirement accumulated under different fund designs in DC plans is of interest to sponsors, members, regulators, and policy makers. This distribution depends on two key factors: the income profile over the life cycle of the plan participant, which determines contributions to the plan, and the risk and return of the asset classes included in the fund.

Following Poterba and others (2005, 2009), this section utilizes a simulation approach to obtain this distribution for a representative country, Chile, for which there is ready availability of data on life-cycle earnings and a relatively long data series for domestic interest rates and stock returns. This exercise provides a sense of the performance of different funds over the working life cycle of the member of a mandatory DC pension system facing realistic life-cycle earnings growth, earnings uncertainty, and capital markets' expected return and risk.

### Labor Income Profile

Studies of labor income profiles over the life cycle (Hubbard, Skinner, and Zeldes 1995; Carroll 1997; Gourinchas and Parker 2002) find that the typical earnings profile is hump-shaped, subject to random shocks. On average, labor earnings tend to grow in the early part of the life cycle of the employee, reach a maximum around middle age, and experiment a decline afterward. This shape is driven by a combination of increasing wages and labor supply early in life and a decline in labor supply late in life (French 2005; Low 2005; Gomes, Kotlikoff, and Viceira 2008).

In their study of plan participants in the Chilean pension system, Berstein, Larraín, and Pino (2006) find a similar inverted-U shape for a typical contributor to the system. Figure 7.6 reproduces their estimated life-cycle earnings profile for a typical Chilean male participant in constant Chilean pesos of 2004. This profile is the basis for the simulation of labor income histories in this study.

Of course, as noted in earlier sections of this chapter and in other chapters, labor earnings are not deterministic. They are subject to random shocks that make future labor income uncertain for individuals and result in considerable dispersion in the realized labor income profiles of working populations, as discussed in greater detail by Mitchell and Turner in chapter 5. Labor earnings are subject to random shocks, which have a permanent effect on the level of earnings achieved by the individual, and shocks whose effect on earnings is only transitory.

Labor economists find that labor earnings over the life cycle can be modeled as

$$y_t = f(t) + v_t + \varepsilon_t$$
$$v_t = v_{t-1} + u_t$$

**Figure 7.6    Estimated Live-Cycle Labor Earnings of Chilean Males**

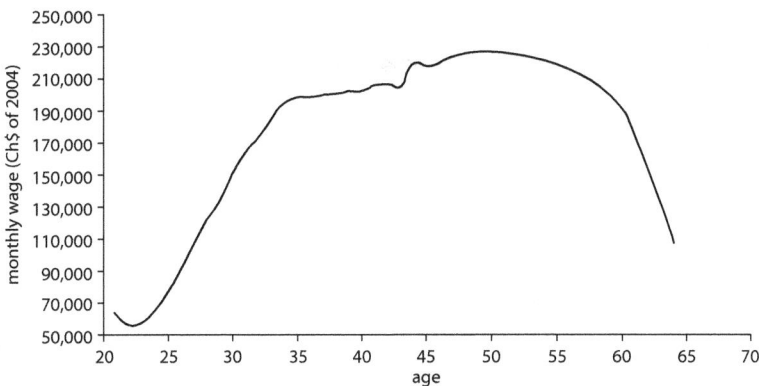

Source: Author's calculation based on data in Bernstein, Larraín, and Pino (2006).

where $f(t)$ describes the deterministic age-dependent component of earnings with an inverted-U shape (figure 7.6), $v_t$ describes the permanent shock to labor earnings, and $\varepsilon_t$ describes the transitory shock. Both shocks are assumed to be uncorrelated both longitudinally and temporally, as well as normally distributed.

Currently no studies have been done about the size of these shocks for plan participants in mandatory pension funds in developing economies. However, empirical evidence is available about their size for U.S. workers. Cocco, Gomes, and Maenhout (2005) estimate the annual standard deviation of these shocks at 10.95 percent and 13.89 percent, respectively, although half of that is attributed to measurement error. The simulations included in this study use these magnitudes with no downward correction for measurement error to provide a rough proxy for the volatility of the shocks to working investors in developing economies. Thus the simulations effectively assume that labor income uncertainty is much more pronounced in developing economies. This is deemed to be a reasonable assumption given the more precarious nature of employment and earnings in these economies.

Figure 7.7 shows the impact of this uncertainty on the distribution of annual labor income in the final year of employment before retirement. This simulation is based on 100,000 replications of the labor income process with the age-profile $f(t)$ shown in figure 7.6, assuming that the individual joins the labor force (and starts contributing to the plan) at age 21 with a starting salary of Ch$62,500 every year and that he or she retires at age 65.

This shows that the impact of labor income uncertainty on final salary is highly significant. The median of the distribution of final

Figure 7.7    Distribution of Labor Earnings in Final Working Year (Ch$)

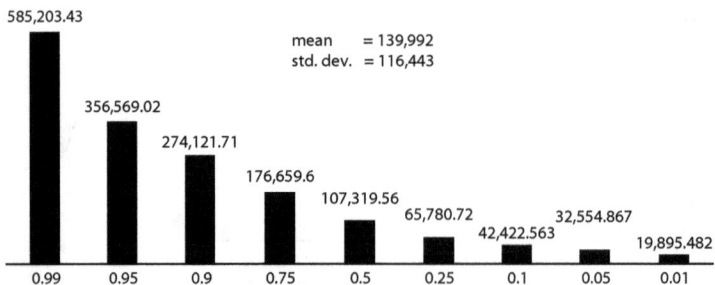

Source: Author.

salary is about Ch$107,000, and the mean is about Ch$140,000. The standard deviation of the distribution is, at Ch$116,500, larger than the median, and it implies a large dispersion in potential outcomes. The fifth percentile of the distribution is about Ch$32,500, and the first percentile is about Ch$20,000, or less than one-third and one-fifth of the median final salary, respectively. At the right side of the distribution, the 95 percentile and the 99 percentile are Ch$356,600 and Ch$585,200, respectively.

Because pension plan contributions are typically proportional to earnings, this implies that the range of potential outcomes in pension assets at the end of the working life is going to be very large, even if these contributions are invested with no risk at all. Thus income uncertainty will generate sizable uncertainty about asset accumulation in retirement, regardless of whether the plan takes investment risk or not.

### Capital Markets

The simulations consider four asset classes. The first one is domestic stocks, which in the simulations is proxied by the MSCI Chile Total Return Stock Index. The second is the world stock market portfolio, which, consistent with the above discussion about currency hedging, is proxied by the MSCI World Total Return Stock Index in dollar terms and is unhedged. The third is domestic government inflation-linked bonds, and the fourth is domestic nominal government bonds.

The simulation of the performance of these asset classes assumes that their returns are uncorrelated over time and lognormally distributed. The assumption of temporal independence is a conservative assumption because it ignores the possibility that stock returns might be predictable or mean reverting (Campbell and Viceira 1999). Mean reversion in return implies that risk is smaller at long investment horizons than at short horizons, whereas temporal independence means that risk is independent of investment horizon (Campbell and Viceira 2005).

Table 7.2 presents the capital market assumptions. Specifically, it presents the mean, standard deviation, and correlation structure of continuously compounded (or log) real returns on the four asset classes. These moments are consistent with the historical experience.

The mean and standard deviation of returns in the MSCI World unhedged portfolio correspond to the period January 1984–April 2008, whereas the moments for the MSCI Chile portfolio correspond to a somewhat shorter period, January 1993–April 2008. This period excludes

**Table 7.2    Capital Markets Assumptions**

| Asset class | Mean | Std. dev. | Correlations | | |
|---|---|---|---|---|---|
| MSCI World | 7.70 | 16.16 | 1.00 | 0.34 | 0.00 |
| MSCI Chile | 7.58 | 22.08 | 0.34 | 1.00 | 0.25 |
| Nominal bonds | 3.00 | 10.00 | 0.00 | 0.25 | 1.00 |
| Inflation-indexed bonds | 2.80 | 0.00 | n.a. | n.a. | n.a. |

*Source:* Author.
*Note:* n.a. = not applicable; std. dev. = standard deviation.

the Pinochet regime and the period of high inflation that Chile experienced in the 1980s but includes events of extreme volatility, such as the emerging markets crisis at the end of the 1990s, the global stock market crash early in this century, and important capital markets reforms in Chile. The mean log real return on the world stock market portfolio and the domestic stock market portfolio are very similar at 7.7 percent and 7.6 percent, respectively. However, at 22 percent the volatility of the domestic stock portfolio is about 30 percent higher than the volatility of the world stock market portfolio, with a correlation with the world stock market portfolio of 34 percent.

The higher volatility of the domestic stock market portfolio relative to the world stock market portfolio implies that, although the mean log returns are about the same for both stock portfolios, the expected mean simple real return on the domestic portfolio is larger than the expected return on the world stock market portfolio. Specifically, the capital market assumptions in table 7.2 imply that the expected simple real return on the domestic portfolio is 10 percent, but the expected return on the world stock market portfolio is 100 basis points lower at 9 percent. The average log real return on inflation-indexed bonds is assumed to be 2.8 percent, roughly the current yield on Chilean long-term inflation-indexed bonds. The simulations assume that investors can get this return with zero volatility. Of course, in practice inflation-indexed bonds have nonzero volatility at short horizons. Because we are interested only in the long-run performance of the asset class, this assumption is a simple way of capturing the fact that inflation-indexed bonds are riskless at long horizons.

Mean simple returns and mean continuously compounded returns are different when returns are volatile. Under the assumption of lognormality, the mean simple return is equal to the mean log return plus one-half the variance of the log return, and approximately equal at small intervals otherwise. The mean simple return determines the expected future return.

The historical average real return on nominal bond instruments in Chile has been negative in most periods, reflecting large inflationary surprises. However, it is unlikely that investors expected a negative real return at issuance of these bonds. Consistent with the idea that investors should demand a positive risk premium on long-term nominal bonds, the simulations assume a mean log real return on nominal bonds of 3 percent every year, with a standard deviation of 10 percent, zero correlation with the world stock market, and a 25 percent correlation with the domestic stock market.

### Investment Strategies

To understand the implications of labor income uncertainty and capital market risk for asset accumulation over the life cycle, this study considers 16 different investment strategies or hypothetical funds. The first four strategies are pure investments in each asset class: government nominal bonds, government inflation-indexed bonds, domestic stock market portfolio, and world stock market portfolio (unhedged).

The next four strategies are lifestyle or balanced funds, each one investing 60 percent in bonds and 40 percent in stocks. The bond portfolio is either 100 percent invested in nominal bonds or 100 percent invested in inflation-indexed bonds. The stock portfolio can be either the domestic stock market portfolio or the world stock market portfolio.

The next eight strategies are life-cycle funds, with two main life-cycle investing strategies. Life cycle 1 considers a stock-bond portfolio that is invested in a 90–10 percent stock-bond portfolio for the first 20 years of the fund and gradually changes this mix until it reaches a 50–50 percent stock-bond portfolio at retirement age. Life cycle 2 considers a strategy that starts with a 90–10 percent stock-bond portfolio and starts reducing immediately the stock allocation until it reaches a 50–50 percent stock-bond portfolio at retirement. All lifestyle and life-cycle funds are rebalanced on an annual basis.

The investment strategies are simulated under three assumptions about labor earnings. First, labor income is assumed to be nonstochastic, so that $yt = f(t)$. Second, labor income is assumed to be stochastic and subject to permanent and transitory shocks that are uncorrelated with stock market returns and nominal bond returns. Third, labor income is assumed to be stochastic, and subject to permanent and transitory shocks, with permanent shocks to income exhibiting a 50 percent correlation with domestic stock returns and uncorrelated with world stock returns and domestic bond returns.

In each case the contribution rate is set at 10 percent of the monthly salary. Setting the contribution rate as a percentage of labor income reflects the standard practice in mandatory pension plans. When labor earnings are stochastic, it also helps to capture in the simulations the impact on asset accumulation of episodes of low or extremely low labor earnings of varying length.

Table 7.3 presents a summary of the main results of the simulation exercise, with a focus on the pure strategies and the lifestyle and life-cycle

**Table 7.3    Summary Table of Simulation Results**

|  | Labor income process | | | | | |
|---|---|---|---|---|---|---|
|  | Nonstochastic | | Uncorrelated | | Correlated | |
| Strategy | Mean | Std. dev. | Mean | Std. dev. | Mean | Std. dev. |
| 100% ILB | 13.2 | 0.0 | 11.6 | 5.2 | 11.5 | 5.2 |
| 100% nominal bond | 15.7 | 7.0 | 13.6 | 8.7 | 13.6 | 8.7 |
| 100% MSCI Chile | 95.0 | 158.4 | 79.0 | 135.1 | 79.0 | 144.6 |
| 100% MSCI World no-hedge | 69.9 | 67.5 | 58.6 | 61.5 | 58.5 | 61.4 |
| 40% MSCI Chile, 60% ILB | 23.4 | 9.7 | 20.1 | 11.9 | 20.1 | 13.1 |
| 40% MSCI World no hedge, 60% ILB | 22.6 | 6.7 | 19.4 | 10.0 | 19.4 | 9.9 |
| Life cycle 1 (90–10 to 50–50 MSCI Chile ILB starting after 20 years) | 38.3 | 30.7 | 32.5 | 29.6 | 32.5 | 32.0 |
| Life cycle 1 (90–10 to 50–50 MSCI World ILB starting after 20 years) | 34.2 | 18.4 | 29.1 | 19.8 | 29.1 | 19.7 |
| Life cycle 2 (90–10 to 50–50 MSCI Chile ILB starting immediately) | 38.3 | 29.5 | 32.3 | 27.9 | 32.3 | 30.9 |
| Life cycle 2 (90–10 to 50–50 MSCI World ILB starting immediately) | 34.1 | 17.6 | 28.9 | 18.7 | 28.9 | 18.6 |
| Final income (monthly) | 107,500 | 0 | 140,260 | 117,068 | 139,992 | 116,443 |

*Source:* Author
*Note:* Statistics presented as multiple of expected income in final year. ILB = inflation-linked bond; std. dev. = standard deviation.

strategies that use inflation-indexed bonds as the basis for the fixed-income allocation. To facilitate interpretation, the table reports the mean and the standard deviation of accumulated assets at retirement under each investment strategy as a multiple of the final annual salary expected at the time that the participant starts working and joins the plan at age 21. The expected final salary is also reported in the bottom row of the table. Tables 7.4, 7.5, and 7.6 present the full distribution of expected final salary multiples for all 16 strategies.

The first two rows of table 7.3 show the results generated by the pure bond strategies. The first row of the table shows that investing in an inflation-indexed bond fund leads on average to an asset accumulation equal to about 13 times expected final salary when labor earnings are nonstochastic, and about 11.5 times when they are. This implies that a plan participant with mean realized earnings in his final year of work, and a life expectancy of 15 years at retirement, would have accumulated under this option enough assets to finance annual spending during retirement equal to about 70 percent of his or her final salary. With a life expectancy of 20 years after retirement, the assets accumulated at retirement would be enough to finance spending equal to about 50 percent of his or her final salary.

Interestingly, despite this being a fully riskless strategy, assets at retirement exhibit considerable dispersion in the case of uncertain labor income. The standard deviation of asset accumulation as a multiple of the expected final salary is slightly above five. Of course, this dispersion is entirely attributable to uncertainty in labor income outcomes, not to investment outcomes, and it is consistent with the dispersion of final salary shown in figure 7.6. Table 7.5 shows that this standard deviation implies that the fifth percentile of the distribution is 5.5 times the expected final salary. This is about 24 times the fifth percentile of the final salary distribution (Ch$32,555). Therefore, a member who ends up in the left tail of the distribution in labor income outcomes would still have accumulated enough assets to finance annual consumption equal to 100 percent of his or her final salary for 24 years.

A strategy of investing contributions in nominal bonds leads to a slightly higher average multiple of expected final salary (13.6 times in the case of stochastic labor income) but at the cost of a much larger standard deviation of outcomes (8.7 times). Of course, this is the result of the assumption that the expected return on nominal bonds is larger than the expected return on inflation-indexed bonds, with a much larger standard deviation. This higher volatility tries to capture the fact that nominal

**Table 7.4   Simulation Results for Investment Strategies When Labor Income Is Nonstochastic**
*(multiple of expected income in final year)*

| | Mean | Std. dev. | Max. | 99% | 95% | 75% | 50% | 25% | 5% | 1% | Min. |
|---|---|---|---|---|---|---|---|---|---|---|---|
| **a. Inflation-Indexed Fixed-Income Portfolio** | | | | | | | | | | | |
| 100% ILB | 13.2 | 0.0 | 13.2 | 13.2 | 13.2 | 13.2 | 13.2 | 13.2 | 13.2 | 13.2 | 13.2 |
| 100% MSCI Chile | 95.0 | 158.4 | 7252.8 | 691.2 | 317.0 | 105.4 | 50.5 | 25.3 | 10.2 | 5.6 | 1.3 |
| 100% MSCI World no hedge | 69.9 | 67.5 | 1409.0 | 335.9 | 189.3 | 85.8 | 50.1 | 30.0 | 15.0 | 9.4 | 2.6 |
| 40% MSCI Chile, 60% ILB | 23.4 | 9.7 | 122.8 | 55.0 | 41.6 | 28.1 | 21.5 | 16.6 | 11.6 | 9.1 | 4.3 |
| 40% MSCI World no hedge, 60% ILB | 22.6 | 6.7 | 73.7 | 42.8 | 34.9 | 26.3 | 21.6 | 17.8 | 13.7 | 11.4 | 6.7 |
| Life cycle 1 (90–10 to 50–50 MSCI Chile ILB starting after 20 years) | 38.3 | 30.7 | 778.0 | 154.7 | 94.7 | 47.2 | 29.7 | 19.2 | 10.7 | 7.3 | 2.4 |
| Life cycle 1 (90–10 to 50–50 MSCI World ILB starting after 20 years) | 34.2 | 18.4 | 253.8 | 98.8 | 69.2 | 41.9 | 29.9 | 21.6 | 13.9 | 10.3 | 4.7 |
| Life cycle 2 (90–10 to 50–50 MSCI Chile ILB starting immediately) | 38.3 | 29.5 | 730.1 | 148.9 | 92.0 | 46.9 | 30.2 | 19.9 | 11.4 | 8.0 | 2.8 |
| Life cycle 2 (90–10 to 50–50 MSCI World ILB starting immediately) | 34.1 | 17.6 | 246.5 | 95.4 | 67.3 | 41.5 | 30.1 | 22.0 | 14.6 | 11.0 | 5.2 |
| Final income (monthly) | 107,500 | 0 | 107,500 | 107,500 | 107,500 | 107,500 | 107,500 | 107,500 | 107,500 | 107,500 | 107,500 |

## b. Nominal Fixed-Income Portfolio

| | | | | | | | | | | | |
|---|---|---|---|---|---|---|---|---|---|---|---|
| 100% Nominal bond | 15.7 | 7.0 | 110.2 | 39.5 | 29.0 | 18.8 | 14.2 | 10.8 | 7.4 | 5.7 | 3.1 |
| 40% MSCI Chile, 60% nominal bond | 26.2 | 15.4 | 253.7 | 81.4 | 55.1 | 32.1 | 22.5 | 15.9 | 9.9 | 7.2 | 3.1 |
| 40% MSCI World no hedge, 60% nominal bond | 24.4 | 10.2 | 148.8 | 58.1 | 43.7 | 29.3 | 22.4 | 17.3 | 12.1 | 9.5 | 5.0 |
| Life cycle 1 (90–10 to 50–50 MSCI Chile nominal bond starting after 20 years) | 41.2 | 37.1 | 1133.4 | 184.2 | 107.2 | 50.5 | 30.6 | 19.0 | 10.1 | 6.6 | 2.3 |
| Life cycle 1 (90–10 to 50–50 MSCI World nominal bond starting after 20 years) | 35.6 | 20.6 | 312.8 | 110.1 | 74.4 | 43.8 | 30.6 | 21.6 | 13.6 | 9.9 | 4.4 |
| Life cycle 2 (90–10 to 50–50 MSCI Chile nominal bond starting immediately) | 41.2 | 36.3 | 1138.6 | 180.6 | 105.2 | 50.4 | 31.0 | 19.5 | 10.6 | 7.1 | 2.6 |
| Life cycle 2 (90–10 to 50–50 MSCI World nominal bond starting immediately) | 35.5 | 19.9 | 336.6 | 106.4 | 73.0 | 43.5 | 30.7 | 22.0 | 14.1 | 10.4 | 4.6 |
| Final income (monthly) | 107,500 | 0 | 107,500 | 107,500 | 107,500 | 107,500 | 107,500 | 107,500 | 107,500 | 107,500 | 107,500 |

*Source:* Author.

*Note:* ILB = inflation-linked bond; max. = maximum; min. = minimum; std. dev. = standard deviation.

Table 7.5  Simulation Results for Investment Strategies When Labor Income Is Stochastic and Uncorrelated with Stock Returns
(multiple of expected income in final year)

| | Mean | Std.dev. | Max. | 99% | 95% | 75% | 50% | 25% | 5% | 1% | Min. |
|---|---|---|---|---|---|---|---|---|---|---|---|
| **a. Inflation-Indexed Fixed-Income Portfolio** | | | | | | | | | | | |
| 100% ILB | 11.6 | 5.2 | 88.3 | 29.3 | 21.4 | 13.9 | 10.4 | 7.9 | 5.5 | 4.3 | 2.2 |
| 100% MSCI Chile | 79.0 | 135.1 | 5798.1 | 593.1 | 267.7 | 86.9 | 40.6 | 19.6 | 7.2 | 3.7 | 0.6 |
| 100% MSCI World no hedge | 58.6 | 61.5 | 1746.0 | 298.3 | 166.1 | 71.7 | 40.3 | 22.8 | 10.4 | 5.9 | 1.2 |
| 40% MSCI Chile, 60% ILB | 20.1 | 11.9 | 212.2 | 62.5 | 42.5 | 25.0 | 17.3 | 12.0 | 7.1 | 4.9 | 1.8 |
| 40% MSCI World no hedge, 60% ILB | 19.4 | 10.0 | 141.1 | 53.3 | 38.2 | 23.9 | 17.2 | 12.5 | 7.9 | 5.7 | 2.4 |
| Life cycle 1 (90–10 to 50–50 MSCI Chile ILB starting after 20 years) | 32.5 | 29.6 | 788.3 | 145.5 | 86.0 | 40.2 | 24.0 | 14.5 | 7.1 | 4.4 | 1.0 |
| Life cycle 1 (90–10 to 50–50 MSCI World ILB starting after 20 years) | 29.1 | 19.8 | 409.6 | 100.3 | 66.5 | 36.4 | 24.1 | 15.9 | 8.8 | 5.9 | 2.0 |
| Life cycle 2 (90–10 to 50–50 MSCI Chile ILB starting immediately) | 32.3 | 27.9 | 685.8 | 139.0 | 83.3 | 40.1 | 24.4 | 15.1 | 7.5 | 4.8 | 1.2 |
| Life cycle 2 (90–10 to 50–50 MSCI World ILB starting immediately) | 28.9 | 18.7 | 330.4 | 95.6 | 64.3 | 36.1 | 24.2 | 16.3 | 9.3 | 6.2 | 2.3 |
| Final income (monthly) | 140,260 | 117,068 | 2,840,192 | 585,203 | 356,569 | 176,660 | 107,320 | 65,781 | 32,555 | 19,895 | 3,730 |

## b. Nominal Fixed-Income Portfolio

| | | | | | | | | | | | |
|---|---|---|---|---|---|---|---|---|---|---|---|
| 100% nominal bond | 13.6 | 8.7 | 166.6 | 44.8 | 30.0 | 17.0 | 11.4 | 7.7 | 4.4 | 3.0 | 1.0 |
| 40% MSCI Chile, 60% nominal bond | 22.4 | 16.4 | 341.7 | 83.0 | 53.1 | 28.0 | 18.1 | 11.7 | 6.3 | 4.1 | 1.1 |
| 40% MSCI World no hedge, 60% nominal bond | 21.0 | 12.5 | 240.1 | 65.0 | 44.5 | 26.1 | 18.0 | 12.5 | 7.3 | 5.1 | 2.0 |
| Life cycle 1 (90–10 to 50–50 MSCI Chile nominal bond starting after 20 years) | 34.9 | 34.9 | 951.9 | 169.4 | 96.7 | 42.8 | 24.7 | 14.4 | 6.8 | 4.0 | 0.9 |
| Life cycle 1 (90–10 to 50–50 MSCI World nominal bond starting after 20 years) | 30.3 | 21.5 | 495.0 | 109.5 | 70.7 | 37.8 | 24.6 | 16.0 | 8.7 | 5.7 | 1.8 |
| Life cycle 2 (90–10 to 50–50 MSCI Chile nominal bond starting immediately) | 34.8 | 33.5 | 902.1 | 164.0 | 94.3 | 42.8 | 25.1 | 14.9 | 7.1 | 4.3 | 1.0 |
| Life cycle 2 (90–10 to 50–50 MSCI World nominal bond starting immediately) | 30.1 | 20.6 | 484.5 | 105.1 | 69.2 | 37.6 | 24.7 | 16.3 | 9.0 | 6.0 | 1.9 |
| Final income (monthly) | 140,260 | 117,068 | 2,840,192 | 585,203 | 356,569 | 176,660 | 107,320 | 65,781 | 32,555 | 19,895 | 3,730 |

Source: Author.

Note: ILB = inflation-linked bond; max. = maximum; min. = minimum; std. dev. = standard deviation.

**Table 7.6  Simulation Results for Investment Strategies When Labor Income Is Stochastic and Correlated with Stock Returns**
*(multiple of expected income in final year)*

| | Mean | Std. dev. | Max. | 99% | 95% | 75% | 50% | 25% | 5% | 1% | Min. |
|---|---|---|---|---|---|---|---|---|---|---|---|
| **a. Inflation-Indexed Fixed-Income Portfolio** | | | | | | | | | | | |
| 100% ILB | 11.5 | 5.2 | 83.4 | 29.1 | 21.3 | 13.9 | 10.4 | 7.9 | 5.5 | 4.3 | 2.1 |
| 100% MSCI Chile | 79.0 | 144.6 | 7654.6 | 625.1 | 275.9 | 85.5 | 38.4 | 17.7 | 5.9 | 2.9 | 0.4 |
| 100% MSCI World no hedge | 58.5 | 61.4 | 1960.5 | 298.8 | 165.9 | 71.7 | 40.4 | 22.8 | 10.4 | 6.0 | 1.2 |
| 40% MSCI Chile, 60% ILB | 20.1 | 13.1 | 280.5 | 67.6 | 44.9 | 25.1 | 16.8 | 11.2 | 6.3 | 4.2 | 1.4 |
| 40% MSCI World no hedge, 60% ILB | 19.4 | 9.9 | 169.6 | 53.6 | 37.9 | 23.9 | 17.2 | 12.5 | 7.9 | 5.8 | 2.5 |
| Life cycle 1 (90–10 to 50–50 MSCI Chile ILB starting after 20 years) | 32.5 | 32.0 | 1001.2 | 156.5 | 89.9 | 40.1 | 23.1 | 13.4 | 6.1 | 3.6 | 0.8 |
| Life cycle 1 (90–10 to 50–50 MSCI World ILB starting after 20 years) | 29.1 | 19.7 | 464.4 | 99.6 | 66.2 | 36.3 | 24.0 | 15.9 | 8.9 | 5.9 | 2.0 |
| Life cycle 2 (90–10 to 50–50 MSCI Chile ILB starting immediately) | 32.3 | 30.9 | 979.9 | 153.2 | 88.0 | 39.9 | 23.3 | 13.7 | 6.3 | 3.8 | 0.9 |
| Life cycle 2 (90–10 to 50–50 MSCI World ILB starting immediately) | 28.9 | 18.6 | 374.7 | 94.8 | 64.0 | 36.1 | 24.2 | 16.3 | 9.3 | 6.2 | 2.0 |
| Final income (monthly) | 139,992 | 116,443 | 2,451,932 | 575,713 | 355,055 | 176,025 | 107,368 | 66,123 | 32,499 | 19,801 | 4,124 |

## b. Nominal Fixed-Income Portfolio

| | | | | | | | | | | | |
|---|---|---|---|---|---|---|---|---|---|---|---|
| 100% nominal bond | 13.6 | 8.7 | 163.6 | 44.6 | 30.0 | 16.9 | 11.4 | 7.7 | 4.4 | 3.0 | 0.7 |
| 40% MSCI Chile, 60% nominal bond | 22.4 | 17.6 | 376.1 | 88.2 | 55.1 | 28.1 | 17.7 | 11.1 | 5.7 | 3.6 | 0.9 |
| 40% MSCI World no hedge, 60% nominal bond | 20.9 | 12.4 | 217.2 | 64.9 | 44.2 | 26.0 | 18.0 | 12.4 | 7.4 | 5.1 | 1.8 |
| Life cycle 1 (90–10 to 50–50 MSCI Chile nominal bond starting after 20 years) | 34.9 | 37.4 | 1143.1 | 181.7 | 100.2 | 42.7 | 23.8 | 13.4 | 5.9 | 3.3 | 0.7 |
| Life cycle 1 (90–10 to 50–50 MSCI World nominal bond starting after 20 years) | 30.2 | 21.5 | 572.1 | 109.4 | 70.3 | 37.9 | 24.6 | 16.1 | 8.7 | 5.7 | 1.9 |
| Life cycle 2 (90–10 to 50–50 MSCI Chile nominal bond starting immediately) | 34.7 | 36.6 | 1214.9 | 178.1 | 98.9 | 42.5 | 24.0 | 13.6 | 6.0 | 3.5 | 0.7 |
| Life cycle 2 (90–10 to 50–50 MSCI World nominal bond starting immediately) | 30.0 | 20.5 | 462.7 | 104.7 | 68.4 | 37.6 | 24.7 | 16.4 | 9.0 | 6.0 | 1.9 |
| Final income (monthly) | 139,992 | 116,443 | 2,451,932 | 575,713 | 355,055 | 176,025 | 107,368 | 66,123 | 32,499 | 19,801 | 4,124 |

*Source:* Author.

*Note:* ILB = inflation-linked bond; max. = maximum; min. = minimum; std. dev. = standard deviation.

bonds are subject to inflation risk, which in developing economies can be significant. Episodes of large unexpected inflation may result in very low or even negative realized returns on nominal bonds. For example, as has already been noted, in the case of Chile, nominal instruments with maturities of more than one year have delivered average negative returns during most periods in the last 30 years.

All other strategies under consideration include investments in stocks, either the domestic stock market or the unhedged world stock market. In general, every strategy involving the domestic stock market results in an average asset accumulation that is larger than the twin strategy that replaces the domestic stock market component of the strategy with the unhedged world stock market portfolio.

However, this comes at a significant cost in terms of higher volatility. The increase in volatility is particularly significant in the case in which labor income is positively correlated with the domestic stock market, which arguably is the most plausible characterization of labor income uncertainty in developing economies. This essentially models the case in which deterioration in local macroeconomic conditions leads to both a fall in domestic stock market valuations and a fall in individual labor earnings. This results in both lower returns and lower contributions, which together have an important negative compounding effect on asset accumulation.

The third and fourth rows of table 7.3 help illustrate the impact of international diversification on asset accumulation. These two rows report the outcomes of investment funds fully invested in either the domestic stock market or the unhedged world market portfolio. A strategy fully invested in the domestic stock market results in the largest average asset accumulation of all strategies under consideration at 79 times the expected final salary in the case of stochastic labor income. Of course, this higher mean asset accumulation is a direct effect of the assumption that the domestic stock market has the largest expected return of all four asset classes. The fund that is 100 percent invested in the world stock market portfolio also produces a large average asset accumulation at 58.5 times expected final salary.

However, the strategy of investing in the domestic stock market comes at the cost of a very high dispersion in outcomes. The standard deviation of asset accumulation at retirement is almost 145 times the expected final salary with correlated labor income. By contrast, by investing instead in an internationally diversified portfolio of equities, plan participants can reduce the volatility of asset accumulation at retirement more than 55 percent (61.5 times versus 145 times), while still achieving significant average asset accumulation.

Interestingly, the benefits of international diversification are most apparent in lifestyle and in life-cycle funds, where equity portfolios are combined with fixed-income portfolios. In those funds replacing domestic equities with the unhedged world stock market portfolio leads to a significant reduction in the volatility of asset accumulation (about 30 percent), with a proportionally much smaller reduction in expected asset accumulation.

The rows in the bottom half of table 7.3 allow for a comparison of lifestyle funds and life-cycle funds from the perspective of asset accumulation at retirement. Both types of funds provide plan participants with a vast reduction in the volatility of assets at retirement relative to the pure equity strategies, while providing plan participants with substantial expected assets relative to their expected final salary. Life-cycle funds provide plan participants with higher expected assets at retirement, and thus with the possibility of having higher replacement ratios for their earnings once they retire. However, they do so at the cost of increased dispersion of the possible outcomes. Note, however, that the higher volatility and higher expected asset accumulation of life-cycle funds relative to lifestyle funds is driven to a large extent by the specific portfolio mix and glide paths for these funds considered in the simulations. At 40 percent, the equity allocation of the lifestyle funds is more conservative than the average equity allocation of the life-cycle funds, which starts at 90 percent and converges to 50 percent in the final year before retirement.

Interestingly, table 7.3 shows that whether the life-cycle fund starts deinvesting in equities uniformly from the first year of contributions or after 20 years does not appear to make a significant difference in the distribution of assets accumulated at retirement.

Portfolio optimization considerations of the sort explained earlier strongly favor the adoption of life-cycle funds for DC plan participants. This section illustrates through simulation that these funds do not perform worse and in most cases perform better than other plausible alternatives in terms of the expected asset accumulation at retirement that they can provide and the volatility associated with this outcome. This is particularly true when they are properly structured with inflation-indexed bonds and an internationally diversified equity portfolio.

In practice, policy makers need to consider which life-cycle structure is more appropriate for the population of participants in the fund. Gomes, Kotlikoff, and Viceira (2008) examine the welfare implications of adopting lifestyle funds and life-cycle funds in DC pension plans. They find that, controlling for risk tolerance, life-cycle funds dominate lifestyle funds in the sense that they are closest to the optimal portfolio strategy that a rational expected utility maximizing working investor would choose.

However, they also find that the optimal design of the glide path for life-cycle funds is sensitive to the risk tolerance of the individual. In particular, participants with very low risk tolerance experience significant welfare losses if they are forced to adopt life-cycle funds with the average high-equity allocations that are standard in the industry, which are optimal for participants with medium risk tolerance. For plan participants with low risk tolerance, life-cycle funds with allocations heavily tilted toward inflation-indexed bonds are optimal. Bodie and Treussard (2007) find similar results, although they focus only on the expected utility of wealth at retirement instead of expected lifetime utility.

## Concluding Remarks

Global competition and aging demographic trends are leading to the widespread adoption of DC plans as the most important vehicle for retirement savings in both developed and developing economies. However, the experience of how the members of these funds choose to save and invest through these plans has been mixed, particularly for those workers at the lower end of the distribution of education and income levels, where poor saving and investing choices appear to be common.

Mandatory participation with appropriately designed default investment options can go a long way to help DC plan participants improve expected asset accumulation at retirement, and consequently their ability to sustain consumption levels in retirement.

The emerging theory of long-term asset allocation provides guidance for the design of saving and investing vehicles that can help investors save for retirement and save themselves from their own "investing maladies" or psychological biases. In particular, it provides support for the adoption of age- and risk-based investing strategies as the basis for the construction of default investment options in DC plans. Simulations show that lifestyle funds and life-cycle funds help improve average asset accumulation at retirement relative to pure bond funds, while drastically reducing the dispersion of outcomes relative to pure stock funds.

The theory also provides strong support for tilting fixed-income allocations in DC plans toward inflation-indexed bonds, as well as equity allocations toward internationally diversified stock portfolios. Empirical research on the correlation of global stock markets and currencies shows that reserve currencies, such as the U.S. dollar, the euro, and the Swiss franc, tend to be negatively correlated with global stock markets, implying that exposures to those currencies in equity portfolios should not be hedged from a portfolio risk-minimizing perspective.

For individuals whose labor earnings are not too volatile and not highly correlated with stock returns, life-cycle funds are better default investment choices than lifestyle funds, money market funds, or pure stock funds. However, making a single life-cycle fund for each retirement horizon the only available choice will not be optimal if there is heterogeneity in the risk tolerance or in the human capital characteristics among plan participants. In particular, individuals with very low risk tolerance or highly uncertain labor earnings are likely to be better off with life-cycle funds that are heavily tilted toward inflation-indexed bonds. Thus, offering life-cycle funds that provide choices that vary by risk tolerance or specifically consider occupation-related risks of earnings volatility through a range of equity allocations could further enhance the welfare gains of implementing such an approach to the design of required investment options, default choices, and by extension the establishment of performance benchmarks for DC pension systems.

## References

Adler, Michael, and Bernard Dumas. 1983. "International Portfolio Choice and Corporation Finance: a Synthesis." *Journal of Finance* 38: 925–84.

Berstein, Solange, Guillermo Larraín, and Francisco Pino. 2006. "Chilean Pension Reform: Coverage Facts and Policy Alternatives." *Economía* 6: 227–79.

Bodie, Zvi, Robert Merton, and William Samuelson. 1992. "Labor Supply Flexibility and Portfolio Choice in a Life Cycle Model." *Journal of Economic Dynamics and Control* 16: 427–49.

Bodie, Zvi, and Jonathan Treussard. 2007. "Making Investment Choices as Simple as Possible, but Not Simpler." *Financial Analysts Journal* 63: 42–47.

Calvet, Laurent E., John Y. Campbell, and Paolo Sodini. 2007. "Down or Out: Assessing the Welfare Costs of Household Investment Mistakes." *Journal of Political Economy* 115: 707–47.

———. 2009. "Measuring the Financial Sophistication of Households." *American Economic Review: Papers and Proceedings* 99: 393–98.

Campbell, John Y. 2006. "Household Finance." *Journal of Finance* 61: 1553–1604.

Campbell, John Y., Karine Serfaty-de Medeiros, and Luis M. Viceira. 2010. "Global Currency Hedging." *Journal of Finance* forthcoming.

Campbell, John Y., Adi Sunderam, and Luis M. Viceira. 2009. "Inflation Bets or Deflation Hedges? The Changing Risks of Nominal Bonds." NBER Working Paper 14701, National Bureau of Economic Research, Cambridge, MA.

Campbell, John Y., and Luis M. Viceira. 1999. "Consumption and Portfolio Decisions When Expected Returns Are Time Varying." *Quarterly Journal of Economics* 114: 433–95.

———. 2001. "Who Should Buy Long-Term Bonds?" *American Economic Review* 91: 99–127.

———. 2002. *Strategic Asset Allocation: Portfolio Choice for Long-Term Investors.* Oxford: Oxford University Press.

———. 2005. "The Term Structure of the Risk-Return Tradeoff." *Financial Analysts Journal* 61: 34–44.

Campbell, John Y., Luis M. Viceira, and Joshua White. 2003. "Foreign Currency for Long-Term Investors." *Economic Journal* 113: C1–C25.

Carroll, Christopher. 1997. "Buffer Stock Saving and the Life Cycle/Permanent Income Hypothesis." *Quarterly Journal of Economics* 112: 3–55.

Cocco, Joao F., Francisco J. Gomes, and Pascal J. Maenhout. 2005. "Consumption and Portfolio Choice over the Life Cycle." *Review of Financial Studies* 18: 491–533.

Dimson, Elroy, Paul Marsh, and Mike Staunton. 2002. *Triumph of the Optimists: 101 Years of Global Investment Returns.* Princeton, NJ: Princeton University Press.

French, Eric. 2005. "The Effects of Health, Wealth, and Wages on Labor Supply and Retirement Behaviour." *Review of Economic Studies* 72: 395–427.

French, Kenneth R., and James M. Poterba. 1991. "Investor Diversification and International Equity Markets." *American Economic Review* 81: 222–26.

Goetzmann, William N., Lingfeng Li, and K. Geert Rouwenhorst. 2004. "Long-Term Global Market Correlations." Yale ICF Working Paper No. 08–04, Yale University, New Haven, CT.

Gomes, Francisco J., Laurence J. Kotlikoff, and Luis M. Viceira. 2008. "Optimal Life-Cycle Investing with Flexible Labor Supply: A Welfare Analysis of Life-Cycle Funds." *American Economic Review: Papers and Proceedings* 98: 297–303.

Gourinchas, Pierre-Olivier, and Jonathan Parker. 2002. "Consumption over the Life Cycle." *Econometrica* 70: 47–89.

Hubbard, Glenn, Jonathan Skinner, and Stephen Zeldes. 1995. "Precautionary Saving and Social Insurance." *Journal of Political Economy* 103: 360–99.

Low, Hamish W. 2005. "Self-Insurance in a Life-Cycle Model of Labour Supply and Savings." *Review of Economic Dynamics* 8: 945–75.

Mottola, G., and S. Utkus. 2009. "Red, Yellow, and Green: Measuring the Quality of 401(k) Portfolio Choices." In *Overcoming the Saving Slump: How to Increase the Effectiveness of Financial Education and Saving Programs*, ed. Annamaria Lusardi, 119–39. Chicago: University of Chicago Press.

Munell, Alicia H., and Anika Sundén. 2006. "401(k) Plans Are Still Coming Short." Issue in Brief no. 43, Center for Retirement Research, Boston College, Chestnut Hill, MA.

Perold, André F., and Evan C. Schulman. 1988. "The Free Lunch in Currency Hedging: Implications for Investment Policy and Performance Standards." *Financial Analysts Journal* 44: 45–50.

Poterba, James, Joshua Rauh, Steven Venti, and David Wise. 2005. "Utility Evaluation of Risk in Retirement Savings Accounts." In *Analyses in the Economics of Aging*, ed. David A. Wise, 13–52. Chicago: University of Chicago Press.

———. 2009. "Lifecycle Asset Allocation Strategies and the Distribution of 401(k) Retirement Wealth." In *Developments in the Economics of Aging*, ed. David A. Wise, 15–50. Chicago: University of Chicago Press.

Solnik, Bruno H. 1974. "An Equilibrium Model of the International Capital Market." *Journal of Economic Theory* 8: 500–24.

Thaler, Richard H., and Shlomo Bernartzi. 2004. "Save More Tomorrow: Using Behavorial Economics to Increase Employee Savings." *Journal of Political Economy* 112: S164–87.

Viceira, Luis M. 2001. "Optimal Portfolio Choice for Long-Horizon Investors with Nontradable Labor Income." *Journal of Finance* 56: 433–70.

———. 2007a. "The U.S. Retirement Savings Market and the Pension Protection Act of 2006." HBS Note no. 207-130. Boston: Harvard Business School Publishing.

———. 2007b. "Vanguard Group, Inc., in 2006 and Target Retirement Funds." HBS Case no. 207-129. Boston: Harvard Business School Publishing.

———. 2009. "Life-Cycle Funds." In *Overcoming the Saving Slump*, ed. Annamaria Lusardi, 140–177. Chicago: University of Chicago Press.

Walker, Eduardo. 2008. "Strategic Currency Hedging and Global Portfolio Investments Upside Down." *Journal of Business Research* 61: 657–68.

# CHAPTER 8

# Future Directions in Measuring the Financial Performance of Pension Funds: A Roundtable Discussion

## Commentary by Keith Ambachtsheer[*]

The financial performance of pension systems is to a large extent determined by more fundamental issues of system design and operational efficiency. Before delving into the finer points of measurement metrics and the effects of the recent financial crisis, it is therefore useful to consider these more basic questions.

### What Are the Key Challenges?

The design and implementation of "good" retirement income systems enhances economic welfare in countries at all levels of development. The designation of "good" requires achieving high scores on four criteria: (1) population/workforce coverage, (2) income replacement adequacy, (3) intra- and intergenerational fairness, and (4) system efficiency. Performance metrics can be developed for each of these four major criteria. The first three relate to the effectiveness of pension accumulation design, and the fourth to the effectiveness of institutional implementation design.

The main focus of the chapters in this volume is on the fourth criterion: measuring system efficiency. In a broad sense, this is the question of the conversion ratio of units of input (that is, retirement savings) into units of output (that is, pension payments). This overall system efficiency metric is driven by four factors: (1) the long-term risk-free real interest rate (Rrf), (2) the gross risk premium (RP) on risky investments less the cost of passive implementation, (3) the gross value-added (VA) from active management less the cost of active implementation, and (4) the cost of benefit administration. On an economywide basis, the net value-added of active management should be zero (even negative), unless pension funds are systematically extracting wealth from other market participants, or if they are actively engaged in the wealth-creation process (for example, infrastructure or private equity). In general equation form we can write

$$\text{Pension System Efficiency} = F\{Rrf, (RP - ImplCost), (VA - ImplCost), BenAdmCost\},$$

where ImplCost is the implementation cost and BenAdmCost is the benefit administration cost.

---

[*] Director of the Rotman International Center for Pension Management, Rotman School of Management, University of Toronto.

## Status Assessment on the Pension Design Question

Regarding *pension design*, we are now moving toward a global consensus on what pension arrangements should generally look like. Why? Because there is broad agreement that we have an operationally useful theory on which this can be based. In fact, we have two related theories: (1) the life-cycle theory of personal finance and (2) behavioral finance theory. The former deduces rational savings and investment behavior from the goal of optimizing lifetime consumption subject to a level of risk tolerance. The latter catalogs actual, not-so-rational, savings and investment behavior based on clinical studies. These two theories are driving pension design in the direction of target benefit models with clear property rights, efficient risk pooling, and informed defaults (for example, related to auto-enrollment, contribution rates, age-based investment policy, and annuitization). An important benefit of this emerging consensus is that we can finally cease the nonproductive defined benefit (DB) versus defined contribution (DC) debates. Good pension design contains elements of both.

The three chapters by Mitchell and Turner; Bagliano, Fugazza, and Nicodano; and Viceira support this viewpoint using the lifecycle model as the framework within which to conduct their analyses.

## Status Assessment on the Institutional Implementation Question

Regarding *institutional implementation*, we are also moving toward a consensus as to what optimal institutional arrangements look like, although that consensus is currently still narrow and needs to become more broadly based. An operationally useful theory has evolved here as well. Integrative investment theory (IIT) posits the following:

$$\text{Stakeholder Value} = F\{A, G, IB, R, S\}.$$

The five drivers of stakeholder value are the following

A = Agency costs: for example, implementation costs can be higher than required for the purpose in the form of unnecessary third-party fees and commissions of various sorts

G = Governance quality: for example, better-managed funds should outperform poorly managed funds

IB = Investment beliefs: for example, funds with well-thought-out views on how capital markets function and where they may have comparative advantages should outperform those without such views

R = Risk management: for example, providing the right context/framing, which would be different for a collective DB arrangement than for a target benefit arrangement with individual pension accounts and a collective annuity balance sheet

S = Scale: for example, there are significant scale economies in both the investment and benefit administration functions.

IIT hypothesizes that large funds that are managed on an arm's length basis, with good governance, sensible investment beliefs, and sound risk management practices, will generate greater stakeholder value than funds that do not have these characteristics. Empirical research findings are consistent with this hypothesis.[1]

The efforts to use available pension fund gross returns to assess fund performance across a number of countries with privately managed pension funds presented in the chapters by Antolín and Tapia and Walker and Iglesias are based on the standard metrics of gross returns and standard deviation, which are then used to derive initial Sharpe ratios. These appear to indicate that over the periods measured, most fund Sharpe ratios (gross) were positive when the risk-free rate proxy was based on short-term interest rates. The authors of both papers warn that these findings should be treated with caution because of data quality and availability limitations. Chapter 4 on fund management by Castañeda and Rudolph focuses on the behavior of fund managers in competitive situations. Its major message is that any legal structure that is not arm's length, and lacks alignment of economic interests with plan participants, is likely to incur material agency costs.

## Future Directions

The efficiency and value creation assessment framework sketched out above points to the directions that pension fund performance measurement must take if it is to eventually provide operationally useful information and knowledge for policy makers and pension plan or fund trustees and managers,

The *Pension System Efficiency* equation recognizes the separate functional activities of investment management and benefit administration, as well as the importance of capturing the costs associated with each activity. Within the investment function, it points to the need to capture the performance of the risk-minimizing strategy, as defined by the financial characteristics of future streams of pension payments. Relative to this risk-minimizing strategy are two sources of potential excess returns: (1) undertaking systematic mismatch risk and (2) undertaking idiosyncratic mismatch risk. Ideally, the necessary data to calculate the related metrics are captured at the individual pension plan or fund level, and the net payoffs from both types of mismatched risk exposures are measured regularly over time.

The *Stakeholder Value* equation requires that value creation be defined in a measurable manner. For example, it could be defined as the risk-adjusted net return from undertaking idiosyncratic (that is, active) mismatch risk. If fund data are regularly captured as described above, such a metric can be calculated. This performance measurement specification structure for pension plans or funds has been accepted as representing "best practice" for quite some time. Data availability has been the barrier to implementation, but as noted below, this barrier is now being overcome.

## A "To Do" List for Researchers

Given these status assessments of the pension design and institutional implementation questions, where should research activities go from here? Below are some suggestions.

*Pension Design:* The chapters in this volume identify several promising directions, largely focusing on how to further adapt the life-cycle model so that it becomes an operationally useful guide to building better pension systems. The need to deal more creatively with the decumulation phase of the life cycle underlies much of this analysis. Somehow a post–work life annuity element must be engineered into the design of smart decision defaults. Another default element discussed is age-based investment risk exposure. Although it is intuitively obvious that young workers can place their early retirement savings "at risk," it is less obvious that a 65-year-old might still have 60 percent equity exposure, as some of the model simulations appear to suggest. It would seem that either the return distributions used in the simulations, or the risk tolerance of a 65-year-old is misspecified, or possibly both.

*Institutional Implementation:* A critical element here is the creation and availability of micro- (that is, at the individual plan or fund level) databases that permit research to be conducted along the lines set out above. The only databases of which this author is aware that contain the necessary degree of detail are those maintained by CEM Benchmarking Inc. Pension industry associations, such as the VB in the Netherlands and Committee on the Investment of Employee Benefit Assets (CIEBA) in the United States, have contracted with CEM to provide performance analytics for their entire memberships. Academic researchers, such as Ken French with Dartmouth College (United States), Rob Bauer with Maastricht University (the Netherlands), and Kees Koedijk with the University of Tilburg (the Netherlands), have completed or are in the process of performing extensive studies on pension fund performance using the CEM databases.[2]

## A "To Do" List for Policy Makers, Policy Advisers, and Policy Implementers

Moving pension reform agendas forward around the world requires the combination of good theory, good information and knowledge, and the political will to move ahead. Countries such as Australia and the Netherlands place a high priority on optimal pension system design and efficient institutional implementation. Australia actually has a cabinet position titled Minister of Pensions. Countries that make such conscious, proactive pension priority decisions will continue to lead the world in innovation in retirement income systems. The question is whether, and at what rate, other developed and developing countries will follow.

## How Does the Financial Crisis Influence Our Thinking?

Let's start with a thought experiment. Consider a world where everything we know about good pension system design and implementation was implemented many decades ago. Now superimpose the current financial crisis on this hypothetical world. What has happened? Younger workers will have lost money in their personal pension accounts but have many years of retirement saving ahead of them. They now have the opportunity of investing those savings in risky assets at significantly lower prices and higher expected returns. Older workers and retirees have most of their retirement wealth in the form of safe current and deferred annuities and are thus largely sheltered from the current financial markets turbulence. Large, arm's length, expert pension institutions managing the financial affairs of these younger and older workers, as well as retirees, communicate regularly and effectively with their constituents as the financial crisis plays out, and eventually ends.

Contrast this benign, but unfortunately hypothetical, world with current realities. The most obvious shortcoming of all is the continued lack of widespread pension coverage. Many of the DC arrangements that do exist are high cost, rather than low cost. Further, these arrangements do not have well-engineered decumulation "back ends" with significant annuitization components. As a result, many older workers and even retirees have suffered significant reductions in their accumulated retirement savings. They have limited prospects for recovery, and no trusted institutions that they can turn to for advice.

So a painful lesson that current reality teaches is that good pension design and implementation matter. Well-designed and managed retirement income systems can alleviate much financial pain in times of financial crisis. Thus building such systems should be assigned a high priority.

## Notes

1. See Ambachtsheer (2005, 2007), Ambachtsheer and Bauer (2007), Ambachtsheer, Capelle, and Lum (2008), Bauer and others (2007), Bauer and Kicken (2008), Bogle (2008), Fear and Pace (2008), and Sy (2008) for further IIT elaborations and empirical confirmations. The Discussion Forums and Research Funding Program of the Rotman International Centre for Pension Management are built around this IIT framework. See www.rotman.utoronto .ca/icpm for more.

2. I am willing to facilitate controlled access to the CEM databases to other qualified researchers and possibly involve CEM in the creation of new databases. CEM Benchmarking Inc. was founded in 1991 by Keith Ambachtsheer and John McLaughlin. Both continue to be associated with CEM co-owners and board members. See www.cembenchmarking.com for more information. CEM currently has 340 funds participating in its DB investments database, 155 funds in its DC investments database, and 124 funds in its pension administration database. Participant organizations are based in Europe, North America, and the Pacific Rim. See www.cembenchmarking.com for more information.

## References

Ambachtsheer, K. 2005. "Beyond Portfolio Theory: The Next Frontier." *Financial Analysts Journal* 61 (1): 29–33.

———. 2007. *Pension Revolution: A Solution to the Pensions Crisis.* New York: Wiley.

Ambachtsheer, K., and R. Bauer. 2007. "Losing Ground: Do Canadian Mutual Funds Produce Fair Value for Their Customers?" *Canadian Investment Review* 20 (1) (spring): 8–14.

Ambachtsheer, K., R. Capelle, and H. Lum. 2008. "The Pension Governance Deficit: Still with Us." *Rotman International Journal of Pension Management* 1 (1) (Fall): 14–21. www.rotman.utoronto.ca/icpm. Available at doi:10.3138/rijpm.1.1.14.

Bauer, R., and R. Frehen, H. Lum, and R. Otten. 2007. "The Performance of U.S. Pension Funds: New Insights into the Agency Costs Debate." ICPM Working Paper, April. www.rotman.utoronto.ca/ipcm.

Bauer, R., and L. Kicken. 2008. "The Pension Fund Advantage: Are Canadians Overpaying Their Mutual Funds?" *Rotman International Journal of Pension Management* 1 (1) (Fall): 64–71. www.rotman.utoronto.ca/icpm. Available at doi:10:3138/rijpm.1.1.64.

Bogle, J. 2008. "Bringing Mutuality to Mutual Funds." *Rotman International Journal of Pension Management* 1 (1) (Fall): 54–63. www.rotman.utoronto.ca/icpm. Available at doi:10:3138/rijpm.1.1.54.

Fear, J., and G. Pace. 2009. "Australia's 'Choice of Fund' Legislation: Success or Failure?" *Rotman International Journal of Pension Management* 2 (2) (Fall): 26–34. www.rotman.utoronto.ca/icpm. Available at doi: 10.3138/rijpm.2.2.26.

Sy, W. 2008. "Pension Governance in Australia: An Anatomy and an Interpretation." *Rotman International Journal of Pension Management* 1 (1) (Fall): 30–37. www .rotman.utoronto.ca/icpm. Available at doi:10:3138/rijpm.1.1.30.

# Commentary by Olivia Mitchell[*]

The question that motivates the research in this volume is how policy makers might seek to evaluate the performance of funded pensions, particularly in light of the recent financial market turmoil that poses deep challenges for those charged with managing retirement systems. There are two goals that most economists believe are appropriate and proper for a pension system: consumption smoothing over the lifetime and delivery of adequate of resources in retirement. Pension systems should therefore be judged by more clearly defined and measured pay-out benchmarks if policy makers are to judge sensibly when and why a retirement system will succeed or fail.

## Pension System Goals

Generally speaking, a retirement program can be judged by how well it helps workers achieve retirement security. In the case of a funded pension, this will require workers to defer consumption via saving to invest and reap the rewards of a future payout in old age. One part of this is to manage risks and generate strong investment earnings on the assets. Recent work on behavioral economics and finance has had a worldwide beneficial impact by influencing pension systems to move toward automatic enrollment and default investments that utilize target date maturity funds, as well as increasing efforts to encourage the conversion of account balances to lifetime annuities to pool longevity risk.[1] As a result, along many dimensions, retirement systems are becoming more resilient to political and economic shocks than in the past (Mitchell 2000, 2004).

Many people would also agree that an equally critical component of the task is to help the retiree protect against longevity risk and insure against indigence in old age. However, this requires the policy maker to stipulate and measure the performance criteria against which outcomes will be judged. In the case of the consumption smoothing goal, a pension system would be deemed successful if it paid higher benefits to those experiencing economic or health shocks—providing an insurance function transferring resources from the rich to the poor. Yet in many countries it is notoriously difficult to obtain consumption data to determine whether, in

[*] Director of the Pension Research Council, The Wharton School, University of Pennsylvania.

fact, consumption smoothing takes place before and after retirement. To the extent that one can assume that income and consumption are highly correlated, it will be sufficient to compare pre- and post-retirement income to see if they seem closely related. This has led policy makers to focus on replacement rate notions, to determine whether a pension benefit amounts to a relatively high fraction of income during the working life. As Meier and others (1980, p. 1) put it, a well-run pension system has as an "implicit or explicit goal—the maintenance of preretirement standards of living." The recent work of OECD (2007) and Whitehouse (2007) provide an excellent measurement of this replacement rate concept across several dozen nations.

The advantage of this approach is that it uses relatively easy to get data on stylized average (or low/high) income workers, and the methodology does not require detailed individual earnings histories or administrative records. Nevertheless, recent research has questioned the replacement ratio approach. One reason is that, in many developing nations, informal work is widespread, so people do not contribute to their pension programs, sometimes for many years. For example, in Chile many workers have extremely uneven patterns of attachment to the pension system (Berstein, Larraín, and Pinto 2005). Similar results have been found for the United States using administrative records (Mazumder 2001; Mitchell and Phillips 2006). As a consequence, projected replacement rates that assume a full lifetime of contributions will generate quite high projected benefits, which indeed are much higher than most people actually receive.

An even more profound critique of the replacement rate measure is that it does not actually measure consumption, even if this is the target outcome of interest. Aguiar and Hurst (2005) and Scholz, Seshadri, and Khitatrakun (2006) show both empirically and theoretically that retirees reduce their consumption substantially after leaving the workforce, often because of changes in household composition. Yet most replacement rate measures do not take this into account, which means that using replacement rate measures could substantially overstate retiree needs.

Instead of using replacement rate, an alternative (or additional) policy objective would be benefit adequacy.[2] From this perspective, a well-performing retirement system would be one that ensured that retirees had at least some minimum socially agreed on subsistence or poverty-line income level. This notion, however, is also subject to debate because it can be measured in many different ways. One concept might focus on what is needed to purchase a minimum food budget, consistent with the U.S. approach to defining poverty. A different one, used, for example, in Chile, sets a minimum pension amount as a percentage of the national minimum wage level. Other variants on this approach compare payouts to average economywide earnings. Despite controversy over exact measurements, most policy makers would concur that maintaining a minimum benefit amount is a necessary if not a sufficient condition for pension system success.

## Pension System Pillars

Inevitably the question arises as to whether funded pension systems can and should be asked to meet both benefit adequacy and the consumption smoothing goals. Indeed, in many influential World Bank projects that have been conducted over the past 20 years, it was often argued that multiple pillars or tiers could best meet these needs.

Thus the "safety net" objective would be served by an unfunded pay-as-you-go (PAYGO) tax-financed program, and the consumption smoothing need would be met by a funded earnings, insurance-type plan. It is interesting that both DB and DC plans can and often are both held to this standard: for instance, Chile's mandatory DC plan is often judged in terms of the replacement rate objective (Arenas de Mesa and others 2008). Naturally, having separate pillars also provides more transparency and more readily measured performance outcomes for each pillar.

## Impact of the Financial Crisis

The recent collapse of the global financial system has brought to light several deep concerns about pension performance that are likely to force a profound reassessment of what funded pensions are being asked to accomplish.

First, although many workers have amassed substantial pension accumulations over the past several decades, these accruals are not always as large as they should be. One explanation is that benefit accumulations have too often been eroded by investment fees and commissions, meaning that workers may arrive at the doorstep of retirement with much less savings than anticipated.[3] More attention must surely be paid to mechanisms to hold down administrative costs of funded pensions systems in the future.

A related reason for inadequate accruals is that workers in many nations suffer under the burden of substantial financial illiteracy,[4] which impairs their saving ability and detracts from sensible investment strategies. As an example, in the U.S. Health and Retirement Study, one finds that consumers in their mid-50s fail to correctly answer simple questions about compound interest calculations, inflation, and investment risk. Similarly, using the Chilean Encuesta de Proteccion Social, one finds that workers report pension contributions and accumulations inaccurately, do not know how much they pay in commissions, are unaware of the rules for minimum pensions, and cannot say how their funds are invested. This level of financial illiteracy is also concentrated among lower-educated and lower-paid workers, women, and minority groups. Inevitably, plan sponsors and policy makers must reassess their role in educating and advising pension participants, to better incentivize and protect pension savings.

A second consideration is that many funded pension systems have not focused enough attention on how benefits are paid out over the retirement period (Antolín 2009). That is to say, both DB and DC programs can and often do pay out lump sums rather than annuitizing the benefit payments, which then exposes the retiree (and his or her spouse) to longevity risk (the risk of running short of money in old age). Much more effort will have to be devoted to ensuring that pension programs actually deliver lifelong benefits if the systems are to be deemed successful at ensuring old-age retirement security. In an interesting policy development on this front, in Singapore the government has recently announced a minimum retirement subsistence level and required DC plan participants to save enough to pay themselves this minimum consumption level in retirement. Most relevant is the fact that the funded plan is being held to a minimum income standard, illustrating how DC programs are being asked to take on DB-type tasks.

Third, some retirement programs have recently been forced to greatly enhance their minimum benefit levels. For instance, Chile has recently instituted a large new publicly financed minimum benefit guarantee called the Pilar Solidario that does not require workers to have contributed to the program at all. This is a rather expensive means-tested PAYGO benefit estimated to cost an estimated 3 percent of gross domestic product. The issue that arises from this approach is that guaranteed benefits paid to those who fail to contribute to the program will boost adequacy but also increase the incentives for evasion of contribution requirements while working. Given the recent downturn in equity markets, it is likely that more governments will be pressed to enhance minimum benefits, which will both increase financing costs and undercut contribution and work incentives.

The fourth and perhaps most critical concern for pension managers in the future is how they can do a better job of risk management. This is a broad topic, but the financial crisis has revealed that pension plan managers have too often tended to ignore explicit or implicit benefit targets when making asset allocation choices. In turn, this has exposed participants to severe shortfalls. An alternative and better-informed approach would be to use simulation models to quantify the conditional Value-at-Risk of pension costs and determine the optimal contribution rate and portfolio asset allocation while controlling investment risk (for example, Maurer, Mitchell, and Rogalla 2008). The general point, of course, is that asset management should be done with liabilities in mind, even in the case of DC pension programs.

## Conclusions

Funded pension systems around the world have built a respectable track record along many dimensions and in many countries. Yet the financial market challenges of the recent past will require plan sponsors and policy makers to be far more explicit about the appropriate and affordable roles of the various components in a multipillar retirement system. This will require some difficult discussions of what is affordable in terms of subsistence benefits and how to manage the potentially negative incentives. Furthermore, such judgments on pension performance will clearly require far better data and models than we have had in the past. Information is needed to better model pension system liabilities—which require data on worker earnings and contribution histories as well as consumption patterns—with saving, investment, and capital market information. Only by advancing is these area can policy makers move beyond a narrow focus on pension investment to take into account the very important and much broader spectrum of pension performance outcomes.

## Notes

1. See, for instance, Mitchell and Utkus (2004).
2. This section draws on McGill et al. (2005) and Mitchell and Phillips (2006).
3. See, for instance, Bateman and Mitchell (2004); Mitchell (1998); and Koh et al. (forthcoming).
4. See, for instance, Lusardi and Mitchell (2007) in the United States and Arenas de Mesa et al. (2008) for Chile.

## References

Aguiar, Mark, and Erik Hurst. 2005. "Consumption versus Expenditure." *Journal of Political Economy* 113 (5): 919–48.

Antolín, Pablo. 2009. "Policy Options for the Payout Phase." Paper presented at the International Conference on Annuity Markets: Structure, Trends and Innovations, Institute of Economic Research, Hitotsubashi University Collaboration Centre, Tokyo, January.

Arenas de Mesa, Alberto, David Bravo, Jere R. Behrman, Olivia S. Mitchell, and Petra E. Todd. 2008. "The Chilean Pension Reform Turns 25: Lessons from the Social Protection Survey." In *Lessons from Pension Reform in the Americas,* ed. Stephen Kay and Tapen Sinha, 23–58. Oxford: Oxford University Press.

Bateman, H., and O. S. Mitchell. 2004. "New Evidence on Pension Plan Design and Administrative Expenses." *Journal of Pension Finance and Economics* 3 (1): 63–76. www.journals.cambridge.org. Available at doi:10.1017/ S1474747204001465.

Berstein, S., G. Larraín, and F. Pino. 2005. "Cobertura, Densidad y Pensiones en Chile: Proyecciones a 20 años plazo." SAFP Documento de Trabajo no. 12, Santiago, Chile.

Koh, B. S. K., O. S. Mitchell, and J. H. Y. Fong. 2008. "Cost Structures in Defined Contribution Systems: The Case of Singapore's Central Provident Fund." *Pensions: An International Journal* 13 (1–2): 7–14. www.palgrave-journals .com/pm. Available at doi:10.1057/pm.2008.3.

Lusardi, Annamaria, and Olivia S. Mitchell. 2007. "Baby Boomer Retirement Security: The Roles of Planning, Financial Literacy, and Housing Wealth." *Journal of Monetary Economics* 54 (1): 205–24.

Maurer, Raimond, Olivia S. Mitchell, and Ralph Rogalla. 2008. "The Victory of Hope over Angst? Funding, Asset Allocation, and Risk-Taking in German Public Sector Pension Reform." In *Frontiers in Pension Finance,* ed. Dirk Broeders, Sylvester Eijffinger, and Aerdt Houben, 51–81. Cheltenham, U.K.: Edward Elgar.

Mazumder, Bhashkar. 2001. "The Mismeasurement of Permanent Earnings: New Evidence from Social Security Earnings Data." Working Paper 2001-24, Federal Reserve Bank of Chicago.

McGill, Dan, Kyle N. Brown, John J. Haley, and Sylvester J. Schieber. 2005. *Fundamentals of Private Pensions.* 8th ed. Oxford: Oxford University Press.

Meier, E., C. Dittmar, and B. Torrey. 1980. "Retirement Income Goals." Report prepared for the President's Commission on Pension Policy, Washington, DC, March.

Mitchell, Olivia S. 1998. "Administrative Costs of Public and Private Pension Plans." In *Privatizing Social Security,* ed. M. Feldstein, 403–56. National Bureau of Economic Research. Chicago: University of Chicago Press.

————. 2000. "Building an Environment for Pension Reform in Developing Countries." In *Foundations of Pension Finance*, ed. Zvi Bodie and E. Phillip Davis, 480–503. London: Edward Elgar.

————. 2009. "New Directions for Pension System Performance Measurement." Presentation for International Association of Pension Fund Administrators (FIAP), Lima, Peru.

Mitchell, Olivia S., and John W. R. Phillips. 2006. "Social Security Replacement Rates for Alternative Earnings Benchmarks." *Benefits Quarterly* (fourth quarter): 37–47.

Mitchell, Olivia S., and S. P. Utkus. 2004. "Lessons from Behavioral Finance for Retirement Plan Design." In Olivia S. Mitchell and Stephen P. Utkus (eds.), *Pension Design and Structure: New Lessons from Behavioral Finance*. Oxford: Oxford University Press, pp. 3–41. www.oxfordscholarship.com. Available at doi:10.1093/0199273391.001.0001.

Organisation for Economic Co-operation and Development (OECD). 2007. *Pensions at a Glance: Public Policies across OECD Countries*. Paris: OECD.

Scholz, John Karl, Ananth Seshadri, and Surachai Khitatrakun. 2006. "Are Americans Saving 'Optimally' for Retirement?" *Journal of Political Economy* 114 (4): 607–43.

Whitehouse, Edward. 2007. *Pensions Panorama: Retirement Income Systems in 53 Countries*. Washington, DC: World Bank.

## Commentary by Luis Viceira[*]

The studies contained in this volume, in addition to the considerable volume of related work, make it clearly apparent that there is a need to develop far more appropriate benchmarks for measuring the performance of DC pension funds around the world.

Although preliminary and limited by the scope and the quality of the data, the initial studies comparing reported returns offer some interesting insights into the industrial organization and the design of pension fund systems. In particular, they suggest that introducing competition in privately managed pension systems may be beneficial for their performance. A distinctive aspect of pension fund regulation in many mandatory DC pension funds in developing economies is the existence of minimum return guarantees that typically punish asset managers whose performance falls below the medium performance of their peers by requiring that they make up for investment shortfalls out of their own capital. This provides incentives for herding behavior that might affect the efficiency of the system negatively, as pension managers become overly concerned about their performance relative to that of their peers, and might end up colluding in a single portfolio strategy that may not be optimal for pension plan participants.

Castañeda and Rudolph study the implications for portfolio choice of the existence of such minimum return guarantees by assuming that private portfolio managers with relative performance concerns will act strategically. They find that the more prone that portfolio managers are to relative performance concerns, the closer is the asset allocation of the whole pension system to the optimal growth portfolio, or the portfolio that maximizes the geometric mean return on assets. This suggests that pension fund regulators should consider carefully the adverse effects of minimum return guarantees on competition, performance, and efficiency.

Although the optimal growth portfolio maximizes asset accumulation, it does so by assuming a level of risk that might be excessive relative to the risk optimal for long-term risk-averse investors. The study by Viceira develops this point in more detail. Another important and related aspect of pension fund regulation has to do with costs. In many developing economies, pension fund managers are required to charge a one-time fee to plan participants for the ongoing investment and administrative

---

* The George E. Bates Professor, Harvard Business School, Harvard University.

services that they must provide as long as the participant remains in the plan. This creates incentives for plan participants to avoid switching managers, which, in turn, limits competition in the system, and for managers to charge hidden fees through, for example, excessive portfolio turnover or some other means.

Costs are one of the most important determinants of the long-run efficiency of a pension system. For example, a system that runs at an annual cost equivalent to 1 percent of assets—which is the fee typically charged by most active mutual funds—and has an expected return gross of costs of 7 percent will cost plan participants 39 percent of their assets over an investment horizon of 35 years. This investment horizon is typically the time a worker will participate in a plan contributing and accumulating assets. In other words, the gains from saving just 1 percent in annual costs can be enormous given the long horizons of DC pension plan participants.

An obvious way of achieving considerable cost reductions and improve long-run performance is to incentivize the use of indexed investment options in the style of the U.S. Federal Employees Retirement System DC individual account component known as the Thrift Savings Plan, which has an average investment management cost of just seven basis points, or 0.07 percent. Pension programs in the Netherlands are also well known for achieving considerable cost savings for their participants.

Unfortunately, there is very little transparency about the overall costs of running most pension systems or the total direct and indirect fees that they charge to participants and sponsors. It is therefore unclear whether the returns that pension funds report are gross of fees—or, as some would put it, "paper returns"—or net of fees—what plan participants effectively receive. Ideally, information on fees and costs should go beyond aggregate figures. A better understanding of the efficiency of pension fund systems could be achieved with more standardized and disaggregated information on different cost components—reporting these in well-defined categories such as pure investment management costs, administration costs, and marketing expenses.

The studies by Antolín and Tapia and Walker and Iglesias also note other potential important problems and biases with the existing data and capacity to measure the performance of pension systems around the world. Perhaps the most important concerns the aggregation of the performance of the privately managed pension funds operating in a given country to provide a system-wide national performance figure. This will require a more comprehensive approach to fees and common methodology to provide meaningful comparative information, and more work needs to be done on this front. Beyond consistent aggregation figures, however, it would be desirable to have a disaggregated database of individual pension fund returns free of survivorship bias. This would allow researchers to decide how to best aggregate results depending on the objective of the research they are conducting.

The exploratory empirical analyses of pension fund performance that use Sharpe ratios and attribution analysis (noting the inherent limitations of these methods) provide interesting evidence that many privately managed funds have produced an average risk premium against short-term investment alternatives. Of course, the results of this study should be interpreted with caution because the study is limited by data availability in its scope and in its ability to measure performance even using simple performance metrics.

Risk premia and Sharpe ratios computed using averages of simple returns are very noisy estimates of true risk premia and are extremely sensitive to the choice of sample period. For example, emerging markets have outperformed developed markets over most of the sample period available in the data. Given the bias built into most national pension system regulations in developing economies toward investing in their own domestic markets, one might conclude from these data that the best performing funds are those in developing economies that invest in their own domestic markets. Yet, as Viceira notes, this is precisely what pension systems in developing economies should perhaps try to avoid. With improved information about asset class composition of pension funds, one might improve on the measurement of these particular performance metrics by using the data to compute volatilities, correlations, and betas and replacing sample period averages of returns in each asset class with long-term averages or some other less noisy measure of risk premia.

Attribution analysis is an attempt to avoid this issue by computing the exposure of a given portfolio to traded portfolios that reflect fundamental sources of risk, and then finding how much value the portfolio has added relative to the average return that the investor would have obtained by investing in a passively managed portfolio with the same risk exposure. Interestingly, the attribution analysis in the studies suggests that privately managed pension funds appear to have added value over the sample period available, although perhaps the value-added is not economically significant.

The overall theme of the studies in this volume raises a more fundamental question: how to measure the performance of a pension system. Arguably, the goal of a performance metric is to measure performance of an investment strategy relative to a passive implementable benchmark that properly reflects the objective of the strategy. Therefore, a question that precedes how to measure performance is how to determine an appropriate benchmark that is aligned with the particular objectives and relevant risk parameters related to supporting consumption in retirement.

Measuring performance in a specific asset class is conceptually straight-forward. For example, if the goal is to measure the performance of an active portfolio manager in the large capitalization equity market space in the United States, one might want to compare the performance of a man-ager relative to that of a passive investment, through an index fund or exchange-traded fund on the Standard & Poor's 500 or some other index. If the manager uses tilts (such as growth or value, large capitalization, or small capitalization) or leverage, we can still measure relative perform-ance using attribution analysis.

However, measuring the performance of a DC-based pension system is much more complex. This problem is conceptually akin to measuring the performance of the overall portfolio of an investor or, rather, a group of investors: plan participants. Thus, measuring the performance of the sys-tem requires first understanding the objectives of the participants or at least defining the objectives that the regulator or policy maker wants to achieve for those participants.

Traditional portfolio theory—mean-variance analysis—which Harry Markowitz formulated about 50 years ago, shows investors how to allocate assets when there is no uncertainty about future investment opportunities and investors rely exclusively on traded wealth to finance their spending needs. This analysis shows that in the parsimonious world of constant risk and return, it is optimal for investors to act myopically, ignoring the long term. The resulting insights into optimal portfolio composition are rela-tively simple, yet of enormous value, particularly the principle of portfo-lio diversification to eliminate exposure to risk that is not rewarded.

In a world where interest rates, risk premia, and risk are all constant, and all wealth is tradable, investors should choose the asset allocation that max-imizes the Sharpe ratio of their portfolios. In this world, investment hori-zon is irrelevant. Cash (or short-term bonds) are riskless at all horizons, and all risky assets are equally risky at all horizons. Accordingly, investors should assume portfolio risk only if they can improve the expected return per unit of risk on their portfolios relative to what they can achieve with riskless investments in cash instruments. Thus the short-term interest rate, which by assumption is also the long-term interest rate, defines a good benchmark against which to measure performance, and the Sharpe ratio that utilizes this is a useful measure. Therefore, under the assumptions that constant investment opportunities and tradability of all wealth constitute a good approximation of reality, the Sharpe ratio provides a good benchmark to measure performance

However, as the study by Bagliano, Fugazza, and Nicodano as well as the study by Viceira emphasize, the assumptions that investment opportunities are constant and that all wealth is tradable do not constitute a good approximation of the reality of pension fund members. In particular, real interest rates and nominal interest rates vary systematically over time, making cash and nominal government bonds risky at long horizons. Also, long-term working investors, as nearly all pension plan participants are, have an important source of wealth—their human capital—which is nontradable and interacts in important ways with their financial assets (savings). Both studies emphasize that accounting for these factors has profound implications for personal investing over the life cycle. The study by Viceira explores in more detail the implications for the design of DC pension funds and more generally for financial products for individual investors.

For working investors with long-term spending plans and liabilities, expected future investment opportunities are as relevant as current investment opportunities for investment decisions. Integrating both current and future investment opportunities into a coherent investment plan requires careful modeling of investment opportunities, human capital characteristics, and investors spending plans. Both studies provide insights on how to conduct such modeling and on how to evaluate its performance.

These useful insights include how to define benchmarks against which to measure the performance of DC pension funds. Performance is perhaps best measured against a passive benchmark that reflects the life-cycle investment policy of a typical participant in the plan. One relatively straightforward way to implement such an approach would be to utilize a commission of independent experts to formulate benchmarks for specific groups of pension system members, differentiating them in terms of a relatively limited set of income, age, and occupational categories for which there are distinguishable differences in the correlations with the relevant asset categories. Within these categories a differentiation by risk tolerance might also be feasible and desirable.

Creating a set of such benchmarks would enable the regulator to measure performance of various funds against the individual benchmarks to provide meaningful performance information to members with varying characteristics. As individuals progress through their working lives they would transition through the benchmarks applicable to their individual circumstances. This, of course, would require an ongoing effort to collect data on the relevant characteristics of the population, as discussed in the Mitchell and Turner study. The study by Viceira and references therein provide guidance toward how to build that benchmark or a set of benchmarks.

A benchmark thus defined would define the risk exposures that are relevant to the fund, and its passive implementation would provide managers with a minimum performance that they might try to improve upon through active investment. Regulators could limit the level of "active bets" that managers could take in their effort to improve upon the performance of the benchmark by defining maximum tracking errors, just as institutional investors do with the active managers they hire. This would enable the pension system to remain within the overall risk level that is deemed appropriate.

Alternatively, the benchmark could be defined as the riskless alternative at the relevant investment horizon and the performance of the fund measured against the performance of such a benchmark. This could also be the relevant investment objective if the goal of the plan is to offer insurance in the spirit of traditional DB plans, or if the typical plan participant is deemed too risk averse to assume any risk in his portfolio. The study by Viceira emphasizes that in such a case the riskless alternative is a portfolio of inflation-indexed funds with a duration that properly reflects the investment horizon of the population of plan participants.

In summary, the work by Bagliano, Fugazza, and Nicodano, the work by Viceira, and the research summarized in these two studies suggest that there is probably ample room for improvement in pension fund design, particularly in developing economies. Their studies also provide important insights about how to define benchmarks against which to measure pension fund performance. This information provides a useful step forward and, it is hoped, will motivate further developments in an area of obvious importance around the world.

# Commentary by Zvi Bodie*

A country's pension system is the set of formal institutions that provide income to the elderly. The most important social objective in their design is to ensure that everyone has sufficient resources to maintain an acceptable standard of living after they can no longer work. Beyond that is the question of how to sustain standards of living and economic security as the population as a whole ages. Among the many complicating factors is the reality that people often lack the knowledge or self-discipline to act rationally in their own best interest. People routinely make errors in judgment, and even when they know what they ought to do, they often fail to do it.

The natural point of departure for the study of pension plan design and performance measurement is the theory of optimal decisions regarding saving, investing, and risk management over a consumer's lifetime. The economic principle that underlies the theory of consumer choice over the life cycle is that consumers should manage their human capital and financial wealth to achieve the most satisfying standard of living under all possible contingencies. This principle, for risk-averse individuals, is called consumption smoothing.

An ideal pension system from an individual point of view allows households to achieve their desired consumption pattern throughout retirement. Such a plan must deliver the necessary resources for that purpose at retirement time under all contingencies that might arise. It must also specify the financial transactions needed during retirement to finance the optimal consumption. A pension plan with these properties is a dynamic portfolio policy that finances the contingent claims that are best for retirees. Although the general concept is easy to grasp, figuring out the specifics and effectively implementing them is a very difficult intellectual and practical task. Measuring performance ex post is even more difficult, perhaps impossible. Moreover, it may not even be worth undertaking.

In a recent paper, Bodie, Detemple, and Rindisbacher (2009), review the scientific literature on consumer financial decisions over the life cycle and its implications for the design of pension plans. They show that optimal life-cycle portfolios depend on both individual characteristics (investment horizons, age, risk aversion, initial financial wealth, expected growth rate of wages, wage rate volatility) and market factors (interest rate, market price of risk, return volatilities). Optimal retirement products are the

* Norman and Adele Barron Professor of Management, Boston University.

contingent claims generated by these portfolios (see Bodie, Ruffino, and Treussard 2008). It follows from the theory that they differ across households and market structures.

It also follows that implementation of the hedging demands will require a large number of assets. The exact number of securities required for such a synthesis is dictated by the dimensionality of the set of state variables that affect asset returns and the growth rates of wages. This number is potentially very large. Even if individual characteristics are perfectly known, it then follows that optimal hedges, for a given household, involve the constitution and dynamic management of large portfolios. Accounting for diversity across households appears to render fully individualized solutions prohibitively costly to manufacture.

Recent results by Detemple and Rindisbacher (forthcoming) offer hope for a reduction in the complexity of the problem. They show that dynamic hedging can be partially accomplished by holding a suitably specified long-term bond. This bond has a maturity date that matches the household's investment horizon and pays coupons that reflect the specific preferences for consumption and leisure. This single bond obviates the need to hedge fluctuations in the short rate, which requires a dynamic trading strategy with multiple securities when several factors drive the interest rate evolution. Complete spanning of the hedging demands does require additional securities to hedge fluctuations in the forward market prices of risk and in the value of human capital.

However, for investors with large risk aversion or when circumstances for a deterministic forward market price of risk prevail, the long-term bond alone covers most of the hedging needs. Indeed, under these circumstances, the hedge associated with the forward market price of risk vanishes. In fact, in the case of large risk aversion, even the mean-variance demand (that is, the diversification motive) disappears. Under these conditions a single fixed-income security with suitable maturity date and payments covers most of the retirement financing needs of the household.

Target-date funds (TDFs) are an early attempt to provide a product that covers the retirement needs of large classes of households. Funds of these types typically follow a simple investment strategy that consists of reducing the equity proportion with age. Most funds implicitly assume constant interest rates, market prices of risk, expected wage rate growth, and wage rate volatility. As a result, age simply approximates the changing financial-to-human capital ratio over the life cycle (the portfolio rules applied resemble the approximation derived in Cocco, Gomes, and Maenhout 2005).

In the United States, TDFs and closely related life-cycle funds have grown considerably since the early 1990s. Many DC plans now offer life-cycle funds, and these have been accepted by the regulators as permissible default investment options. Equity proportions in TDFs are high but vary widely. In 2008 some TDFs lost up to 40 percent of their value.

Recent performance results suggest that TDFs with high equity proportions might be inappropriate investments for individuals with moderate to high risk aversion. Furthermore, existing life-cycle funds focus predominantly on the retirement date and ignore the retirement phase. However, the optimal allocation during the accumulation phase depends on optimal plans during retirement and vice versa. TDFs should therefore take a comprehensive view and focus on the optimal behavior throughout the life cycle.

As noted by Bodie and Treussard (2007), TDFs are inappropriate for most individuals, in particular for those who face considerable exposure to human capital risk, have a high degree of risk aversion, or both. They stress that the equity proportion for such investors is too high. They also show that substantial welfare gains could be achieved if an age-dependent safe-target fund is offered in the form of a suitably designed inflation-protected bond with horizon-matching maturity date.

To offer optimal retirement vehicles, pension fund investments in theory need to be fully customized to service the needs of each individual household. In practice, various imperfections hinder implementation of optimal strategies. Difficulties that need to be addressed include the following:

1. Full customization is extremely costly: offering fully tailored plans involves information collection costs, database creation and maintenance costs, and individual account management costs. Fully disaggregated solutions may prove infeasible.
2. Implementation requires complete information about individual characteristics: although some characteristics, such as age and education, are easy to identify, others, such as risk aversion and tastes, are difficult to elicit. Even individuals who are well acquainted with notions of risk and return often find it difficult to articulate precise risk preferences.
3. Markets are not complete: severe shocks can introduce discontinuities in prices. Other shocks correspond to risks that are simply not traded. In both cases hedging proves challenging, if not infeasible. For financial intermediaries selling and managing pension plans, the constitution of

adequate capital reserves may be the only solution to absorb risks that cannot be efficiently hedged in the capital markets.

4. Continuous trading is not feasible: transaction costs have shrunk significantly during the last 30 years, but still remain material. This precludes instantaneous rebalancing.

5. Implementation also requires complete information about the model parameters: statistical and econometric techniques are not powerful enough to achieve that goal. Even if the true structure of the model is known, parameter estimates are subject to errors.

Imperfections, such as those listed above, need to be incorporated in the life-cycle model. Research on that front will undoubtedly help to fine-tune the analysis and lead to retirement products that reflect economic realities and serve the best interest of households. In the meantime it might be prudent to adopt a cautious approach to the design of pension plans. A guiding principle should perhaps be one derived from the Hippocratic oath: "First, do no harm." In the absence of precise information or effective hedging vehicles it might be advisable to select default strategies that limit the downside risk exposure for plan participants. As consideration is given to implementing the complex (albeit theoretically superior) optimization approaches suggested by several of the studies, we should carefully evaluate the potential gains in consideration of the implementation costs and errors that may be associated with the outcomes. A useful way to do this is to evaluate the likely results against the outcomes of investing in a simple minimal risk inflation-indexed bond, such as those currently issued by a number of governments. I expect that at least for now this would prove to be a superior investment strategy in the vast majority of cases, perhaps motivating more governments to incorporate the issuance of such bonds into their retirement income provision policies.

## References

Bodie, Zvi, Jérôme Detemple, and Marcel Rindisbacher. 2009. "Life Cycle Finance and the Design of Pension Plans." 2009. Boston University School of Management Research Paper Series No. 2009-5. Available at SSRN: http://ssrn .com/abstract=1396835.

Bodie, Zvi, Doriana Ruffino, and Jonathan Treussard. 2008. "Contingent Claims Analysis and Life-Cycle Finance." *American Economic Review* 98: 291–96.

Bodie, Zvi, and Jonathan Treussard. 2007. "Making Investment Choices as Simple as Possible but Not Simpler." *Financial Analysts Journal* 63 (May–June): 42–47.

Cocco, Joao, Francisco J. Gomes, and Pascal J. Maenhout. 2005. "Consumption and Portfolio Choice over the Life-Cycle." *Review of Financial Studies* 18: 491–533.

Detemple, Jérôme, and Marcel Rindisbacher. Forthcoming in *Review of Financial Studies*. "Dynamic Asset Allocation: A Portfolio Decomposition Formula and Applications."

# Index

Figures, notes, and tables are indicated with *f*, *n*, and *t* following the page number.

www.ingramcontent.com/pod-product-compliance
Lightning Source LLC
Chambersburg PA
CBHW061138220326
41599CB00025B/4286